Amazing Grace

ALSO BY STEVE TURNER

Trouble Man: The Life and Death of Marvin Gaye

A Hard Day's Write: The Stories Behind Every Beatles Song

Jack Kerouac: Angelheaded Hipster

Van Morrison: Too Late to Stop Now

*Hungry for Heaven: Rock and Roll and the
Search for Redemption*

H Y M N   XLI.

Faith's review and expectation.
Chap. xvii. 16, 17.

1 AMazing grace! (how sweet the sound)
    That sav'd a wretch like me!
I once was lost, but now am found,
    Was blind, but now I see.

2 'Twas grace that taught my heart to fear,
    And grace my fears reliev'd;
How precious did that grace appear,
    The hour I first believ'd!

3 Thro' many dangers, toils and snares,
    I have already come;
'Tis grace has brought me safe thus far,
    And grace will lead me home.

4 The LORD has promis'd good to me,
    His word my hope secures;
He will my shield and portion be,
    As long as life endures.

5 Yes, when this flesh and heart shall fail,
    And mortal life shall cease;
I shall possess, within the vail,
    A life of joy and peace.

6 The earth shall soon dissolve like snow,
    The sun forbear to shine;
But GOD, who call'd me here below,
    Will be for ever mine.

Amazing Grace

THE STORY OF

America's Most Beloved Song

STEVE TURNER

ecco

An Imprint of HarperCollinsPublishers

FRONTISPIECES:

TOP: *The only image we have of John Newton. Painted by John Russell (1745–1806).*
COURTESY OF THE CHURCH MISSION SOCIETY, LONDON.

Hymn text as originally published in Olney Hymns, 1779.
COURTESY OF THE BRITISH LIBRARY, LONDON.

Text permissions may be found following page 266.

HarperCollins books may be purchased for educational, business,
or sales promotional use. For information please write: Special Markets Department,
HarperCollins Publishers Inc., 10 East 53rd Street, New York, NY 10022.

First Ecco paperback edition published 2003

Designed by Barbara M. Bachman

Library of Congress Cataloging-in-Publication Data has been applied for.

ISBN 0-06-000218-2

ISBN 0-06-000219-0 (pbk.)

07   08   09   BVG/RRD   10   9   8   7   6   5   4   3   2

Contents

Foreword

BY JUDY COLLINS

It seems to me that I have known "Amazing Grace" all my life. I first learned the song from my maternal grandmother, Agnes Byrd, when I was a young girl. From the beginning, I experienced "Amazing Grace" as a powerful, evocative piece of writing, one that hit the heart like a dose of sunshine, a wave of elation. When I sang "Amazing Grace," my heart soared. My soul seemed to heal, and all the power and strength of those southern Methodists, with their fierce determination to do good, surrender to God, carry the message of hope, and try to make the world better, surrounded me, brought me comfort. I hear a song in its stark and glorious simplicity that speaks, at least on a metaphysical plane, of spiritual and physical unity.

My grandmother was born in Ohio in 1877. Her father had fought for the Union and her family believed in the abolition of slavery. The bloody Civil War was over by then and the country had begun the long path to heal the wounds that slavery had inflicted on black Americans. The fight to overcome the gruesome but previously accepted practice of racial intolerance was only beginning.

When she was just a few years old, Grandma and her family of eleven brothers and sisters moved to Tennessee. Many unhealed scars still survived, and there were some who held to the idea that blacks, freed by the Union victory, still shouldn't live and work, love and sing in the same rooms, the same cities, the same churches as their white brethren. "Separate but equal" was thought by many to be the post-war solution to the many freed slaves who were on the move to the north and to the west to settle, often to scatter.

When she was in her teens, Grandma Byrd married into a family where "brother had often fought against brother" in the Civil War and she was exposed to a good share of prejudice about race. It is strange, I think, that "Amazing Grace" would be one of her most important legacies to me.

My grandmother died in 1972. At that time I didn't know that "Amazing Grace" had a history that would have scalded some of my grandmother's prejudiced contemporaries' views. Surely it would have surprised them, as it did me, when I came upon the song's history to learn that the song had been created by John Newton, the captain of a slave ship that probably brought some of my grandmother's neighbors' ancestors from Africa to the newly formed United States. Agnes could not have known about the bleak chains of Newton's near tomb, of his shipwreck, and his survival. She did not know that the author of "Amazing Grace," reformed in his views after writing his monumental song in 1772, would become a fierce, lifelong opponent of slavery, a fighter for abolition, as well as a writer of hymns. She knew only, as I did, that "Amazing Grace" had a power to transform and give faith—that wrongs can be righted, that light can follow darkness, that healing is a miracle of faith. This was the power instilled in her and her children.

In 1970, two years before Grandma Byrd's death, I recorded "Amazing Grace" on my eighth album, *Whales and Nightingales*. I am so glad my grandma Byrd was able to hear it before she died.

During the sixties, I had been making records, singing folk music, writing my own songs, and finding and recording the songs of other singer-songwriters for ten years. My records had included songs of love, of protest, of personal insight. I had become an interpreter of songs by Joni Mitchell, Bob Dylan, Pete Seeger, Leonard Cohen, and Randy Newman, selling millions of records of my music, as well as the music of others. I had marched against the war in Vietnam and protested against the United States' involvement in the continued fighting in Indochina, in which so many American and Vietnamese were dying for what I felt was an illegal and immoral war. I had prayed and marched for peace and wondered if peace would ever come. The year I recorded "Amazing Grace," American troops were still in Vietnam and would be for another four years.

By the end of the sixties, I had lost hope in much of what the sixties had promised, my life was chaotic and full of pain, complicated with a divorce and the loss of custody of my son. When he returned to me at the end of 1969, a difficult adjustment for both of us followed. I searched for meaning—in therapy and in my career. I was looking for a renewal of my faith, which had faltered and flickered in that danger-ous, violent time. It was into that climate of fear and confusion that my recording of "Amazing Grace" arrived, with a power that reflected the need for the spirituality that is in this song. This powerful hymn, and the other songs I chose for the album, gave me the courage to believe there were solutions that I might not know but could find, for my son and for myself, if I let my faith and my music guide me.

One night after a particularly argumentative meeting of an en-counter group I was part of, I was asked to sing a song that might bring us all back together, a song we could all sing and relate to. I chose "Amazing Grace." Instantly, all disquiet faded from the group. We stood together, singing. Everyone seemed to know at least part of the song. We were transformed to a place that was calm and serene, peace-ful and loving.

My producer, Mark Abramson, with whom I was working on my current album, was at the meeting that night and called me in the morning to tell me "Amazing Grace" was a song that should be in-cluded on the album. I quickly agreed.

I recorded the song at St. Paul's chapel on the campus of Columbia University in New York. The chorus singing "Amazing Grace" was comprised of many close personal friends, including Stacy Keach, Harris Yulin, Yafa Lerner, Janet Young, and even one of my brothers, Denver John. The recording was truly a coming together of family and friends, kith and kin, and was performed in the same way my grand-mother's singing taught me, all those years ago. And it was my grand-mother's song that stood out, and shone among all the other songs like the jewel it was and will always be.

The sound of "Amazing Grace" swept across the country, becoming an instant hit, and for that reason, creating room for other spiritual songs in the pop repertory. The voices of many other singers began to transport a less orthodox audience to the spiritual places many of us have abandoned in our departure from churches and synagogues, tem-ples and the formal architecture of spirituality. I could be on a highway somewhere and hear the sound of "Amazing Grace" or one of the other popular hymns and feel the lift of hope, the soaring of my own wings of desire and elation.

It was only after "Amazing Grace" became a part of my life, my concerts, and my consciousness that I learned the story of how it was written and of John Newton—his mighty yearning, his early spiritual training, and his climactic, life-altering near tragedy. In fact, I, too, wrote a book about the song, in which I told some of the story of Newton's life and struggle and his great gift to all of us. I spoke primarily of the spiritual impact the song had on my life.

Now I have the great pleasure to read this new, wonderful, enlightening book. It bristles with great historical information—details of John Newton and his family, his background, and the great service he performed through his own enlightenment. In light of my intense relationship with "Amazing Grace" and my awe at its power to heal, it is with gratitude and astonishment that I read Steve Turner's deep and extensive history of Newton's life, in which so many more layers are revealed. This song was born out of the soul of a complicated and unique man, and Turner has given us much more of the background for the miracle of lyric and melody that is "Amazing Grace." One of the things I discovered in Mr. Turner's book was the gradual falling away of the presence of this great song in literature and oral tradition until my recording of it in 1970. I am honored to have played a part in making so many people aware once more of something rare and fine, a song that performs magic in people's souls. But my grandmother deserves all the credit, for she carried the song through time and gave it to me to bring to others.

In the months since the tragedy of 9/11, the song has even more poignancy and beauty. In the many years I have been singing "Amazing Grace," I have found it difficult to imagine that more meaning and hope could be communicated in its simple, direct, and heart-healing message. Yet in the aftermath of the tragedy, in the streets of New York as in cities all over the world that need healing, I sometimes hear "Amazing Grace" wafting from the doors of a church or funeral home, played by bagpipers. The melody itself is haunting and healing, even without the transforming words. The book you are about to read is thrilling and enlightening. Steve Turner has given us a gift—the story of the foundation from which this flower of music and healing has sprung.

Acknowledgments

I begin by honoring those who trailblazed the intensive study of single songs. There may well be more who have done so, but those that came to my attention and inspired my interest are the late Nigel Finch, who made a groundbreaking BBC television documentary on "My Way" for the *Arena* series; Bill Nicholson, who gave similar televisual treatment to the hymn "Abide with Me"; and rock critic Dave Marsh, who produced a 246-page book on "Louie Louie" (published in 1993). After I had started the project I became aware of Clinton Heylin's *Dylan's Daemon Lover*, an investigation into the seventeenth-century ballad "The House Carpenter," and David Margolick's *Strange Fruit* (published in 2000), which tackled the song made famous by Billie Holiday.

I began reading about John Newton after a casual remark made by Bono (see prologue), but the first stage of development came when I met Bobette Buster in Los Angeles and attended some of her screenwriting classes at the George Lucas School of Cinema at the University of Southern California. She encouraged me in my conviction that John Newton's life contained all the elements of great drama. Then, just as I was considering writing a John Newton biography to facilitate research for a screenplay, a book editor, Maurice Lyon, persuaded me to think in terms of telling the story of "Amazing Grace" rather than of John Newton on the grounds that the song was better known than its author.

I then have to thank my editor, Dan Halpern of Ecco, who responded so immediately and positively when I first mentioned the idea of a book on "Amazing Grace" to him. Generally I dislike discussing book outlines on the phone because of the danger of misrepresenting my own ideas, but on this occasion I dared to explain and Dan was sufficiently interested to ask me to e-mail a synopsis as soon as I possibly could. After reading it he was keen enough to make an offer to my agent, Kathy Anderson of Anderson Grindberg Literary Management.

Once I had started on the book, the work of four people with a previous interest in "Amazing Grace" helped me enormously. I offer particular thanks to William J. Reynolds, Distinguished Professor of Church Music Emeritus at Southwestern Baptist Theological Seminary, who has carried out a valuable study of the song, tracing the variety of tunes it has been set to and the details of American hymnals that have included it. He kindly sent me a copy of this research, with photocopies of the tunes, and of his lecture "Amazing Grace: A Twentieth-Century Phenomenon," which he had delivered in 1999 at the Southern Baptist Theological Seminary as part of the Hugh T. McElrath Lecture Series.

I first learned about the work of Bill Reynolds from a lecture given by Bruce Hindmarsh at the May 2000 Hymnody in American Protestantism Conference. Titled "Amazing Grace, How Sweet It Has Sounded," it used Reynolds's research as source material but made interesting observations about the song as a cultural phenomenon and the way in which it had been frequently reinterpreted according to the prevailing theological winds. Hindmarsh is also the author of *John Newton and the English Evangelical Tradition* (Oxford: Clarendon Press, 1996), which devotes one of its eight chapters to a sharply focused overview of Newton's hymnody.

Just as I started the book my father gave me a reissued version of Richard Cecil's 1808 biography of Newton, updated by Marylynn Rousse (Fearn, Ross-shire: Christian Focus Publications, 2000). Rousse hadn't tampered with Cecil's text but had comprehensively annotated it and added almost 200 pages of appendixes, including an extensive bibliography, potted biographies of all the key players in Newton's life, and transcripts of pertinent documents.

Her research was fastidious, an obvious labor of love, and was immensely helpful. Most valuable to me was her reproduction of the sermon notes on the verses that were used as the inspiration for "Amazing Grace." With this information I was able to see the original document in Lambeth Palace Library and from that to work out the date it was preached and therefore, for the first time, to put an accurate date on the composition of the hymn. Previously it had only been guessed at within a ten-to-fifteen-year period.

I was helped by Marion Hatchett, Professor of Liturgy and Music at the University of the South in Sewanee, Tennessee, whose entry on "Amazing Grace" in *The Hymnal 1982 Companion* (New York: Church Hymnal Corporation, 1994) was the best published summary of the origins of the hymn that I found. It was Dr. Hatchett who discovered the earliest known printing of the tune we now use with the song, and he very courteously answered my queries and pointed me to articles he had written.

On the musical side I had useful correspondence with Peter van der Merwe, author of *Origins of the Popular Style: The Antecedents of Twentieth-Century Popular Music* (Oxford University Press, 1989), who drew my attention to possible influences on the tune for "Amazing Grace." Noël Tredinnick, organist and director of music at All Souls, Langham Place, London, helped me understand the musical changes that had taken place in the tune over the past two centuries.

When I visited Sierra Leone, I was given invaluable help by Doris Lenga-Kroma, who became my guide and hostess. Kevin McPhillips Travel kindly gave me a ticket from London to Freetown with Sierra National Airlines, and the Cape Sierra Hotel supplied me with accommodation. A number of people on the ground made the trip go smoothly: Cecil Williams and Tamba Sellu of the National Tourist Board of Sierra Leone, Carroll Sahaidak-Beaver, James Lenga-Kroma, Bobby Caulker, Albert Yanker, Hamid Mendu, SLP Sergeant Swaray, Ben Caulker, Sullay Kamara, A. A. Lamin Bangura, Marvin Bailor, Zachariah Bangura, Charles Barlay, Bailor Rendenssa, and Lionel R. Tower.

In general I was helped enormously by library archivists, to whom I was often only a voice on the end of the phone, and the wonderful instrument of the Internet, which, if it didn't give me the answer to my question, at least pointed me to someone who could. Much of the research that produced this book would have been impossible without search engines and e-mails. So, a thank-you to btopenworld for giving me access at a very reasonable price and to google.com for looking things up so thoroughly and speedily.

The following libraries and archives were used:

IN AMERICA: Spartanburg County Public Library (Spartanburg, S.C.), South Carolina Historical Society (Charleston, S.C.), The Hymn Society (Boston, Mass.), Archive of American Folk Song at the Library of Congress (Washington, D.C.), Special Collections Library of Vanderbilt University (Nashville, Tenn.), Chicago Public Library (Chicago, Ill.), Newport Historical Society (Newport, R.I.), Southern Baptist Historical Society and Archives (Nashville, Tenn.), University of Tennessee Library (Knoxville, Tenn.), Transylvania University Special Collections (Lexington, Ky.), Grace Doherty Library at Centre College (Danville, Ky.), University of Virginia Library (Charlottesville, Va.), Russell County Public Library (Lebanon, Va.), Menno Simmons Historical Library at Eastern Mennonite University (Harrisonburg, Va.), Rare Book, Manuscript and Special Collections Library at Duke University (Durham, N.C.), Firestone Library at Princeton University (Princeton, N.J.), American Catholic Press (South Holland, Ill.), Western Historical Manuscripts Collection at University of Missouri (Columbia, Mo.), Public Library of Charlotte and Mecklenburg County (Charlotte, N.C.), and the Gallup Organization (Princeton, N.J.).

IN CANADA: Hudson's Bay Company Archives (Winnipeg, Manitoba).

IN ENGLAND: Bristol City Museum, Bristol Central Library, Bristol Record Office, Society of Merchant Venturers (Bristol), British Library, National Sound Archives, Performing Rights Society, Society of Jesus, Cecil Sharp House, Guildhall Public Library, National Maritime Museum, Public Record Office, Cowper and Newton Museum, Lambeth Palace Library, Chiswick Public Library, Essex County Records Office, Family Records Centre, Liverpool Central Library Record Office, Cambridge University Library, Historical Manuscripts Commission, London Metropolitan Archives, National Meteorological Library and Archive.

IN SCOTLAND: School of Scottish Studies (Glasgow), Glasgow University Archives, The National Archives of Scotland (Edinburgh).

IN SIERRA LEONE: Pool Newspaper (Freetown), National Tourist Board of Sierra Leone (Freetown).

IN PORTUGAL: Instituto dos Arquivos Nacionais (Lisbon).

The following people were interviewed: Joan Baez, Steve Burgay, Shirley Caesar, David Cohen, Judy Collins, Major Tony Crease, Arthur Crume, Dillard Crume, Leroy Crume, Jeff Dexter, Ani Choying Drolma, Harry Eskew, Stuart Fairbairn, Keith Fordyce, Clarence Fountain, Diamanda Galas, Jim Ginty, Arlo Guthrie, Marion Hatchett, Brigadier Melville Jameson, Peter Kerr, Doris Lenga-Kroma, Joe Ligon, Peter van der Merwe, Ras Michael, Sam Mitchell, Bernice Johnson Reagon, Jean Ritchie, Ed Sanders, Annie Sprinkle, Ralph Stanley, Scott Stevenson, Pete Seeger, Ira Tucker, Albertina Walker, Doc Watson, Ronnie Wood, and Maceo Woods.

The following people gave generous assistance either in supplying information, setting up interviews, or sending me copies of out-of-print records: Tim Anderson, John Beecher, Viv Broughton, Roderick Cannon, Ed Clinch, Mary Louise van Dyke, José Maria Furtado, Dr. Christopher Fyfe, Father Michael Gilligan, Judith Gray, Clinton Heylin, Andrew Jackson, Erik James, Bob Laughton, Anne Morton, Rob Orlemans, Glenda Osborne, John Pollock, William J. Reynolds, Ian Samwell, Susan Thoms, Ger Tillekens, Dr. John and Mrs. Wallace, Daniel Wolff, Jerry Zolten.

Finally I owe thanks to Dan Halpern and Patty Fernandez of Ecco for their editorial comments, which helped me strengthen my raw material; to Judy Collins for being so kind as to offer a foreword for a book about a song with which her name will be forever associated; and to my family—wife, Mo; daughter, Lianne; and son, Nathan—for putting up with someone who, since 1999 at least, has had a one-track mind.

Introduction

Despite the enormous popularity of "Amazing Grace," the story behind its writing is not as widely known as might be expected. Many performers who include the song in their repertoires assume that because both the words and music are in the public domain the identity of the author is unknown, just as we don't know who wrote "House of the Rising Sun" or "Barbara Allen." Others assume that it was composed in the 1960s along with "Where Have All the Flowers Gone," "If I Had a Hammer," and "Blowing in the Wind," possibly by Arlo Guthrie or Judy Collins. Where the basics of the story *are* known, they are often reassembled to add support to a particular religious or political view and thereby end up being closer to fiction than fact.

This lack of knowledge may be because previous tellings of the story have been aimed at specialized audiences rather than at the general reader: academic papers for those interested in hymnology, meditations on grace for the religiously minded, and easy-to-read illustrated books for children. The most accessible account in recent years was not a book but a ninety-minute television film produced by Bill Moyers in 1990, and yet documentary demands for action and interview meant that the emphasis was on living performers and their feelings for the words rather than the history of the song.

As soon as I began researching, it became obvious that this book was going to divide naturally into two. The first part would tell the fascinating story of John Newton, the Englishman who wrote the words of "Amazing Grace." The second part, picking up the thread in the years immediately following his death, would tell the story of the song itself as it has spread and developed over the past two centuries.

I felt that there could be no real understanding of "Amazing Grace" without an understanding of Newton's life and no real understanding of Newton's life unless it was covered from birth to death, because at every stage there are occurrences that illuminate the song. Joan Baez, who played an important role in popularizing the song in the 1960s, told me that she thought its unique power came because it was the "song of his life." I wasn't sure whether she meant that it was his magnum opus or his most autobiographical lyric. There was no need to ask. It was both.

The part of the book concerned with Newton's life, which I have called "Creation," isn't an attempt at a full-scale biography. I have deliberately avoided detailing all his activities, so that I could focus on those events and ideas that contributed most directly to the theme of the song; events and ideas that when understood could deepen our appreciation of his words. For this reason I thought it worth lingering over his upbringing, his life at sea, and his participation in the African slave trade but quickly passing over his time spent on land as a tide surveyor in Liverpool and his day-to-day parish work in Olney.

I could have left his life story at the point that he penned the words of "Amazing Grace" and turned my attention immediately to the life of the song, but I felt it was important to stay with him through his years in London, when he allied himself with the movement to abolish slavery, because for many people this has been the hard evidence that grace worked in his life. At the same time, in order to correct the assumption that "Amazing Grace" was a song of remorse over his involvement in the slave trade, it was necessary to point out how slow he was in condemning it.

I have, of course, relied on earlier publications for the details of Newton's life, particularly his autobiography and slave ship journals, the nineteenth-century biographies by Richard Cecil and Josiah Bull, and the twentieth-century biography by Bernard Martin, but have supplemented these with original research into contemporary newspapers, wills, legal documents, maps, logbooks, weather reports, church registers, and correspondence as well as Newton's own handwritten journals, diaries, letters, and sermon notes.

I was particularly keen to know the identities of people that Newton referred to but didn't name or named but gave no further details of. It was therefore satisfying to be the first author to discover who rescued him from the coast of Africa in 1748, the identity of the company that sold his first "parcel" of slaves in America, and the background to Mr. Clow, the slave trader who has been demonized in recent writing about Newton. I was also privileged to trace previously unseen letters written by his father when employed by the Royal African Company and by Joseph Manesty, the Liverpool merchant and shipowner who offered him work as a teenager, arranged his rescue from Africa, and set him up as a captain in the slave trade.

In the second part of the book, which I have called "Dissemination," where the song itself moves center stage, two centuries of history are covered in roughly the same number of words used for the eighty-two years of Newton's life. This has naturally meant being selective, writing only about significant stages in the development of "Amazing Grace" and bearing in mind the key questions How did the song change during this period? and In what way did the cultural climate contribute to this change?

Between Newton's death and the start of the Civil War, the words had crossed the Atlantic from England and had been set to the now familiar tune by a singing instructor from South Carolina. Between the end of the Civil War and the start of the First World War, the song had spread across America through revival campaigns, the tune had been slightly embellished, and a new verse had been added. This long period is covered in two chapters because other information about the song in the nineteenth century, such as a list of hymnals that included it, wouldn't have advanced the story or deepened our knowledge of the song's evolution.

During the twentieth century, mainly because of the advent of recorded sound, the changes were rapid, and I have dedicated chapters to the main musical genres within which "Amazing Grace" grew, even though the periods covered often overlap. For example, its use in gospel affected the urban folk movement, just as folk usage spilled over into pop and rock. I decided against devoting chapters to jazz, blues, white gospel, or country, either because there weren't enough recordings to justify a separate discussion, or because they fitted better as subgenres inside other chapters.

For the second part of the book, there were no previously published studies to draw on. Each era and style of music had its own literature, none of which was exclusively concerned with "Amazing Grace." Books on gospel music, for example, would mention the song, but no one had published a study of "Amazing Grace" as a gospel song. Again, I tried as often as possible to go to primary sources—letters, journals, newspaper articles, and best of all, interviews with many of the main artists who have recorded the song over the past fifty years.

I ended the book by surveying the different ways in which grace has been understood since the publication of "Amazing Grace." Despite lyrical pruning and musical decoration over the last two and a quarter centuries, the core message remains surprisingly the same. However, interpretations of that message have changed, and these offer interesting indicators of sociospiritual trends.

A discography is included not only because it's rewarding to survey all the major artists who have recorded it but also because it wasn't possible to mention everyone in the text without making it sound like a long-winded acceptance speech at the Grammys. It isn't comprehensive. I have deliberately restricted it to the more well-known artists and the more significant or unusual recordings. The other lists were added for the same reasons.

Following one song down the ages has been as interesting and invigorating an experience as I thought it would be, taking me (in my thoughts if not in person) from the banks of the River Thames to the slopes of Mount Kilimanjaro, from revivalist preachers on the sawdust circuit to self-help gurus, from the Civil War to the Twin Towers, from shape-note singing to reggae, rap, and rock. As the Grateful Dead once said, "What a long, strange trip it's been," and I now leave you to embark upon that trip at the point where I began.

Amazing Grace

Since thou waſt precious in my ſight,
thou haſt been honourable,
Iſaiah XLIII. 4.th
BUT,
Thou ſhalt remember that thou waſt
a bond-man in the land of Egypt,
and the LORD thy God redeemed thee
Deu.my XV. 15.th

Bible verses that Newton had painted over his study fireplace at Olney. PHOTO BY STEVE TURNER.

The vicarage at Olney. "Amazing Grace" was written in the room behind the attic window to the right.

PHOTO BY STEVE TURNER.

Prologue

I believe our hearts are all alike, destitute of
every good, and prone to every evil. Like money
from the same mint, they bear the same impression
of total depravity. But grace makes a difference,
and grace deserves the praise.
—*John Newton*, LETTER TO MRS. T., 1777

I am a singer and a songwriter but I am also a father,
four times over. I am a friend to dogs. I am a sworn enemy
of the saccharine, and a believer in grace over karma.
—*Bono*, SPEECH TO HARVARD STUDENTS, 2001

When it got to the "wretch" part of it, I said, wait a minute!
He's in the wretch-saving business? I said,
I qualify. I qualify.
—*Sherman Whitfield*, 2001

*I*t began in 1991 with a chance remark made to me by
Bono, lead singer of the Irish rock band U2 and political activist. We
had been discussing the merits of Catholic and Protestant artists in
Western culture when Bono said that, in his opinion, some of the
greatest works of art made by Protestants in England were the hymns
of people like Charles Wesley. I said something about the intriguing
nature of the stories behind some hymns, thinking in particular of
"When Peace Like a River" by Horatio Gates Spafford, which I knew
was written while the author was sailing from Liverpool to New York
having heard that his four daughters, who had preceded him on another ship with his wife, had been drowned after a collision with a vessel off the coast of Newfoundland. Apparently, as Spafford sailed into

the area where his children had been lost and looked out over the ocean, the opening lines of the hymn came to him:

When peace, like a river, attendeth my way,
When sorrows, like sea-billows, roll,
Whatever my lot, Thou hast taught me to say,
It is well, it is well with my soul.

I also had a vague memory that "Rock of Ages" had been written by someone (Augustus Toplady) who had taken shelter in the cleft of a rock in Cheddar Gorge, Somerset, England, to avoid a violent thunderstorm, and had been reminded of the biblical metaphor "God is my rock, in whom I take refuge":

Rock of Ages, cleft for me,
Let me hide myself in Thee;

These were the types of stories that preachers sometimes told, and when I was a child they enhanced hymns that would otherwise have seemed dull.

Then Bono mentioned "Amazing Grace." "Do you know that one?" Of course I did and I knew something of the story. Author: John Newton. Background: Slave trader who converted after terrible storm at sea. Became vicar. Wrote hymn. Hymn became Top-10 hit in 1971. I even had a paperback copy of Newton's autobiography, which I think I'd borrowed from my dad and never read. For this modern printing, it was called *Out of the Depths* and had a garish cover of a ruddy-cheeked mariner at the helm of a sinking ship, waves breaking over his ankles and tattered sails flapping in the wind.

Three years later I was fishing around for film ideas. On a flight from London to Los Angeles I started reading *Out of the Depths*, which I had taken with me as possible source material, and found the story of this sailor and slave trader absolutely compelling. It seemed to have all the elements of great drama: a rebel hero, a love interest, quests, escapes, obstacles, conflicts, ordeals, reversals, a crisis, climax, resolution, and personal transformation. When I got back to London I called

Bono and told him what a great idea he'd turned me on to. "Really?" he said. "I never knew the story behind the song. I just thought there must be a good one." So I gave him the plot synopsis. He listened quietly. "You've got me hooked right there," he said. "You've got me hooked."

For the next few years I casually researched Newton's life story before focusing my attention on a book rather than a movie, and on the song rather than the author. I was well into the writing stage on September 11, 2001, after which "Amazing Grace" became the song that people turned to most often to express their faith, hope, and solidarity. One of the most poignant images of the shock and grief was that of people of all ages joining hands or linking arms and softly singing the words. When Columbia released the album *God Bless America* ("a collection of songs of hope, freedom and inspiration"), which went straight to the top of the Billboard charts, Tramaine Hawkins's rendition of "Amazing Grace" was heard alongside Frank Sinatra's "America the Beautiful," Mariah Carey's "Hero," and Pete Seeger's "This Land Is Your Land."

The song was used at church services, memorial gatherings, tribute concerts, and funerals. It was played on Manhattan's Fourteenth Street by a Salvation Army ensemble as volunteers loaded trucks of supplies for helpers at Ground Zero. Pipers from the NYPD piped it at the commencement of the Prayer for America service held at Yankee Stadium. Red Cross workers sang it at the site at Shanksville, Pennsylvania, where United Airlines flight 93 had plunged into a field after its hijackers were apparently overwhelmed by courageous passengers.

It was played at the many funerals of New York City firefighters, a large proportion of whom were of Irish descent. The FDNY Emerald Society Pipes and Drums, now seventy strong, was formed in 1962, and it has become a tradition for them to play for the five to eight colleagues who die each year in the line of duty. In the sixties they would play "Will Ye No Come Back Again," but after the success of the pipe version of "Amazing Grace" by the Royal Scots Dragoon Guards in 1972, they began playing "Amazing Grace" as the coffin was brought into the church and "Going Home" as it was brought out.

"Amazing Grace" was heard not only around America after September 11, but around the world. A local school choir performed it at

Singapore's National Stadium in front of fifteen thousand people; British soul star Mica Paris delivered an unaccompanied version at a service of remembrance held in London's Westminster Abbey; at the Brandenburg Gate two hundred thousand Berliners hummed its tune; Canadian MPs joined in song at the Parliament Building in Ottawa; and at Lakenheath, America's largest military air base in Europe, where F-15 bombers waited in readiness to be sent to the Middle East, a lone piper played it to signal the end of a three-minute silence.

Appropriately it was already the favorite hymn of President George W. Bush. In his 1999 autobiography, *A Charge to Keep*, he described his Christian commitment in phrases borrowed from the song. "I was humbled to learn that God sent his Son to die for a sinner like me," he wrote. "I was comforted to know that through the Son, I could find God's amazing grace, a grace that crosses every border, every barrier, and is open to everyone." During his inauguration in Washington, D.C., it was performed three times by New Orleans high school student Tiffany Ameen.

The most spine-chilling "Amazing Grace" moment for me came not during the events of September 11 but on one Sunday when I was with my sixteen-year-old son at All Souls Church in London's West End. My son, I have to point out, was wondering why his father was spending so much time diligently scrutinizing a song that was so, well . . . *old*. He would have been far more interested in a dissertation on something currently in the charts. Something *relevant*.

That Sunday morning, before the sermon, a church member went to the lectern to give a brief account of how he had become a Christian. His name was Sherman Whitfield. He was a tall, muscular black American with a shaved head, a wide grin, and a voice that actors would die for. I had seen him around before and had been impressed at his readings of the Bible, which were so dramatic that I'd be left feeling that I'd never read the book before.

Sherman Whitfield was from Arkansas, working in England for a chemical company. His story, as he told it, was that he was from a family of six children and that his father had walked out when he was young. No one in his family went to church, although his grandmother was a faithful Christian. He'd fought his way up through school and college, earning a good degree followed by a well-paying job. He became proud of his achievements: "I felt pretty good about Sherman Whitfield," he said. "I felt that I had pulled myself up by my own bootstraps, that I was the captain of my soul, that I was the Man."

He married two years after leaving the university and his work prospered, but then things started to go wrong. His marriage foundered and his wife sought the counsel of a local preacher. Sherman returned home one afternoon to discover them being intimate with each other. The preacher upped and ran out of the house with Sherman in hot pursuit. "I had heard about this preacher's one-to-one sessions," he said, "but I hadn't realized just how personal they were."

As a result of this discovery his life went into free fall. His marriage broke up, he began drinking heavily all day every day, and his work performance deteriorated. The self-assurance that had built steadily over the years was rapidly eroding. "I no longer felt in control of the ship. I no longer felt in control of my life. I was devastated, I was hurt. I was broken." It was then he remembered things his grandmother had told him about a Jesus who could heal the sick, raise the dead, and give sight to the blind. Could this Jesus do anything for Sherman Whitfield? "I told my running buddies that I was thinking of going to church and they said, no Sherman, it couldn't have got *that* bad."

He set out for church, still unsure that he was doing the right thing. "There was a mind telling me, Sherman, you don't have to go tonight. Don't go. Go back home. There was another mind saying, no, you must go. So I went into church that night and I heard the word of God preached and at the end of the sermon the choir got up and they started singing the song:

Amazing grace! (how sweet the sound)
That saved a wretch like me!
I once was lost, but now am found;
Was blind, but now I see.

"When it got to the 'wretch' part of it, I said, Wait a minute! He's in the wretch-saving business? I said, I qualify. I *qualify!* I was not used to going to church and so I didn't understand all the protocol of how you get saved yet when they got through singing the song I was sitting right at the back and I stood up and raised my hand. The preacher looked at me. I don't know if he thought the church was on fire or what but he said, sir, can I help you? I said, I want that Jesus that you're talking about. I want the one that can save a wretch. So he asked me to come on down. I gave my hand to the preacher and I gave my heart to God.

"Since that time 'all things have become new.' God has sent me a new wife, sent me a new life and a couple of years after that I ran into this preacher, the one that I had run after when he was with my wife, and all the hate, all the anger, all the things I imagined I was going to do to him, just melted away. I went up to him and I shook his hands. I hugged him. I loved him. Only a Jesus can make that kind of difference."

Sherman's story felt to me like a confirmation. It was as though God had put his hand on my shoulder. Here were words written one frosty December day in the attic room of an English vicarage in the late eighteenth century that were still having a life-changing impact; words that in the twenty-first century were still encouraging, challenging, comforting, and even stopping people in their tracks.

A few weeks later I was in that vicarage, standing in the small room where Newton first put *grace* next to *amazing* in the words of a song that touched on the peaks and troughs of his life. The house no longer belongs to the church, but there is an agreement that whoever owns it at any given time will not make alterations to the room that was once his study.

From this window can be seen the site of the long-demolished Great House, where Newton first presented his freshly composed hymns at Sunday night meetings. Next to it stands the fourteenth-century church of St. Peter and St. Paul, with its 185-foot-tall spire, where for sixteen years he was the curate in charge. At the far side of the church is his grave. Over the fireplace, painted directly onto the wall, are two Old Testament verses that Newton wanted to be constantly in his gaze as a reminder of the grace that had invaded his life.

Since thou wast precious in my sight,
thou hast been honourable,
  Isaiah XLIII. 4th.
    BUT
Thou shalt remember that thou wast
a bond-man in the land of Egypt,
and the Lord thy God redeemed thee.
  Deu. XV. 15th.

The first verse was a reminder of how far he had come and the change that had taken place both in his circumstances and his behavior. The second verse reminded him of where he had come from and he never let himself forget that. He never forgot the time he spent enslaved on an African island, the time when he realized that he was not the captain of his soul, that he was not the Man. That these verses have remained intact on this wall through more than two centuries of frequently changing inhabitants is testimony to the respect given to John Newton and his story.

Alone in that room it was impossible not to want the floorboards or the fireplace to yield up their secrets and tell me exactly what happened the day that Newton wrote what would become one of the best-known songs in history. Did he work at a desk or sitting back on a sofa? As it was winter, and a cold winter at that, with temperatures hovering around the freezing point, he would almost certainly have had a fire in the grate. He may have been smoking his long pipe, with which he used to relax. Did the verses come to him almost fully formed, or was he balling up his failed attempts and tossing them in the flames before he found the right words?

The idea of grace seasoned Bono's thinking even as I was working on this book. Performing the U2 classic "I Will Follow" while on tour in America, he was adding the couplet "I was cased in amazing grace / I was lost but now am found," and then for the album *All That You Can't Leave Behind* he wrote his own song "Grace." Being a singer, he is interested in the connection between the sweet sound and grace, between music and spiritual transformation. The day that Joey Ramone died in April 2001, the band was in Portland, Oregon, and Bono sang an unaccompanied version of "Amazing Grace" in honor of the New York singer whose work with the Ramones had inspired him as a teenager in Dublin. Reporting on the performance for a U2 Web site, a fan wrote: "The audience joined in, and the sound of ten thousand people singing in tribute was a sobering but uplifting moment for us all. True magic can't be rehearsed, and this was it."

"It's a powerful idea, grace. It really is," Bono told launch.com in October. "We hear so much of karma and so little of grace. Every religion teaches about karma and what you put out you will receive. And even Christianity, which is supposed to be about grace, has turned redemption into good manners, or the right accent, or good works, or whatever. I just can't get over grace."

PART ONE

Creation

Eighteenth-century caricature of an English press gang in action.

Chapter 1

PRESS-GANGED

In a man of war, you have the collected filth of jails.
Condemned criminals have the alternative of hanging
or entering on board. There's not a vice committed
on shore, but is practised here.
—*Edward Thompson*, A SAILOR'S LETTERS, 1767

Sent Lieutenant Ruffin with 31 men on board
the *Betsy* tender to impress seamen.
—*Captain Philip Carteret*, LOGBOOK ENTRY,
FEBRUARY 6, 1744

I am going from England with a good prospect of
improving my fortune, and please myself with hopes of
being one day able to make you proposals of certainty if
I find you undisposed when I come back.
—*John Newton*, LETTER TO MARY CATLETT, 1744

*J*ohn Newton, *a seventeen-year-old sailor, was standing* on the deck of a ship anchored off Venice in the Spring of 1743. The sun was just slipping beneath the horizon. Out of the shadows came a figure that stopped in front of him and held out a ring, urging him to take it. If he was to accept it, and treasure it, his life would be crowned with happiness and success. If he was to refuse or lose it, he would be dogged by trouble and misery. Newton accepted the challenge. He had always been attracted to the idea of having total mastery of his destiny.

As the bearer of the ring slipped back into the shadows, a second anonymous figure came to him, this one pouring scorn on the promises that had just been made and accusing him of being ignorant and naive. How could blessings emanate from something so small and insignificant? How could he have placed such trust in someone who didn't back up his claim with evidence? He advised Newton to shun such superstition and get rid of the ring. Newton jumped to its defense but his arguments weren't sufficient and so he slipped the gold band from his finger and threw it in the Gulf of Venice.

The moment it disappeared beneath the water, a wall of fire shot into the air around the city, lighting up the night sky. It was as if a mechanism had been triggered to unleash a terrifying power. Seeing the look of panic spreading across Newton's sweating face, his accuser, with a smug grin, revealed that what he had thrown away was not a mere gold ring, which could easily be replaced, but all the mercy that God had stored up for him. His sins could now never be forgiven. John Newton had just thrown away his only chance of salvation.

As the implications dawned on him, a third visitor approached. The face was obscured by shadow, making it difficult for him to tell if it was someone new or whether, as he suspected, it was the original ring bearer. Newton admitted what he had done and accepted that he had done it voluntarily and knew what the terrible consequences would be. The visitor, surprisingly, was sympathetic and asked him if he would handle things differently if given a second chance.

Before Newton could reply the man dove into the water and surfaced with the ring. The flames around the city were immediately extinguished, and the accuser, who it now became clear had been lurking in the background throughout, slunk away defeated. Relieved beyond words, Newton stepped forward to reclaim the ring. But the visitor sharply withdrew it, saying, "If you should be entrusted with this ring again, you would very soon bring yourself into the same distress. You are not able to keep it, but I will preserve it for you. Whenever it is needful, I will produce it on your behalf."

Thinking about this dramatic dream many years later Newton could see the spiritual allegory. It was the story of his life; the golden gift of gospel truth handed to him as a child, that gift given up in the face of taunts and tempting arguments, the destructive effects of this abandonment and the opportunity, eventually, to begin again. In retrospect he saw that it had been "a last warning" but at the time he had seen it only as a disturbing and graphic vision, one that was powerful enough to rob him of sleep and appetite for a few days but not powerful enough to arrest his moral and spiritual decline.

The dream came to him when he was actually on a ship in the Mediterranean, Venice having been a recent port of call. The image of the ring thrown in the water was almost certainly suggested by the annual Venetian ceremony *sposalizio del mare,* in which decorated barges full of nobles sailed out to drop a consecrated ring into the sea. It was a symbolic marriage of city and ocean, acknowledging Venice's dependence on the surrounding sea and its need to be on good terms with an element that could bring it wealth or wash it away.

Whether Newton had seen the ceremony, which took place on Ascension Day, he never said. He may simply have heard about it in Venice or he may have been aware of Canaletto's painting *The Bucintoro Returning to the Molo on Ascension Day,* which had been completed just thirteen years before. He was aware of the ritual because he later mentioned it in a letter, referring to it as "a foolish ceremony or marriage between the republic and the Adriatic."

Newton had been born on July 24, 1725, in Wapping, London, close to the Tower of London and on the north bank of the River Thames. It was an area dominated by Britain's then-flourishing shipping industry. Five years before, Stow's updated *Survey of London* said that Wapping was "chiefly inhabited by seafaring men, and tradesmen dealing in commodities for the supply of shipping and shipmen. It stands exceeding thick with buildings, and is very populous having been very much improved by human industry."

Newton's father, also John Newton, was one such seafaring man. He worked as the commander of various merchant ships trading in the Mediterranean, and each voyage would take him away from home for up to three years. Despite having been educated by Jesuits in Spain he was not, according to his son, "affected by religion" and was rather pompous and aloof. Newton's mother, Elizabeth, seems to have been his opposite. She was frail and inward-looking, a devout Christian who worshiped at a Nonconformist meetinghouse in nearby Gravel Lane.

Captain Newton was away so often that John Newton's early up-bringing was almost entirely at the hands of his mother. Her Christian convictions meant that she made his moral and spiritual education her priority. By the age of four he could read in English, and a year later he was learning Latin. Her dream was that he could become a preacher like her minister, Dr. David Jennings. Because she was not a member of the Church of England she knew that her son wouldn't be able to en-roll at an English university, so she planned that, like Dr. Jennings, he would go to St. Andrew's University in Scotland.

Elizabeth Newton trusted in the proverb "Train up a child in the way he should go: and when he is old, he will not depart from it." Be-fore Newton could talk Dr. Jennings preached a sermon based on the verse "And give unto Solomon my son a perfect heart" from 1 Chron. 29. "Did you ever pray this prayer for your children in good earnest?" he challenged his congregation. "Lord, give them a perfect heart. What pains have you taken to instruct and teach them the good ways of holi-ness . . . ? O! be earnest and importunate with God, be daily interces-sors with him for the souls of your dear children. Beg it of him, who is the God of grace, that he would give your children a perfect heart."

Elizabeth read Bible stories to her son until they were as familiar to him as the tales his father brought back from sea. To reinforce the un-derlying teachings, she would test his knowledge with the 107 ques-tions and answers of the *Shorter Catechism*.

QUESTION 1: What is the chief end of man?
ANSWER: Man's chief end is to glorify God, and to enjoy him for
    ever.
QUESTION 2: What rule hath God given to direct us how we may
    glorify and enjoy him?
ANSWER: The word of God, which is contained in the scriptures of
    the Old and New Testaments, is the only rule to direct us how we
    may glorify and enjoy him.

She also taught him the children's verse of Isaac Watts, another Nonconformist minister and coincidentally a friend of Dr. Jennings's. Besides *Divine Songs Attempted in Easy Language for the Use of Children*

(1715), one of the first books of English poetry written specifically for children, Watts had written *Hymns and Spiritual Songs* (1707), now regarded as the foundation of English hymnody. Some of the hymns in this collection, such as "Our God, Our Help in Ages Past" and "When I Survey the Wondrous Cross," are still sung today.

Like every innovative hymn writer, Watts felt that the available church music was inadequate. The prevailing belief that only adaptations of Psalms were appropriate for congregational singing was severely limiting. Watts wanted to write songs that used "the common sense and language of a Christian." Yet he was aware that such writing could become trite. It was difficult, he admitted, "to sink every line to the level of a whole congregation, and yet to keep it above contempt."

Newton's home education was not unusual at the time—Watts learned Latin at four and Greek at nine—but it may have made him more reflective and bookish than other children in Wapping. This introspection would have been intensified by the teachings of the catechism and the poems of Watts both of which encouraged self-examination. In later life he described his boyhood self as "sedentary," "not active," and "not playful." He found his pleasure in reading, watching, and thinking. "I had little inclination," he once said, "to the noisy sports of children."

In 1732, not long before his seventh birthday, his mother developed tuberculosis (then called consumption), one of the most potent diseases affecting Londoners. The airborne bacilli spread quickly in unventilated homes and there was no medical cure. Unable to care for herself, she was taken to the home of a long-standing friend, Elizabeth Catlett, and her husband, George, who lived in Chatham, Kent. The Catletts had two children, Mary, aged three, and John, aged one, and the mothers had a private joke that their firstborn, separated by only four years, might one day become husband and wife.

At the Catlett home, the ailing Elizabeth Newton would have been put to bed in a room with all the windows and cracks sealed to prevent the feared disease from spreading. She may even have been given a twice-daily spoonful of a broth made from snails, hyssop, and sugar, as recommended by Hannah Woolley's book of home hints *The Queen-Like Closet*. But nothing worked. On July 11, 1732, she died.

With no relations nearby, the effect on the already sensitive New-ton must have been traumatic. His father continued to be away for long periods; and after not very long as a widower he got remarried to a woman known only as Thomasina, moved to Aveley in Essex, and started a second family. During this time Newton was sent for two years to a boarding school near Stratford, also in Essex. It was to be the unhappiest period of his life so far. The gentle, loving instruction of his mother was replaced by the "imprudent severity" of a schoolmas-ter who ended up breaking not only his spirit but his love for books. His memory began to fail him. He forgot the basic rules of arithmetic and felt that he had been turned into a "dolt."

Partial relief came in his second year through the teaching of a new master who "observed and suited my temper." Aware of Newton's sen-sitive nature, this teacher began to develop his new pupil's apprecia-tion of language and literature, introducing him to the prose of Cicero and the poetry of Virgil, both of which were taught in Latin. School hol-idays were spent in Aveley with his new stepmother and here he was now "permitted to mingle with careless and profane children, and soon began to learn their ways."

This distaste reflected the religious values he had absorbed from his mother. According to Isaac Watts's catechism, profanity was "Abusing or despising anything that is holy or that belongs to God." This meant not only blasphemous talk but not keeping the Sabbath special or mocking the Christian faith, a teaching that would have a profound effect on Newton later in life by shaping his idea of sinful behavior.

There were few occupations less suited for such a mild-mannered boy than that of a sailor, but there were no alternatives open to him when he left school, and so he went to sea with his father. "The day I was eleven years old," he told his first biographer, Richard Cecil, "I went on board my father's ship in Longreach [an area of the Thames close to Purfleet, Essex]."

The book of Mediterranean passes kept at London's Public Record Office confirms this. On July 22, 1736, his father came to London to register his forthcoming journey on the *Valentia Pacquet* with a crew of twenty. The return date, added in the right-hand margin, was October

6, 1738. Assuming that Newton didn't return on another ship this means that he would have been thirteen years old before he saw England again.

Being on a relatively small ship and sharing the captain's cabin softened the impact of the transition from land to sea, from school to ship, but his father remained a remote figure to him. Newton praised his "remarkable good sense" and "great knowledge of the world" but added that he had "an air of distance and severity in his carriage which overawed and discouraged my spirit. I was always in fear before him. . . ."

Newton's feelings about religion were now becoming confused. During several voyages with his father he swung between intense religiosity and utter lack of interest. When he became devout it was usually as a reaction to a period of excess. He would try to win back God's approval by showing that he could control his appetites. When the self-discipline lapsed, as it inevitably did, he would feel guilt, then fear, and the cycle would begin again.

Brushes with death had a temporarily sobering effect on him. Once he was dramatically thrown from a horse and landed perilously close to a row of sharpened stakes in a hedgerow. The escape led to a reorganization of his life, and yet, "it wasn't long before I declined again. These struggles between sin and conscience were often repeated, and every relapse sank me into still greater depths of wickedness."

Another time he and a friend had been promised a guided tour of a warship moored in the Thames near Purfleet. Newton arrived late to meet the tender that would take them across the river. It wasn't there and he cursed himself for his poor timekeeping, but as he drew closer to the water's edge he realized that the boat, which had already collected his friend and some other boys, had overturned, and all its passengers had drowned.

As with the riding accident, his immediate feeling was relief followed by the sense that God must be protecting him in a special way. Maybe he had been chosen for an important mission. These thoughts, and the sight of his friend's grieving family at the funeral, chastened him. But, he later commented, "this likewise was soon forgotten."

Specific books at times had a similar effect. *The Family Instructor,* written by Daniel Defoe in 1715 with the aim of improving behavior, made him "see the necessity of religion as a means of escaping hell," he wrote, "but I loved sin, and was unwilling to forsake it." *The Christian Oratory* by Benjamin Bennett reached even deeper. After reading it he began to study the Bible, keep a journal detailing his spiritual development, and arrange a disciplined prayer life. But this, too, eventually "passed away like a morning cloud."

The most deep-seated change lasted for two years. He became a ship-bound ascetic. He prayed, meditated, and read the Bible for what he said was "the greatest part of every day," turned vegetarian, went on fasts, and avoided all conversation so that he wouldn't be guilty of saying anything foolish or sinful. Abstinence made him feel extremely religious but it didn't bring love, joy, and peace. "It was poor religion," said Newton. "It left me, in many respects, under the power of sin. It tended to make me gloomy, stupid, unsociable, and useless."

Then, at the age of seventeen, while anchored outside the Dutch port of Middleburg, he picked up a book that was to have a decisive effect on his life, breaking the cycle of indulgence and asceticism. The book was Volume II of the Third Earl of Shaftesbury's *Characteristicks*, a collection of philosophical essays first published in 1711. Shaftesbury, not to be confused with his evangelical descendent the Seventh Earl of Shaftesbury, had been educated under the supervision of the English empirical philosopher John Locke and later became his patron.

For a short period during the first half of the eighteenth century, Shaftesbury's ideas were fashionable because he questioned church teachings and mocked religious "enthusiasts," as the devout were called. He wasn't an athiest but a deist, accepting the possibility of God's existence but discounting most Christian teachings. In particular he attacked the commonly held belief that high moral standards or "virtue" depended on the Christian faith. He was in turn attacked by the church. William Warburton, bishop of Bristol, reported that "Mr. (Alexander) Pope told me that, to his knowledge, the *Characteristicks* had done more harm to Revealed Religion in England than all the works of Infidelity put together."

For Newton, who had read very little philosophy or theology, the idea that it was possible to believe in God and live a virtuous life without being guided by the teachings of Jesus seemed liberating. *Characteristicks* discussed "piety" and "true religion" but drew unexpected conclusions. It argued that true morality must be rooted in human instinct rather than divine laws. Doing the right thing through fear of God's punishment was selfishness not righteousness, because the motivation was self-preservation rather than love.

This small palm-sized book became Newton's new catechism. He carried it with him at all times and almost learned by heart the second section, a 178-page "philosophical rhapsody." He felt released from the demands of orthodox faith but without the attendant fear of judgment. Understanding Shaftesbury's lofty ideas made him feel superior to those who meekly accepted the teachings of the church.

He wasn't in love with seafaring life but without a trade or an appetite for business he had no option but to keep sailing. His father was concerned about his lack of ambition, so to develop his self-reliance, found him work with a merchant friend in Alicante, a port on the southeastern coast of Spain. Newton, however, couldn't stomach the discipline. He showed, as he later put it, "unsettled behaviour" and "impatience of restraint" and was sent home.

These character traits were the cause of all his early problems. He resisted organization, bristled at discipline, and was only truly happy when left to his own devices. Poor working relationships, antisocial behavior and broken contracts were the result. As he summarized it himself when older, "I was fond of a visionary, contemplative life, a medley of religion, philosophy and indolence; and was quite averse to the thought of industrious application to business."

When Captain Newton retired from the sea in order to spend time with his second family, the need to settle his son became urgent. He turned to a friend, Joseph Manesty, who like him had been a captain but was now a successful merchant and shipowner in Liverpool. Manesty had some interests in the Caribbean, possibly part ownership of a plantation, and offered Captain Newton a job in Jamaica for his recalcitrant son. The placement would last for five years and his ship would be leaving Liverpool in December 1742.

It was a good offer for someone yet to prove himself. Newton would be twenty-two by the time he returned and would have enough money saved to marry comfortably. There was also the opportunity to vindicate himself in the eyes of his father, to prove that he had matured out of his early fecklessness. But the path to a settled life was to be a lot more circuitous than he could ever have anticipated.

Unexpectedly, an invite came asking him to visit the Catlett family in Chatham. Under normal circumstances, he would have politely declined because, although the Catletts had cared for his mother when she was dying, there had been no contact since. But it came just as he was about to deliver a package to an uncle in nearby Maidstone. To return home via Chatham wouldn't involve a detour.

On December 12, 1742, he arrived at the Catlett home and was welcomed by George and Elizabeth and their three older children. Mary—sometimes known as Polly—was now a vivacious fourteen-year-old with a talent for putting others at ease. Newton never described her physically and rarely referred to her character, but whatever it was that she had, it held him in thrall. When she was in the room he couldn't keep his eyes from her. When she left, he couldn't stop wondering where she was. On the spur of the moment he decided not to go to Liverpool to join Manesty's ship bound for Jamaica but to remain in Chatham and bask in the presence of Mary. It would be three weeks before he packed his bags and returned to Aveley to face his father.

He expected a severe talking-to for breaking his promise to Joseph Manesty, but his father surprised him by being understanding and patient, even going so far as to find him work on a merchant ship trading in the Mediterranean. This time though he wouldn't be able to take refuge in the captain's cabin. He was out on his own for the first time, working alongside the world-weary sailors who would have little time for his interests in Virgil and mathematics. Samuel Johnson's comment on life at sea during this period was "No man will be a sailor who has a contrivance enough to get himself into jail; for being in a ship is being in a jail, with the chance of being drowned." A contemporary proverb said much the same thing: "He who would go to sea for pleasure, would go to hell for a pastime."

It was during this trip that he had his dream of the gold ring being offered him in Venice. It could have resulted from a vivid imagination collaborating with a disturbed conscience, or it could have been as he later thought, a spiritual intervention. Newton was to attach significance to dreams, believing that just as God spoke to Joseph and Jacob as they slept, he could so speak today. In a song entitled "On Dreaming" he wrote the following lines:

> But though our dreams are often wild,
> Like clouds before the driving storm;
> Yet some important may be styl'd,
> Sent to admonish or inform.

"However, though I saw not these things, I found the benefit," he said of his Venetian dream. "I obtained the mercy."

This Mediterranean voyage ended on November 10, 1743. Newton disappointed his father yet again by going directly from the dock at Rochester to see Mary rather than returning home. His last visit to the Catletts had changed the course of his life by nixing his Caribbean adventure, and this visit would alter it in yet another way.

For such a major event, Newton was surprisingly brief when dealing with it in his autobiography, saying only, "Before anything suitable was offered again, I was pressured, owing entirely to my own thoughtless conduct, which was all of a piece, and put on board a tender." Chatham was close to the River Medway, and fleets of the Royal Navy often anchored in the river mouth off the coast of Sheerness. Small boats with press-gangs would go out to the local towns to forcibly enlist men into the navy, preferably men with seafaring experience. In February 1744, Newton was one of those unfortunate men.

He didn't specify his "thoughtless conduct." It could have been the mistake of staying in an area known to be popular with press-gangs. It could have been his unguardedness when out and about—his clothes and gait signaling his being a sailor. One of the most familiar pressing techniques was to get men drunk in public houses and then arrest them when they were incapable of resisting. Was Newton tricked in this way?

The gang that arrested him was led by First Lieutenant Thomas Ruffin, sent out from HMS *Harwich* by its captain, Philip Carteret. During a three-week trawl of Medway towns on the tender *Besty*, 8 men were collected for the newly built 976-ton warship, bringing its crew numbers up to 350. England and France were on the verge of war, and the navy needed experienced sailors.

Newton's prospects were bleak. There had been no time for farewells and the length of his service would be indefinite. The Admiralty could dispatch the *Harwich* anywhere at a moment's notice. In desperation he wrote to his father, now land-based as an agent for the Royal African Company, the Crown-chartered organization guaranteed a monopoly of British trade with Africa, to ask if he could get him out or at least have him transferred to a merchant ship. Although he was in regular contact with the Admiralty by post, Captain Newton's influence wasn't that great. The fragile situation between England and France didn't allow for favors. The best that he could sort out was promotion to the quarterdeck as one of ten midshipmen.

When war did break out the *Harwich* was assigned to protect convoys in the English Channel. She traveled up to Scotland and across the North Sea to Ostend in Belgium, Gothenburg in Sweden, and Helsingor in Denmark. The conflict didn't directly affect Newton until September 1744, when the *Harwich* opened fire on the French ship *Solide* and captured her after a two-hour battle. The sails and rigging of the *Harwich* were damaged and one of its crew was killed, but seven of the *Solide*'s men died and twenty were seriously injured, including the captain, who lost a leg. The rest of the French crew were taken as prisoners of war.

Newton made two close friends on the quarterdeck. Job Lewis, a quiet youth, had a simple Christian faith, but the other sailor, whom Newton didn't name, considered Christianity to be no more than an enduring superstition. As a "freethinker" he was familiar with *Characteristicks* but thought that Newton had misunderstood Shaftesbury. Slowly and yet meticulously he began to work away at Newton's residual Christian beliefs.

Some biographies have identified this man as James Mitchell,

Captain Carteret's clerk, but Mitchell's private journal, unknown to any of them, shows this to be unlikely. In contrast to Shaftesbury, Mitchell saw a connection between moral behavior and religious belief. After a violent storm the sailors became conscious of their mortality and arranged a thanksgiving service. But, Mitchell noted, "as soon as the service was over and the danger past, the impression was entirely effaced and the crew proceeded to get drunk, swear and to [perform] every act of impiety as formerly." He called them "ungrateful, unthinking creatures" and bemoaned the fact that "they seem only to have a notion of a Superior Power while danger is impending."

The freethinker, whoever he was, who tried to remove the remaining fragments of faith from Newton, felt that he was mistakenly creating an unsustainable synthesis of Shaftesbury's deistic ideas and New Testament Christianity, and like the shadowy accuser in the dream of the gold ring he persuaded him to give up. Many years later, in a letter to Mary, Newton referred to this person as "a shrewd man who robbed me of my principles and poisoned me with infidelity."

Before encountering Shaftesbury's work he would probably have sympathized with Job Lewis's sincerely held but untested faith, because it must have been so much like his own when younger. But now, emboldened by his newfound secular beliefs, he dished out ridicule. Lewis would eventually abandon his faith and the knowledge of this would always haunt Newton. When he composed his epitaph, he mentioned Christianity as the faith "he had long laboured to destroy," and Job Lewis was his first victim.

The *Harwich* had a chaplain, Robert Topham, but neither Newton nor Mitchell ever mentioned him. From the little that's said of him in official records he seems to have been a man of the cloth who was better known for his comfortable and indulgent lifestyle than for his dynamic faith. When he first came to the ship, he complained to Captain Carteret about the size of his cabin. He expected something larger and more luxurious than he had been allocated. Later in the voyage he had to be disciplined for drunkenness.

On December 5, 1744, while anchored off the town of Deal on the southeast coast of England, the *Harwich* had instructions to sail. The mission was to accompany a convoy of Royal African Company ships to Gambia and then go on to India with ships from the East India Company. The journey, including a long stay in India, would last just over five years. The agent responsible for preparing the Royal African Company ships and liaising with the Royal Navy fleet happened to be Captain Newton.

Newton, Jr., who was expecting to be away a maximum of twelve months, was alarmed by news of the five-year journey. At the earliest opportunity he took shore leave and rode to Chatham, hardly able to believe that he might not see Mary again until she was twenty-one. He should have returned to the ship within twenty-four hours, but, in a repeat of his earlier behavior, extended it to several days, not returning until New Year's Day, 1745. "This rash step," he admitted, "especially as it was not the first liberty I had taken, highly displeased [Captain Carteret], and lost me his favour, which I never recovered."

Three weeks later, at one o'clock in the morning while performing a watch, he wrote a letter to Mary, encapsulating the turbulent feelings he felt unable to express in person.

There is I know not what within me, that bears me up, and assures me that I shall certainly come home again; but whether it will be to any purpose; whether I shall be happy in you, or no, is what I long to know, yet should dread to be resolved in. I will not mortify myself to think I shall return to find you in another's possession, before I have an opportunity of showing what I could do to deserve you. . . . The first day I saw you I began to love you. The thoughts of one day meriting you (and I believe nothing less could have done it) roused me from a dull insensible melancholy I had contracted, and pushed me into the world. Had it not been for you, I had till this time remained heavy, sour, and unsociable.

It is now more than two years since, from which time till now I have been almost continually disappointed in whatever I have undertaken. My designs are now bent to one point that is this voyage, which I seriously believe will either make or mar me. It's true I hope to succeed; but I take Love to witness, it is not wholly on my own account for I shall not value riches but for the opportunity of laying them at your feet, and if deprived of that I can be indifferent to the other; for I am certain could enjoy them with no relish without you. . . .

Your most devoted admirer,

John Newton.

Captain Newton had been lodging at a house in East Street, Portsmouth Point, Devon, since October, when his five Royal African Company ships—the *Loyal Judith, Katherine, Happy Deliverance, Expedition,* and *Cape Coast*—arrived from Deal. His responsibility was ensuring that they were fully manned, loaded, stocked with provisions, and ready to be escorted under the protection of the naval fleet. He wrote regularly to Thomas Corbett at the Admiralty in London and to Captain Patrick O'Hara, whose ship, HMS *Gosport,* would be in charge of the Royal African Company ships once they set sail.

The fleet that was being assembled off the south coast of England was huge, made up of 116 warships, merchant ships, and store ships. It was to leave from Portsmouth Sound before dividing up for Newfoundland, Lisbon, India, and Africa. Bad weather had hindered them. Captain Newton had to organize repairs, and then one of his captains fell ill and needed to be replaced. Once these problems were resolved several sailors deserted the *Katherine,* and on January 15, 1744, Captain Newton wrote to the Admiralty requesting six sailors from the navy, eventually being given four from HMS *Gosport.*

In February the cold weather brought heavy sleet and snow. On February 27, 1745, while the fleet was anchored in Torbay, a hurricane struck, forcing many of the ships to cut their anchor cables. "Much confusion ensued from such a numerous fleet turning out of the bay," wrote Mitchell in his journal. "A storeship for Gibraltar and a ship for Mahon were stranded on the rocks and most of the crews perished. Two vessels were run abroad and dismasted and the *Royal George* lost her bowsprit and returned to Spithead to refit."

The *Tiger,* a troop ship bound for the West Indies carrying 170 soldiers recruited from Devon and Cornwall, was hurled onto the rocks at

Berry Head near Brixham, killing everyone on board. Three of Captain Newton's ships—*Expedition*, *Cape Coast*, and *Katherine*—were badly damaged and couldn't be repaired immediately. Two days later HMS *Winchester* was driven into the path of HMS *Ipswich*, breaking off its foremast and killing twenty-eight of its sailors who were furling the foretopsail.

To prevent further damage and loss of life, Rear Admiral Henry Medley, who was on the *Ipswich*, ordered the fleet into the protected waters of Plymouth Sound, where Newton learned for the first time of his father's role and that he was on his way to Brixham from Portsmouth to attend to the damaged ships.

Since his father was now in communication with high-ranking officers in the fleet, it occurred to Newton that he might be able to arrange a transfer from the *Harwich* to one of the Royal African Company ships. There wasn't time to send him a letter, so it would have to be discussed in person. He took his opportunity when escorting sailors to Plymouth. Instead of looking after them on shore, as he'd been charged, he himself deserted, taking off on foot. He wasn't sure that he was on the right road to Brixham but obviously couldn't ask for directions, and it might have been this hesitancy that revealed him as a deserter. A group of soldiers noticed him, and he was arrested, taken back to Plymouth, and put in a prison cell for the night. Desertion, especially during war, was a serious offense.

Newton was returned to the *Harwich* in chains, tied to a grating, and flogged in front of the whole crew. A flogging like this wasn't unusual. A diary kept by George Ratcliffe, an able seaman on the *Harwich*, refers to several floggings that took place later in the journey. For abusing a boatswain's mate, James Wood and James Casberry were given a dozen lashes each. For abusing an officer, John Welch was court-martialed and given forty lashes plus a further twenty lashes in front of each of the other navy ships in the area.

Ratcliffe didn't begin his journal until the *Harwich* sailed, and so Newton's punishment isn't mentioned. He was probably given twelve lashes, the maximum allowed to be ordered by a captain without a court-martial, and more than enough to severely lacerate his skin. To avoid infection, salt water would have been poured on the wounds by the ship's surgeon and he would have been swathed in white bandages before being carried down to his hammock.

To literally add insult to injury, he was demoted from the quarter-deck. This marked an end to his fine conversations about theology, philosophy, and morals and also an end to the comparative comfort of living alongside the ship's officers. All midshipmen were instructed not to speak to him.

On April 14, 1745, the fleet finally set sail from Plymouth Sound. The next day, turning away from Lizard Point in Cornwall, the sailors had their last glimpse of the English coastline. James Mitchell wrote in his journal: "A pleasant gale across the bay. Nothing else remarkable." John Newton, reflecting on the same day many years later, wrote: "I cannot express with what wishfulness and regret I cast my last look upon the English shore. I kept my eyes fixed upon it till it disappeared. When I could see it no longer, I was tempted to throw myself into the sea. According to the wicked system I had adopted, this would put a period to all my sorrows at once. But the secret hand of God restrained me."

Map of the "Guinea Coast" as it was then known, used in the
second edition of Newton's autobiography. Plantain Island
(here called Planting Island) is just below Yawry Bay.

Chapter 2

CAPTIVE IN AFRICA

I must say the life of a seaman is no ways agreeable to a
man of quiet disposition, but he that is wild and rakishly
inclined, turbulent in his manners and loves liquor and
bad company, shall very often have the upper
hand in a ship's crew.
—*Nicholas Owen*, JOURNAL OF A SLAVE DEALER, 1755

. . . To spots remote and corners of the isle
By the seaside, and draw his diagrams
With a long stick upon the sand, and thus
Did often beguile his sorrow, and almost
Forget his feeling . . .
—*William Wordsworth*, THE PRELUDE, 1805

The dreary coast of Africa was the university to which
the Lord was pleased to send me, and I dare
not acknowledge a relation to any other.
—*John Newton*, IN A LETTER TO "D. W.," 1793

*T*he further south the Harwich sailed, the deeper Newton
sank into gloom. Although forbidden to communicate with him, the officers from the quarterdeck had shielded him from ill treatment, but as
time passed so did their concern. Captain Carteret, responsible for
promoting him to the quarterdeck after Captain Newton had inter-
ceded, felt bitter that his trust had been betrayed and pointedly showed
his resentment.

Yet far from seeing his fall as a natural consequence of his impulsive behavior, Newton felt that he was a victim of injustice. He contemplated suicide, restrained only by his feelings for Mary and the thought that if he ended his life he wouldn't be able to take revenge on Captain Carteret, whom he claimed he seriously thought of murdering. This cocktail of love and hate gave him the will to live. "I think nothing I either felt or feared distressed me so much as to see myself thus forcibly torn away from the object of my affections under a great improbability of seeing her again, and a much greater [improbability] of returning in such a manner as would give me hopes of seeing her mine."

Freethinking had freed him from the worry of divine retribution. Without heaven or hell, death was mere extinction. There was nothing to fear either from suicide or capital punishment. "My love was now the only restraint I had left. . . . This single thought, which had not restrained me from a thousand smaller evils, proved my only and effectual barrier against the greatest and most fatal temptations."

Life on board the *Harwich,* as on any other warship, depended on rank. For James Mitchell, Captain Carteret's clerk, it provided an illuminating and cultivating experience. He had the time to marvel at cloud formations and identify species of flying fish. There was even time for fun, games, and dancing. One entry in his journal records: "Engaged in a variety of amusements [by day] such as Storm the Castle, The Miller, King Arthur, The Judge, A Rude Harlequin and Cudgels. At night singing, telling humorous stories—many of them indelicate or laughable—or [stories about] feats of heroism."

George Ratcliffe, serving belowdecks with Newton, never commented on the flying fish or the games. Life for the lowest-ranking sailors was tedious and often brutal. He mentioned a sailor being whipped for "striving to commit sodomy with ye carpenters boy." Two days later the same man had to "run ye gauntlet for striving to commit sodomy with a black man. He run three times round ye lower deck. Peter de Cruse, a black Portigee, had ye same punishment for committing sodomy with a sheep."

The demoted Newton had to live in these conditions. "I was as miserable on all hands as could well be imagined. My breast was filled with the most excruciating passions, eager desire, bitter rage, and black despair. Every hour exposed me to some new insult and hardship, with no hope of relief or mitigation, no friend to take my part or to listen to my complaint."

On April 27, the *Harwich*, along with the *Winchester, Scarborough, Lincoln, Kent*, and *Admiral Vernon*, reached Madeira, a Portuguese island colony to the west of Morocco, and dropped anchor outside the capital of Funchal. It was the only port of call before Africa, and the main tasks were to take on board water, wine, and wood and to make minor repairs.

James Mitchell went ashore to explore, commenting on the variety of wines and fruits and complaining about the quality of the meat. He found the streets of Funchal "narrow and dirty" and the many churches too plain for his taste, although he was intrigued by a visit to a convent where the nuns tried to sell him baskets of artificial flowers and where human skulls and bones decorated the walls and ceiling of the chapel.

Six days after arriving at Madeira, Newton was sleeping late when one of his old companions from the quarterdeck paid him a visit. Realizing that he wasn't yet awake the friend played a prank on him by slashing the rope of his hammock with a knife. He woke as he crashed to the deck. "I was very angry," said Newton with typical understatement, "but dared not resent it."

Reluctantly he dressed and followed his friend up to the main deck, where he noticed a sailor preparing to leave the *Harwich* on a tender. Inquiring why this man was leaving he was told that two merchant seamen had been taken from an English ship anchored nearby in exchange for two of the *Harwich*'s men. This was accepted practice. Life with the Royal Navy was tougher and more disciplined, and so the captains of merchant ships gladly exchanged their unruly crew members.

As Newton recorded it, his heart "instantly burned like fire" when he heard this. He wanted to be the second man to leave the *Harwich* and begged the lieutenant on duty to choose him. There was no good reason for him to be released from service on the *Harwich* but it must have been reckoned that the ship was better off without him, because, after consultation with Captain Carteret, he was discharged. "Though I had been formerly upon ill terms with these officers, and had disobliged them all in their turns, yet they had pitied my case, and were ready to serve me now. . . . In little more than half an hour from my being asleep in my bed I saw myself discharged, and safe on board another ship."

The *Harwich*'s muster confirms Newton's story. On May 3, 1745, while the ship was anchored at the Funchal Road off the coast of Madeira, William Langworthy and John Newton were discharged, and on the same day Archibald Farley and Francis Viera entered service "in lieu," from an unnamed merchant ship.

For Newton the best thing about life on the smaller ship, which was bound for Sierra Leone to buy slaves, was the relief from the hardships of the *Harwich*. What he didn't anticipate was that it was to take him to a place where he would be plunged even further into despair before rising again to joy. "This was one of the many critical turns of my life in which the Lord was pleased to display His providence and care by causing many unexpected circumstances to concur in almost an instant of time," he would reflect when older. "These sudden opportunities were several times repeated; each of them brought me into an entirely new scene of action, and they were usually delayed to almost the last moment in which they could take place."

The name of the ship was omitted by Newton, who said only that it was English and was collecting slaves from the Guinea Coast for sale in the West Indies, and that the captain died before it left Africa. The one ship fitting this description recorded in both the Mediterranean Pass book and the Port Entry book for Jamaica is the *Levant*, a two-hundred-ton ship that left Bristol for Africa in March 1745 under the captaincy of James Phelps and arrived in Jamaica under the captaincy of William Miller in March 1746.

The captain, who apparently knew his father, showed his friendship toward Newton by making him a steward even though the sailor he was replacing had worked on the foremast. Even in his absence, Captain Newton's influence was making life smoother. Yet despite this good fortune, despite being received, in his own words, "very kindly," he had an impulse to spoil things. He needed to create danger and conflict.

He later said that during this period he was "exceedingly vile" but never expanded. This may either have been to protect the sensitivities of the Christian audience likely to read his autobiography or because his conscience grew more tender when he was older. His lack of specific examples of vileness caused some Victorian commentators to assume that he exaggerated his wickedness. Sir James Stephen, writing about Newton in 1860, said, "His mistake was that of transferring to the press the language of the oratory."

The sins he mentioned most frequently were blasphemy and defiance of authority. On this ship he not only refused duties but made up insulting songs about the captain, which he then taught the rest of the crew. The captain heard them and, as Newton put it, "was no stranger either to the intention or the author." He was honing his attacks on the Christian faith. In a letter written in 1754 he said that before he had "reached the age of twenty" (he turned twenty while serving on this ship) he was never an hour in anyone's company "without attempting to corrupt them."

He may have used slave girls for sex. He never said so, but he planted hints. Describing his moral condition at the time, he referred to the words of the apostle Peter: "With eyes full of adultery, they never stopped sinning; they seduce the unstable; they are experts in greed—an unstable brood" (2 Peter 2:14). Elsewhere he wrote of the lusts of sailors as they leered at the young female slaves. "In imagination, the prey is divided upon the spot, and only reserved till opportunity offers. Where resistance, or refusal, would be utterly in vain, even the solicitation of consent is seldom thought of." He told Dr. David Jennings, his childhood pastor, that he had been "a slave to every customary vice"—a strange choice of phrase if his sins were confined to bad language and disobedience.

The ship spent six months sailing down the African coast before she was fully slaved. Then, while anchored off the coast of Banana Island ready to leave for Jamaica, the captain died. Newton panicked because the first mate, who now took command, resented him even more than the captain had. He was sure that he would get rid of him to the Royal Navy at the earliest opportunity. This outcome, "was more dreadful to me than death."

An easier solution presented itself suitable to both parties. Leaving the ship at Banana Island was a resident English trader with a financial stake in the voyage and it was agreed that Newton could continue his service for the company by working in Africa for this man. Most slave ventures were funded by groups of merchants whose partnerships were dissolved after the profits had been shared. The 1745 trip of the *Levant*, for example, was invested in by a group of eight, two of whom, James Laroche and Isaac Hobhouse, were prominent Bristol merchants.

It increasingly made sense for British shipowners to have representatives in Africa who could buy slaves inland and keep them in pens ready for collection. This reduced the length of time ships needed to spend on the African coast. The *Levant*, which managed to complete the triangular journey in a year (England–Africa–Jamaica–England), arrived in the Caribbean with 410 slaves, a good tally for any ship.

The trader impressed Newton. He was powerful, wealthy, and independent. There was no boss breathing down his neck. He lived with an African woman and was about to establish himself off the coast of Sierra Leone on Plantain Island. Inspired by his example, Newton fancied he could become a successful slave trader, eventually able to redeem himself in the eyes of his father and return to England with enough money to marry Mary.

Despite its prime location, when Newton and this unnamed master arrived on Plantain Island, at the end of 1745, it was home to only one other trader. Two miles out at sea, surrounded by shallow water ideal for anchorage, it was accessible to shallops bringing slaves down the nearby rivers and clearly visible to European ships plying the coast for business. It was also secure. The only way to escape was to commandeer a boat, but the reefs were only safely navigable by experienced sailors.

It wasn't picturesque. There were no hills, rivers, waterfalls, or startling vistas. There was a natural cove facing northeast, with a sloping beach, and trees that acted as breakers against the fierce winds. Newton described it as "a low sandy island, about two miles in circumference, and almost covered with palm trees," and Nicholas Owen, an Irish trader who visited seven years later, said, "It has very little produce of anything but rice. It has a good harbour for vessels and a considerable trade with shipping."

Newton and his master began by building accommodations of sticks and mud with a thatched roof. Presuming that they followed the popular European style they would have built a separate cook room and storehouse behind the main building, and then surrounded it with a garden of pumpkins, watermelons, and pigeon peas.

Time on the island was spent planting, buying goods from local traders, and selling slaves to passing ships. Newton enjoyed the life and seemed to hit it off with the man, who welcomed the companionship of a fellow Englishman. However, to his African mistress Newton was an intrusion, and she was immediately "strangely prejudiced" against him for reasons that were never explained.

Known as P. I. (her name sounded like the two letters pronounced separately) she was a Bullom from the ruling Bombo family. The French captain Jean Barbot who traveled to Sierra Leone during this time mentioned meeting a Bullom king, Antonio Bombo, a convert of Portuguese missionaries who favored "the English more than either the Portuguese, French or Dutch." This may have been the father of P. I., because Newton claimed that the trader owed his success to her connections. Elsewhere he mentioned that her brother, Sury Bombo, was a slave dealer. Nicholas Owen drew a picture in his journal of "Surry, King of Sherbrow" who could have been the same person.

Resident English traders often took African mistresses. If these were from local royalty, it had the bonus of increasing their influence in the region. The male mulatto children from such liaisons often became powerful middlemen in the slave trade, doing business with both native kidnappers and British captains. It was an advantage to speak at least two languages, and some were even given a privileged English education. The Caulker family, who controlled land around the Sherbro River close to Plantain Island, were descended from Thomas Corker of Falmouth, one of the earliest agents sent from England on behalf of the Royal African Company. Even today members of the Caulker family have local power in parts of the Sherbro region.

The relationship between P. I. and Newton deteriorated. Newton was to go with his master in the shallop on a slave-gathering trip up the Rio Nuñez but fell ill and had to remain at Plantain Island for several weeks. He had almost certainly contracted malaria, but the disease had only recently been named, and it was common to refer to it simply as the "fever." He would have suffered from chills, headaches, convulsions, muscle pains, nausea, vomiting, diarrhea, and delirium. It was the biggest killer of sailors traveling to Africa and of whites involved in the slave trade.

At first P. I. showed concern, but when his health didn't improve she began to ignore him, not even bothering to feed him properly or supply him with water. When she deigned to give him something, it was the scraps left on her plate. "So greatly was my pride humbled," he wrote, "I received this with thanks and eagerness, as the most needy beggar does an alms."

P. I. lived in style, eating off china and with the latest in European luxuries provided by the captains of visiting ships, her slaves attending to her every need, while Newton had to sleep on a straw mat spread on a board with a rough log sufficing as a pillow. Once she called him in to eat some of her food. He was so weak from fever that it took all his strength to walk unaided to her table. She handed him a meal but he wasn't strong enough to take it, and so the plate slipped from his fingers and fell to the floor. P. I. shrieked with laughter at his feeble attempts to feed himself and let him go hungry.

There was a calculated cruelty in the way that she played on his weakness and vulnerability. Sometimes her attacks were simply verbal, telling him how worthless and lazy he was, but at other times they were physical. She commanded him to get up from his mat and walk, knowing that he could barely stand, and then got her slaves to mimic his faltering steps. She would ask them to throw rocks and rotten fruit at him, punishing them if they disobeyed. Secretly some of them pitied him because they realized that his fate was now worse than theirs.

The loss of dignity he felt would have been acute. Africans were regarded as uncultured, ignorant, lazy, and brutish. Additionally, women were meant to be subservient to men and not challenge their decisions. For an Englishman to be treated in this way by an African woman seemed an offense against natural law. In a letter to Mary he spoke of having to live in an almost naked state, with heat blisters covering his skin, and "where sometimes I have not had half a good meal in the course of a month."

When P. I. wasn't around some of the slaves would pass him morsels from their own meals. At night he would crawl from his hut and tear at cassava roots, which he would then wash in the sea and eat uncooked. Cassava roots made a good meal when boiled or roasted but, as Newton discovered, "were as unfit to be eaten raw in any quantity as a potato."

Plantain Island was to provide the reference point against which he would always measure his spiritual and social progress. If he was ever tempted to feel proud of his natural abilities or his moral caliber, he would think back to the time when he was lower than the slaves. This was the state he had in mind when he referred to himself as a "wretch." To his friend William Bull he wrote in 1795, "It is a part of my daily employment to look back to Africa, and to retrace the path by which the Lord has led me, for about forty-seven years, since he called me from infidelity and madness." It was even mentioned in his will as "that state of misery on the coast of Africa into which my wickedness had plunged me." It was there in the epitaph he prepared for himself where he described himself as having been "a servant of slaves in Africa."

This wretchedness wasn't his fault. He was the victim of P. I.'s jealousy and vindictiveness, more sinned against than sinner. But Newton had a wider angle of vision. He saw that he had ended up in this predicament, just as the prodigal son had ended up feeding pigs, through a succession of wrong choices. If he had honored his agreement with Joseph Manesty, he would have avoided the press-gang. If he hadn't deserted from the *Harwich*, he would not have been demoted. If he hadn't caused dissension on the slave ship, he wouldn't have ended up on Plantain Island anxious to be a successful trader.

Newton was very sure about this chain of events. He never blamed anyone else for his plight. "When, after repeated checks of conscience, I obstinately broke through all restraints of religion, it pleased God for a time to give me up to my own willfulness and folly; perhaps as much so, as ever a poor creature was given up to himself, who did not finally perish. The way of transgressors is always hard. It proved so to me. The miseries into which I plunged myself, could only be exceeded by the dreadful wickedness of my heart and life. At length I was driven to the desperate determination of living upon the coast of Africa."

On Plantain Island it was as though his past had caught up with him. Anxious for wealth and glory he had ended up with poverty and squalor. For the first time his outward appearance matched the deterioration of his inner spirit. What better illustration of a wretch was there than a sunken-cheeked, bent, thin, disheveled, blistered, filthy, barefooted, half-naked man crawling across the sand of an African island in search of food and living in fear of punishment and ridicule? He had only one shirt, which he would wash on the rocks under cover of darkness and wear while he slept to dry it out. When ships visited he would hide himself inside the wood out of shame. Yet, in his estimation, his internal wretchedness was far worse. "My conduct, principles, and heart, were still darker than my outward condition."

In his later writing Newton implied that P. I., because of her connections with the local ruling family, was more powerful than the Englishman who was "much under [her] direction." This was why Newton got nowhere when he complained about P. I. to his master when he came back. "He could not believe me, and as I did it in her hearing, I fared no better for it."

His strength returned in time to take the next trip upriver. He began to get on well with his master until another trader lied about him, saying that while the master was on shore doing business Newton was helping himself to his goods on the shallop. The trader chose to believe this story and so he confined Newton to the shallop by chaining him to the deck and leaving him nothing but a pint of rice in a bowl until he came back.

Sometimes the trader was away for two days or more and Newton had to catch fish with an unbaited hook to supplement his rice diet. It was the start of the rainy season, and without covering he was exposed to the full brunt of the weather's extremes—blistering heat during the day with no shade to offer relief, violent storms at night with no protection from the cold and damp. His only clothes were his shirt, a pair of trousers, and a cotton handkerchief knotted to make a cap. The combination of sun, rain, and sudden drops in temperature broke his already weak constitution and further dimmed his spirit. He developed what appears to have been rheumatoid arthritis, pains that would stay with him for the rest of his life and that he would refer to as "a needful memento of the services and wages of sin."

Although Newton never identified the master who treated him this way, several recent biographers have called him Clow because later in his career he did deal with a trader named Mr. Clow who lived on Plantain Island and knew P. I. Based on the assumption that Clow must have been living there in 1746, he has become identified as the wicked trader who allowed Newton to be abused. In his magisterial study, *The Slave Trade*, historian Hugh Thomas even refers to P. I. as "Mrs. Clow."

A close reading of Newton's account doesn't support this. When he introduces Clow in his later journals there is no mention of any previous relationship, although when he writes of P. I., he pointedly refers to her as his "quondam black mistress." He also, tellingly, says of his master and P. I. in 1747 that "one of them at least" would live to see him return to Africa. As he saw P. I. again in 1750 it has to be deduced that his master was the one who didn't live.

The much maligned Patrick Clow—who Newton even referred to as "the only person whose word I can place any dependence on"—was a Scottish-born trader whose brother James Clow was a professor of philosophy at Glasgow University and would succeed Adam Smith, author of *The Wealth of Nations*, in the Chair of Logic. Patrick Clow dealt with Newton several times in the 1750s, appears to have left Africa by the end of that decade and died in London in 1763.

The abuse didn't end when Newton and the trader returned to Plantain Island. There were still no shoes or fresh clothes. The food he was served was given grudgingly, to fend off starvation but not to rebuild his wasted body. The only break in the routine came when he took himself off to a remote corner of the island with a copy of the only book he had with him, Barrow's translation of Euclid's classic of geometry, *Elements*, where he would copy enlarged versions of the diagrams in the sand with a stick. His description of this practice was later read with interest by the British poet William Wordsworth, who incorporated it into his *Prelude*.

To Mary and to his father he wrote letters that sympathetic slaves agreed to smuggle on board visiting English ships. To Mary he expressed his undying love and reminded her that the hope of them being reunited was all that was keeping him going during this time of suffering. His father he begged to use his influence to arrange a rescue. But there was no way of knowing whether the letters arrived on the ships bound for England or that, if they had, they had ended up in the right hands.

There was now little overt evidence of the arrogance and pride that had led him into so much trouble, but as he later acknowledged this was not because of a moral transformation, merely a lack of opportunity. In his beggarly condition, what did he have to be proud of? In this state of bondage, what would arrogance achieve? His apparent meekness was the result of a broken spirit rather than a renewed heart. "I was no further changed than a tiger tamed by hunger. Remove the occasion, and he will be as wild as ever."

*Newton's ship was beaten so badly by the waves that
the sails ripped and the timbers were pulled away.*

Chapter 3

MID-ATLANTIC CRISIS

Well, I heard that once he was kind of a wayward guy and
that he got sick and wrote that song on his death bed.
—*Ira Tucker*, DIXIE HUMMINGBIRDS, 2001

I once was lost, but now am found,
Was blind, but now I see.
—*John Newton*, "AMAZING GRACE," 1772

The coast of Guinea is a country from whose bourn few
travellers, who have once ventured to settle there, ever
return. But God, against whom I had sinned with a high
hand, was pleased to appoint me to be a singular instance
of his mercy. He not only spared me, but watched over me,
by his merciful providence, when I seemed to be bent upon
my own destruction, and provided for my
deliverance from my wretched thraldom.
—*John Newton*, LETTERS TO A WIFE, 1793

*N*ewton *lived in this way for almost a year until his*
master finally relented and released him to work with a fellow trader
based on Plantain Island. This man (could he have been Patrick Clow?)
ran several "factories," as the trading stations were known, in the
nearby Sherbro area, and "I was soon decently clothed, lived in plenty,
was considered as a companion, and trusted with the care of all his do-
mestic effects, to the amount in money of several thousand pounds."

He was then sent to join an Englishman running one of his factories on a peninsula bounded on one side by the Kittam River and on the other by the Atlantic. Their job was to sail upriver in a shallop to view slaves already captured by natives, buy them with goods from England, return to base with them in chains, and finally to sell them to slave ships. As a trader he had to assess the quality of the slaves and strike good deals with the natives.

In villages deep in the countryside he and his colleague would be entertained by the chiefs to whom they were valued clients, able to supply them with British luxury goods and weapons that would give them immediate superiority over their neighbors. The villagers lived in huts made of wood plastered over with mud and roofed with grass and leaves. The women washed, cooked, planted, reaped, and pounded the rice while the men sat at home smoking pipes or drinking palm wine.

Like many English travelers before him Newton developed an admiration for their way of life. Their local government seemed stable, they cared for their families, and they had rules to restrain them from acting in anger. They appeared to be peace loving and content people. Giving evidence of life in Africa in his old age he said: "The people at Sherbro are in a degree civilised, often friendly, and may be trusted where they have not been previously deceived by the Europeans. I have lived in peace and safety amongst them when I have been the only white man amongst them for a great distance."

Their religious beliefs intrigued him. They acknowledged a form of divinity but had no dogma. At the center of their religious practice were rituals to protect them from evil and deal with the spirits of the dead, who they believed controlled events. Inside small bags made of goat leather they kept their personal idols, which could be anything from a glass bottle to the bone of an alligator. In order to ward off bad spirits, and before making important decisions, they would always consult the spirits of their ancestors. To ensure good harvests and a safe life they offered wine and food to the new moon.

Away from England for almost two years, Newton was sufficiently destabilized to find himself "infatuated" with these beliefs, and he later felt that if he had stayed longer he might have "yielded to the whole." It's ironic that a man who had so recently rejected Christianity as superstition would be tempted by the idea of ancestral spirits and the power of fetishes. Stripped of his childhood beliefs and away from the support structures of British life, he was probably at his most impressionable. As G. K. Chesterton was to say many years later: "When a man ceases to believe in God, he doesn't believe in nothing. He believes in anything."

Newton may have taken short-term African "wives" during this period. He spoke of living as he pleased and said rather ambiguously that he had "entered into closer engagements with the inhabitants." As this statement was followed by an assurance that this didn't mean that he had put Mary out of his mind, he may well have been referring to sexual liaisons. "This is not a subject for declamation," he noted once after inferring that sailors routinely raped slaves. "Facts like these, so certain and so numerous, speak for themselves."

Europeans in Africa felt free from Western civilization's moral codes and welcomed the fact that African women didn't think it immoral to sleep with someone they might never see again. Another traveler to the Windward Coast during the eighteenth century was William Smith, who wrote in his account *New Voyage to Guinea*: "Tell the Guinea of chastity, and of living celibate, and he laughs at it as a chimera, and says that there is neither chastity or modesty in living the life of a monk or a nun, and that the religion which puts on nature such negatives is a religion unreasonable and unnatural. Chastity and modesty, he says, consists in refraining from women when they are pregnant and menstruous, and in not lying with women in the streets, or before another man."

As an esteemed guest Smith found that village chiefs would offer him the pick of their concubines. "This offer has often been made me, especially when I visited a king, for it is a compliment that is always paid a European." Of one such occasion he wrote: "At midnight we went to bed and in that situation I soon forgot the complexion of my bedfellow and obeyed the dictates of all-powerful nature. Greater pleasure I never found, and during my stay, if Paradise is to be found in the enjoyment of a woman, I was then in the possession of it."

By February 1747, Newton was extremely comfortable with his new life in Africa. The surroundings were amenable, he enjoyed being entrusted with important work, and for the first time he was getting

praised from an employer for doing a good job. He could visit the
beach and gaze at the ocean if he wanted, fish in the Kittam, or sit under the shade of the trees either rereading his Euclid, writing to Mary,
or meditating on the world.

Far from his thoughts were the pleading letters to his father, which
he'd slipped to the slaves on Plantain Island. He had long ago assumed
that either they hadn't made it across the ocean to Aveley or that he had
been taken at his word when he had told him "that I had resolved not
to return to England unless he was pleased to send for me." But at least
one of those letters had made it back home and Captain Newton had
contacted Joseph Manesty in Liverpool, who had in turn alerted the
captains of his Africa-bound ships to make enquiries about John Newton wherever they could. Anyone who discovered him was to make certain that he was returned safely to England.

One of the men given this information was Anthony Gother, captain of the *Greyhound*, which had left Liverpool on July 7, 1746, to collect
gold, ivory, wood, and beeswax beginning in Gambia. He had asked
about John Newton when at anchor in the Bay of Sierra Leone and again
at Banana Island but had been given the impression that Newton had
moved up country. It was as he headed past the peninsula one afternoon in February 1747 that he saw smoke coming from a beach; a recognized sign that a trader was signaling for business.

The fire had been lit by Newton's colleague. The two of them had
packed ready to sail upriver in their shallop and had only delayed their
departure to pick up a few more goods to exchange for slaves. Gother
hesitated because he didn't think that he had sufficient time to slow
down and drop anchor, but he managed to do it, and Newton's colleague took a canoe out to meet him.

One of the first things Gother asked this man was whether he knew
anything of John Newton. Learning that this same Newton was on the
beach beside the fire he came ashore to personally deliver the message
entrusted to him by Joseph Manesty but was shocked to find that Newton was indifferent to being rescued. He was no longer desperate to
leave Africa. Life was going well, he enjoyed his work, and pleasure was
easy to come by. What could possibly entice him back to England? Only
one thing. Mary Catlett.

Worried now that he might lose Newton, Gother fabricated a story about a small fortune having been left him by someone who had recently died and a bundle of letters awaiting him in Aveley. Newton reasoned that there was slim possibility of being remembered in a will but was finally persuaded to return to the *Greyhound* with Gother by "the remembrance of my loved one, the hope of seeing her, and the possibility that accepting this offer might once more put me in a way of gaining her hand."

Including the captain and his first mate, Richard Jackson, the ship already had a full crew of ten, and so Gother was able to take Newton as a passenger rather than as a working sailor, accommodating him in his cabin and giving him time to read books, write letters to Mary, and ponder his extraordinary life. Yet even then he didn't show signs of gratitude and seemed oblivious to the remarkable nature of his rescue. "So blind and stupid was I at that time, I made no reflection. I sought no direction in what had happened. Like a wave of the sea driven with the wind, and tossed, I was governed by present appearances, and looked no further. But he who is eyes to the blind, was leading me in a way that I knew not."

The voyage along the African coast, sailing east through the Gulf of Guinea and crossing the equator to Cape Lopez, in what is now Gabon, took almost a year. There were many stops on the way but monotony had set in. More sea, more trees, more sun, more beaches. The variety and depth of conversation would have been limited for Newton because only three of the crew were English. He responded to the boredom by creating disturbances, falling back on his old practice of cursing and blaspheming.

Degrees of blasphemy are hard to determine. Is the worst blasphemer the one who blasphemes most often or the one who blasphemes with more imagination and daring? Should it be gauged by the number of offending words or the degree of offense caused? Newton always reckoned himself to have been a great transgressor in this area, saying, "I know not that I have ever since met so daring a blasphemer." When the power of commonplace oaths waned he invented new ones, presumably graduating from what we now call "language intensifiers" to verbal attacks on everything that Christians held sacred. He claimed that Captain Gother, by no means a man of undefiled lips himself, had to "seriously reprove" him for his profanity.

Boredom led him to organize contests drinking gin and rum from a large seashell, the winner being the last man able to stand. Drunkenly whirling and dancing across the deck during a particularly ferocious contest on the Gabon River, Newton lost his hat overboard. Looking over the side of the *Greyhound* by the light of the moon he could see the ship's boat moored beneath. Determined to retrieve the hat he vaulted over the rail intending to drop into the boat below, but, because of his intoxicated state, he had seriously misjudged the distance. It wasn't directly below but twenty feet out at sea. A crew member grabbed him at the last moment and hauled him back. If he hadn't been caught he would have drowned not only because no one else would have been sober enough to rescue him, but for the simple reason that he couldn't swim.

At Cape Lopez he and some others from the *Greyhound* went hunting, killing a buffalo that then proved too heavy to drag back to the ship. They hacked it into manageable parts, took half with them, and left the remainder for collection the next day. When they returned they couldn't locate the spot and, as night fell, realized that they were lost. There were no landmarks to guide them, they had no lanterns, and the moon was blocked by low clouds. Soon they were waist deep in swamps and could hear the sounds of animals.

Newton, who had the most experience in Africa, became the leader of the lost patrol but had no idea which direction they should be headed in. Their minds were full of rumors about strange man-eating beasts and they knew that without food, drink, and guns they were unlikely to survive for long. The thought occurred to Newton that they were probably the first humans ever to tramp this spot of God's Earth.

Just at the point that they were coming to accept their ignominious end the clouds began to disperse, and with the light of the moon they could make out a glint of sea in the distance. Their worst fears were confirmed. They had been walking deeper into the jungle rather than closer to the shore. Without the sudden change of weather they would have perished.

Narrow escapes such as these, which had once caused him to reflect on the wonderful mercy or the awful judgment of God, no longer produced either praise or fear. He remained unmoved. His new philosophy, inherited from Shaftesbury's *Characteristicks* and made his own through months of self-indulgence, didn't allow for such thoughts. "The admonitions of conscience, which from successive repulses had grown weaker and weaker, at length entirely ceased," he wrote. "For a space of many months, if not for some years, I cannot recollect that I had a single check of that sort."

In January 1748 the *Greyhound* finally left the coast of Africa after over a year of trading to make the circuitous voyage back to Britain, following the trade winds across the Atlantic toward the coast of Brazil, then northward to Newfoundland before turning east in the direction of Britain. Gother planned only two stops en route. The first was at the small island of Annobon to take on fresh food and drink, and the second was off the banks of Newfoundland to fish for enough cod that would last the rest of the journey.

Then on March 9, 1748, three months into an otherwise uneventful voyage, there began a chain of events that would become immortalized in the first two stanzas of "Amazing Grace." Newton "carelessly" picked up a book that he found on the ship, an English translation from the Latin by George Stanhope, former Dean of Canterbury, of the devotional classic *The Imitation of Christ* by Thomas à Kempis. It was an unusual choice given his recent rejection of Christianity, but it may have been that he now felt he was immune to such doctrine. He dipped into the book, he said, with "indifference."

Thomas à Kempis (Thomas Haemerken from Kempen near Dusseldorf) was an Augustinian monk who wrote in the fifteenth century, and *The Imitation of Christ*, published anonymously in 1418, was an exploration of the teachings of Christ intended as an instruction book for fellow monks. It's hard to imagine anything less likely to have stirred Newton's conscience at this point in his life.

Presuming that Newton began at the beginning, "Thoughts Helpful in the Life of the Soul," he would have read:

He who would approve himself wise in good earnest, must first by a just contempt of this world, raise himself up to the desires and endeavours after the kingdom of heaven. Vanity indeed it is, with great solicitude to seek, and place our hope and confidence in riches, which are sure to perish. Vanity, to cherish our ambition, and strive, by all possible means to attain a high and honourable station. Vanity, to indulge the flesh, and count those pleasures, which draw after them grievous and lasting pains. Vanity most exquisite, to be infinitely concerned for living long, and perfectly indifferent, or but coldly affected, concerning living well. Vanity most fatal and stupid, to determine our thoughts and cares to this present life, and never look forward to that which is to come: to dote upon things that fly swiftly from us, and cling fast about imaginary and transitory delight; while we suffer ourselves by these to be detained and diverted from the pursuit of substantial and eternal joys. Oh, turn this vehemence of desire upon the right object, and remember, to how little purpose it is placed on that which cannot content, since most true is that observation, which ought to make us wiser, "The Eye is not satisfied with Seeing, nor the Ear filled with Hearing." Use then thy utmost diligence, to wean thy soul from the Love of things that are seen. And set thy affections on things that are not seen. For, be assured, that they, who follow their own sensual appetites, do lose, not only their labour and expectation, but also their innocence and purity, the peace of their own conscience, and the favour of Almighty God.

As he read the words of this fifteenth-century monk "an involuntary suggestion" arose in his mind. It came in the form of a simple question—what if these things are true? What if it was vanity to be preoccupied with this life ignoring the next? What if the pinnacle of wisdom was seeking God rather than seeking knowledge? What if following sinful passions resulted in a loss of grace—"the favour of Almighty God"? The unavoidable answer was that if the things that Thomas à Kempis believed were true then John Newton was doomed. He was without grace.

If he was lost, he told himself, he had to have courage because his choices had been made with full awareness of the supposed consequences. He had weighed the evidence, he had considered the merits, he had asserted his freedom. But more questions lined up to be answered and the only way he could ignore them was to throw himself into lighthearted conversation of the crew and try to forget that they had ever arisen.

While he was sleeping that night, the *Greyhound* was caught in a violent storm and water began gushing into his cabin as planks were wrenched loose. Dressing himself he could hear the shouts of men above him panicking through the fear that their ship was about to sink. As he climbed the ladder up to the deck, Gother urged Newton to return to the cabin to fetch a knife. A crew member who immediately took his place on the ladder was swept to his death.

Ships for the African trade were built with an eye on quick profit rather than endurance. Very few made more than six voyages before being scrapped because they weren't designed to take such punishment from the elements, in particular the dramatic climate changes which weakened the joints as the timbers expanded, then contracted.

There may be additional reasons why the *Greyhound* found it difficult to withstand the ferocity of the storm. Letters written by Joseph Manesty to Rhode Island merchant Joseph Harrison, whom he had hired to oversee the building of a new ship by John Bannister, show that he was keen to reduce the costs of his ships to bring down the insurance premium and to create space for more slaves. In August 1745 he told Harrison to ensure that the carpenters used sheathing nails and single spikes rather than bolts because he thought bolts were "quite needless" and besides "as insurance is very high [I] would have as little money laid out on the vessels as possible."

Even if these letters were not referring specifically to the *Greyhound* they are proof that during this period Manesty sacrificed safety and durability for immediate profit and encouraged cost-cutting construction methods. His frugality may have played an important part in Newton's story, and therefore to "Amazing Grace," because when Newton went back up on deck he realized that the reason the ship was filling with water was because the waves had torn away the upper timbers on one side of the ship. Pumping the water out with foot pumps and bailing it out in hand buckets was fruitless. In desperation they plugged the gaps with bedding and clothing, nailing timbers over the top to keep them in place. As Newton put it, the ship had been turned into "a mere wreck in a few minutes."

The wind dropped by the following morning and while speaking to Gother, Newton heard himself comment, "If this will not do, the Lord have mercy on us!" He had said it flippantly, without any consideration of either God or mercy, but was "instantly struck with my own words." Taken literally he had said that when all human effort proves insufficient it is only the mercy of God that can save. This prompted the related thought—what mercy was rightfully his at a time like this? In his Venice dream he had stood on the deck of another ship and seen the destructive fire raging because he had not guarded his inheritance. Of that dream he had remembered: "My tempter, with an air of insult, informed me that all the mercy of God in reserve for me was comprised in that ring, which I had willfully thrown away."

The drop in the wind proved to be temporary. He had to return to the pumps for another three hours, roping himself to an upright beam to avoid being washed away. The ship was now rearing up and then plunging dramatically as if dropped from a cliff. Water poured over the freezing and almost naked bodies of the crew. There were tears from hardened sailors convinced that they were living their last day on Earth. Newton, for the first time in years, felt a sense of dread at the prospect of death. "My heart foreboded the worst if the scriptures, which I had long since opposed, were true." If they were true he accepted that "I could not be forgiven, and [I] was therefore expecting, and almost at times wishing, to know the worst."

'Twas grace that taught my heart to fear.

The next day the storm had still not relented. At one o'clock in the afternoon, following a short nap, he took the helm, steering the *Greyhound* for the next eleven hours. "I had here leisure and opportunity to think of my former religious professions, the calls, warnings, and deliverances I had met with, the licentious course of my life, particularly my unparalleled effrontery in making the gospel the subject of profane ridicule. I thought, allowing the Scripture premises, there never was, nor could be, such a sinner as myself. Then, comparing the advantages I had broken through, I concluded at first that my sins were too great to be forgiven."

He recalled a passage from the Bible that sounded as though it had been written with him in mind: "But since you rejected me when I called and no one gave heed when I stretched out my hand, since you ignored all my advice and would not accept my rebuke, I in turn will laugh at your disaster; I will mock when calamity overtakes you like a storm, when disaster sweeps over you like a whirlwind, when distress and troubles overwhelm you. Then they will call to me but I will not answer; they will look for me but will not find me. . . . For the waywardness of the simple will kill them, and the complacency of fools will destroy them; but whoever listens to me will lie in safety and be at ease, without fear of harm" (Prov. 1:24–33).

After five hours he was told that the ship was finally free of water, the first real sign of hope since the storm began forty hours previously. Newton was so relieved that he offered up a prayer. It wasn't a prayer of repentance. It was, he reflected, like the cry of a hungry raven. More specific thoughts about the Christian gospel followed. He knew the doctrines but now wanted to be assured that they were grounded in fact and not in wishful thinking. It would be self-deceit to turn to Christianity merely because he wanted the story of grace to be true.

Still at the wheel he reasoned that the best way forward was to ask for the power of the Spirit and then to start acting as though the gospel was true. The proof would be in the living. As Thomas à Kempis said, "There are many who hear the gospel but care little for it because they have not the spirit of Christ." Newton's logic was influenced by his reading of Luke 11:13, where it is promised that God will "give the Holy Spirit to them that ask him" and John 7:17, which says that if anyone does God's will "he shall know of the doctrine, whether it be of God."

He felt he had been privileged to see his wretchedness for what it was. Only by catching a vision of himself as helpless did God's grace seem so appealing, so amazing.

How precious did that grace appear
The hour I first believed.

This was the beginning of a process rather than a moment of illumination where every question was answered, every bad character trait straightened out, and every problem resolved. His faith was essentially the faith that he was going to be given faith. "I concluded that though I could not say from my heart that I believed the gospel, yet I would for the present take it for granted, and that by studying it in this light I should be more and more confirmed in it."

He found particular consolation in the conversion of Paul, who, like him, was convinced that he was "the chief of sinners" because he had attacked the faith of Christians. In the letters of Paul he read: "Even though I was once a blasphemer and a persecutor and a violent man I was shown mercy because I acted in ignorance and unbelief. The grace of our Lord was poured out on me abundantly, along with the faith and love that are in Christ Jesus" (1 Tim. 1:13–14).

Although the storm had passed, the *Greyhound* was a floating ruin. Ropes had frayed and snapped, sails were shredded, and the missing planks on one side of the ship meant that they had to make the ship list in the other direction to prevent more water flooding in. Casks of food and drink had been smashed open in the tumult; pigs, sheep, and poultry had been washed away; the rations of fish and bread had been eaten. They thought they sighted land and celebrated by finishing off the brandy rations only to find it was not the coast of Ireland but a distant cluster of clouds. With the death of another crew member, only nine were left on board.

It was on April 7, four weeks after the storm, that they finally saw the coast of Ireland. A day later they turned south into Lough Swilly, a twenty-five-mile-long inlet in County Donegal, and dropped anchor two hours before another fierce storm blew up. If they had arrived any later, they would have been caught by the bad weather and would probably have been sunk because the ruined ship couldn't have withstood another battering. "About this time," said Newton, "I began to know that there is a God who hears and answers prayer."

While the *Greyhound* was being repaired for the last leg of its journey to Liverpool, Newton took a break in the walled city of Londonderry, where he found a church to pray in twice a day, took the sacraments for the first time, and "with the greatest solemnity, engaged myself to be the Lord's forever and only his. This was not a formal, but a sincere surrender, under a warm sense of mercies recently received."

And grace my fears relieved.

Invited on a shooting party by William Lecky, the city's mayor, he managed to almost kill himself when scrambling up a bank and accidentally releasing the hammer of his gun; it fired so close to his body that his hat was singed. After his years of dicing with death at sea and in Africa, the irony wasn't lost on Newton. "When we think ourselves in the greatest safety," he said, "we are no less exposed to danger than when all seems conspiring to destroy us."

Captain Newton, who hadn't heard from his son since 1746, had resigned himself to the fact that he was now dead. In January he had accepted the post of governor at the Hudson Bay Company's Fort York trading post in what is now Canada. His minimum stay in this remote, cold, and hostile location, where he would be responsible for collecting fur from native Indian trappers and defending British interests from the French, was to be three years. His second wife and their three children, William, twelve; Henry, eight; and Thomasina, two, would remain in England.

Newton had written to him from Londonderry, but unfortunately Captain Newton received the letter only a few days before leaving London on board the *Prince Rupert* on April 29, 1748, for his four-month voyage to Hudson's Bay. It was a sad realization for both men. The captain had hoped to invite his son to work with him. Newton had wanted to show his father how much he had changed.

When Newton finally arrived back in Liverpool in the middle of May, it was more than four years since he'd been press-ganged into service on HMS *Harwich* and more than three years since he had seen his beloved Mary. And despite all that had happened, he realized that in the eyes of Mrs. Catlett he would be no more eligible a suitor for her daughter than when he had left England. What had made matters worse was the news that he wouldn't be paid for his time on board the ship that had taken him from Madeira to Africa. The company that owned it—presumably made up of merchant venturers—had declared itself bankrupt.

On May 24 he wrote to Mrs. Catlett's sister, Susanna Eversfield, to explain his situation. Susanna was supportive of the relationship but felt he had to prove himself reliable before going any further.

Dear Madam,

I am now able to acquaint you that I have finished my troublesome, tedious voyage, and am safely arrived at this place. I have no reason to complain of my past failure (though really very severe) since I drew it all upon myself. A particular detail of my adventure would be irksome, both to you and myself. Let it suffice to say that I have gained, if nothing else, some experience, which though painfully bought is not the less valuable, and have the good fortune to find a friend here [Joseph Manesty], by whose assistance I hope to redeem my former misspent time.

The manner of my father's message to me to return from Guinea, gave me some room to hope for a handsome settlement on shore, but I find to my sorrow that he has left the land and I am disappointed. It was giving way to this persuasion that fully resolved in me thoughts which I had for some time endeavoured to stifle but could never extinguish. . . . I have not forgot the terms on which I parted from your house, which though they made against me, I must acknowledge to be highly reasonable. I have not been able to remove the objection yourself and Mrs. Catlett urged against me. I have been confounded and disappointed in all my schemes hitherto and am as far back as ever. . . .

It was an admission of abject failure and yet one that he surely hoped would affect Susanna's sympathies and be communicated to Mrs. Catlett. He refers to Mary as "the principle object of my desires these 5 years past" but admits that his financial situation "does not enable me to make her suitable proposals."

Susanna Eversfield's response to this isn't recorded, but she must have taken pity on him and allowed him to visit Chatham, probably in June. It took him four days to travel down from Liverpool by coach, and then when he finally met Mary after such a long absence, he found himself lost for words. "I scarcely durst look at you," he later wrote. "I was tongue-tied." The best he could do was to get her alone and ask her for permission to send her a letter. He knew that he could far more confidently express the depth of his feelings on paper.

So it was that on June 20, having returned to London, he wrote her an impassioned six-hundred-word letter in which he apologized for his inability to speak to her properly in Chatham and begged her for some indication that his hopes were not in vain. "I believe no one was ever engaged in an Amour with such slender hopes in so long a time as I have been. If (as they say) living upon Love itself is but thin diet, how do you imagine I have subsisted upon the mere shadow and idea of it all this time? I wish you would consider my case with the good nature usual to you in other things and bestow a little of your charity, one morsel for God's sake before I am quite starved. Were you willing you could easily find a way to give me a great deal of pleasure without wronging your own discretion in the least."

He must have felt his sense of failure even more on the way back to Liverpool. So poor was he that he couldn't afford the coach fare of two guineas and had to make the two-hundred-mile journey on foot. As he walked he mulled over the events of the past few days, searching for scraps of encouragement in the tilt of her head, the look in her eye, the inflection in her voice. To Mary's brother Jack he wrote, "I amuse myself on the road with building castles."

Once in Liverpool he waited patiently to hear from Mary. When the letter came he was overjoyed to find that it was not a rejection. "I kept it for some time before I durst open it," he wrote back. "When I did, I was transported to find you kind, for though you wrote in the most cautious terms, I knew it was much in my favour that you would write at all, and that you designed I should understand it so. Then, my dearest Mary, on that very day, I began to live indeed, and to act, in all my concerns, with a spirit of firmness to which I before was a stranger."

Sierra Leone pictured at the time Newton was beginning to work as a slave captain.

SOURCE UNKNOWN.

Chapter 4

SLAVE CAPTAIN

In 1965 I started telling the story of John Newton and the story
is basically that he was at sea with a ship full of people chained
to each other and something happened, a storm or something,
and he promised God that if he was allowed to live he would
turn his life around. And he did. He took the people home,
sailed back to England and started writing songs. It's an
abbreviated version. I don't think it goes *quite* like that.
—*Arlo Guthrie*, FOLKSINGER, 2001

Through many dangers, toils and snares,
I have already come.
—*John Newton*, "AMAZING GRACE," 1772

Disagreeable I had long found it, but I think I should have
quitted it sooner, had I considered it, as I now do, to be
unlawful and wrong. But I never had a scruple upon this head
at the time, nor was such a thought once suggested
to me by any friend. What I did, I did ignorantly,
considering it as the line of life which Divine Providence had
allotted me, and having no concern, in point of
conscience, but to treat the slaves, while under my care, with
as much humanity as a regard to my own safety would admit.
—*John Newton*, THOUGHTS UPON THE
AFRICAN SLAVE TRADE, 1788

*T*he folk myth version of John Newton's life goes something like this: He was a slave captain whose ship was hit by a severe
storm. Terrified by the prospect of death he vowed to abandon the

trade if his life was spared. He avoided death and, true to his word, set his cargo of slaves free, left the trade, and devoted his life to writing songs. His best-known song, "Amazing Grace," is about his rejection of the slave trade and how his eyes had been opened to its evil.

It's a lovely story but is a mixture of telescoped events and untruths. He wasn't the captain of the ship caught in the Atlantic storm, which didn't have slaves on board, anyway, and he didn't return to Africa in this ship. Newton was challenged by the prospect of death but made no vows. He didn't leave the slave trade immediately following his conversion and never organized the release of any Africans that he had been responsible for enslaving. Crucially, his captaincy of slave ships didn't begin until after he had become a Christian.

The changes in his outlook and behavior came slowly and painfully. He slipped back into his old habits almost as often as he surged forward. His understanding of Christian doctrine had remained where it had been when he last read the shorter catechism with his mother and he didn't know of the Great Awakening taking place in America, spearheaded by the preaching of Jonathan Edwards and George Whitefield, or the evangelical revival in Britian under John Wesley. He had never thought about the social implications of the truths he had learned in the form of catechisms and had no Christian friends to debate with and learn from. The substance of his faith was that once he had been lost, but now he was found.

Like almost everyone of his generation he saw nothing inherently wrong with slavery and therefore no inconsistency in participating in it as a follower of Jesus. Of all the Christian denominations only the Quakers and Anabaptists had denounced slavery. Powerful traders belonged to the church—Joseph Manesty owned half a pew at St. George's Church in Derby Square, Liverpool—and some Christians argued passionately that slavery was God's way of rescuing Africans from their barbaric practices and heathen beliefs and introducing them to Christianity. Using this perspective, slavery could easily be harmonized with Christianity. The only improvements a Christian trader might make would be to treat the slaves more compassionately.

Against this background the newly converted Newton saw no reason not to accept Manesty's offer to sail to Africa and South Carolina on the *Brownlow* at the end of July 1748. He was desperately short of money and the indications that Mary had given him were, he admitted, "the most powerful engagement to me to exert myself to the utmost and to condemn difficulty and danger." Manesty had wanted to give him the captaincy, but, conscious of his weaknesses, Newton wanted first to prove that he could submit to authority and so was happy to work as mate to Richard Jackson, whom he had already known on the *Greyhound*, as Captain Gother's first mate.

Competition in the slave trade was increasing. The African coast was being targeted by boats from Holland, France, Spain, and Portugal, and the local traders couldn't keep up with the demand for strong, healthy, young slaves. As a consequence ships were forced to spend more time on the coast to collect their full complements and this of course increased the cost of the journey and reduced profits for the merchants.

Traders on the African coast, flush with newly acquired wealth and aware of their power, lived extravagantly and rejoiced under such names as King Peter and Yellow Will. It was a sellers' market. If the captains wanted the best slaves they had to court and indulge these men. Without good contacts it was hard to do business, and those who tried to take advantage of these native traders would find their boats attacked, burned, or set adrift.

One of the *Brownlow*'s first ports of call on this trip was Plantain Island, the scene of Newton's great humiliation, and here he met P. I. and some of the slaves who had once been forced to torment him. He saw the lime trees that he had planted when his master and P. I. had stood by and mocked him. One incident that he would never forget was when two "black females" (presumably P. I.'s slaves) recognized him and were astonished to see him wearing stockings and shoes, only ever having seen him half naked and barefoot.

For someone who enjoyed revisiting old haunts to gain "profitable impressions" of the "contrast between my situation then, and what it is now," this should have been a particularly poignant visit, but he remained unstirred. With no Christian friends and no guided study of the Bible, his faith had not advanced, while the parts of his nature that had always been problematic were being nurtured every day. What he called "a rain of temptations" fell upon him, finding him "easy prey."

Plantain Island again became a place of trial for him. He fell ill there and was forced to remain on the island. In his weak and delirious state, surrounded by reminders of his captivity, he was able to review his recent past. He knew that he had become profane and frivolous and yet he didn't want to make another resolution because both theology and experience taught him that he needed grace rather than renewed intentions. "I made no more resolves, but cast myself before the Lord to do with me as He should please. . . . The burden was removed from my conscience, and not only my peace but my health was restored, I cannot say instantaneously, but I recovered from that hour."

After eight months of trading, when the ship was at Rio Cestors, to-day in Liberia, Newton again had a narrow escape. As he was about to row up the river, Captain Jackson inexplicably recalled him and sent someone in his place. This had never happened before and took Newton by surprise. Even Jackson had no rational explanation for the switch. That night, the small boat sank, and Newton's replacement was drowned. In contrast to earlier experiences of cheating death he saw this as evidence of God's protective hand. In a letter to Mary he wrote, "Providence has preserved me safe through a variety of these scenes since I saw you last and I hope will continue to do so."

Through many dangers, toils and snares
I have already come.

Filled with 218 slaves, the *Brownlow* set sail for Charleston, South Carolina, stopping over at the island of Antigua. This journey across the Atlantic, known in the trade as "the middle passage," was the most dangerous of the triangular route. It was difficult to maintain proper care of the slaves and there was a constant threat of insurrection. A band of slaves rebelled, and before order was restored four had been killed along with one member of the *Brownlow*'s crew. By the time the ship reached America over sixty slaves, more than a quarter of those who left Africa, had died.

Writing about his voyage in later years Newton didn't describe the sale in Charleston even though it was his first experience of seeing the slaves sold on this side of the Atlantic. The *South Carolina Gazette* reported the arrival of the *Brownlow* in its issue of August 14, 1749, by which time the slaves would have been quarantined on Sullivan's Island. Each slave had to be checked for sickness, disease, or deformity before being released for sale. On August 21, a boxed advertisement in the newspaper, showing an engraving of a black slave with a black child announced: "A choice parcel of healthy slaves, just arrived from the Windward Coast of Africa in the snow *Brownlow*, Captain Jackson, to be sold on reasonable terms, at their store in Broad Street, by Kennan and Campbell, who have a parcel of choice Madeira wines to sell."

Kennan and Campbell was listed at the time as a store dealing in "general goods and food" and was situated on one of Charleston's oldest and most prominent thoroughfares. There is no record of this store selling slaves in Charleston before or after this date. Elizabeth Donnan, editor of the most comprehensive collection of published documents concerning the slave trade to America, observed in 1930, "Most, if not all, of the merchants who advertised Negroes in the *Gazette* were doing a general business, of which their trade in Negroes was but a part."

Henry Kennan and Dougal Campbell were respected Charleston merchants. Kennan later moved to Georgia, where he had a tract of land farmed by slaves, and died in London in 1767. Campbell remained in Charleston and became clerk of the Crown and peace. In their advertisement the slaves have been reduced to yet another exotic foreign product, along with fine wines from Madeira. Slaves from the Windward Coast were highly sought after because, being from a rice-growing region, they were thought to be particularly good as workers on plantations.

The ad ran again in the August 28 issue of the *South Carolina Gazette*. Newton's main interest during this stopover, according to his autobiography, was in finding "serious people" (i.e., Christians) whom he could learn from. He found a Congregational minister named Josiah Smith, a graduate of Harvard, whom he admired as a preacher even though he found himself struggling to understand his sermons.

"My conduct was now very inconsistent," he wrote. "Almost every day I used to retire into the woods and fields and trust I began to taste the sweets of communion with God in the exercises of prayer and praise. Yet I frequently spent the evenings in vain and worthless company."

After six weeks the slaves had been sold and the *Brownlow* cleaned and loaded with goods, and on October 2 she was cleared for departure to Liverpool. On arrival in England Newton immediately rode down to London, from where he wrote to Mary telling her that he was back and expressing fears that she would reject him because of his fluctuating fortunes and unreliable past but insisting that he was now a different person. He admitted that he had been ungraceful, full of "dull, rusty gloominess," but now he was open and happy, "more like other folks."

The time had come to propose marriage face-to-face rather than hint at it by post, and the prospect overwhelmed him. He was frightened that he wouldn't be persuasive enough and even more afraid that she would politely tell him that his feelings were not reciprocated. "My heart was so full it beat and trembled to that degree that I knew not how to get a word out," he confessed. "I sat stupid and speechless for some minutes."

When he finally framed the question, the response was as he had feared. She couldn't marry him, she said. Doggedly he went on until again she refused him, but, he thought to himself, not with such conviction. He sensed that her resistance was weakening. When he asked a third time she confessed her fears, none of which had to do with lack of affection for him or suspicions about his moral character. He was too good for her, she said, and she was worried about leaving the safety and warmth of her family home. Newton consoled her, and eventually she consented.

On February 1, 1750, John Newton and Mary Catlett were married at St. Margaret's Church in Rochester, Kent, and started their life together at the Catlett home. Three months later Joseph Manesty proposed his next trip to Africa, this time as captain. Having just settled into married life, Newton was reluctant to return to sea. If he could have made his living without long separations, he would have done so. He bought lottery tickets, hoping to "gain a considerable prize . . . and be saved from the necessity of going to sea," but luck didn't come to his rescue.

Riding back to Liverpool in May 1750 he was tortured by the thought of leaving Mary but knew that there was no realistic alternative. "I am likely to perform the whole journey alone but I want no company," he wrote Mary during a stop at St. Albans. "It will be always a full entertainment to me to recollect how very happy I have been in yours and to animate myself with the pleasing hope that in due time I shall be so again."

During the three months it took to prepare and load the *Duke of Argyle*, his father unexpectedly died at Fort York. Captain Newton liked to go for a morning swim in the icy waters of the Hayes River, where it flowed into Hudson's Bay, and on June 28 he had rowed out to an anchored longboat, stripped down to a pair of linen trousers, tied a handkerchief around his head, and dived in. He swam well for a while but then got into difficulties and eventually was lost to sight.

His deputy, Samuel Skrimsher, who watched it all from the shore, later reported what he saw in the York Factory journal: "Captain Newton was within sixty or seventy feet of the shore when to our great surprise we had the unfortunate aspect to see him go down at once without any hesitation or signs of distress and immediately appeared again calling for help. . . . Our other small boat went to his assistance but the poor gentleman, never appearing the second time, rendered our endeavours unserviceable. It is thought that the cramp was the cause of his misfortune. His death was regretted by all under his command."

Although the accident had been witnessed, his body couldn't be found. Three days later Skrimsher and some other workers returned "in search of the corpse of Captain Newton" but still found nothing. It wasn't until July 2 that it was seen drifting on the tide in the early morning. They hauled it ashore and were "happy to get him to bury, which we did in as handsome and decent a manner as the country would permit." A simple wooden grave marker was erected.

Newton was deeply affected by the loss. He admired his father for his accomplishments as a sailor and for his sense of morality. He was sure that beneath his cold exterior his father cared for him, and had obviously done his best to use his influence to improve his son's prospects. The chances are that with Newton's wild excesses now in the past, the two men would have grown closer. "I loved and revered him," he told Mary when she wrote to him with the news. "My tears drop upon the paper."

The committee of the Hudson's Bay Company, which was based in London, didn't shed tears over Captain Newton's death. They had found him too independent-minded and accused him of mismanagement. They were particularly concerned that he hadn't done enough to maintain peace between the warring Indian tribes and that this had caused a slump in trade. Captain Newton's attitude was that those sitting in comfort in London, who had never traveled to the outposts, had no idea how to run operations in the snowy wastes. In a letter to his replacement, James Isham, the governor and committee wrote, "We are sorry for the loss of Mr. Newton though we cannot help being greatly displeased at his conduct both with respect to the small care taken of our trade and of the works and repairs necessary to have been done about the factory."

Almost nothing was left to his wife and young children. His personal belongings were put into a trunk and sent back to England on the *Prince Rupert*. Thomasina petitioned the Hudson's Bay Company for an annual stipend "towards the support of herself and three children" because of her "necessitous circumstances," but the committee wasn't persuaded. Instead it paid her a lump sum of almost fourteen pounds, which, when added to what had already been given to her, would amount to a year's salary.

At the very time that Captain Newton was being laid to rest in Hudson's Bay, his son had become the new Captain Newton. This was to be the first of three voyages that Newton would make as commander of a ship, and a great deal is known about them because he kept a detailed ship's journal as well as a spiritual diary, and wrote regular letters to Mary. Taken together these have given historians the most comprehensive insider account of slaving practices on the African coast during this period.

His letters to Mary were characterized by tenderness and deep passion. She was constantly in his thoughts and everything he wrote reminded her of this fact and encouraged her to grow in faith and knowledge. He believed that the drama of their intertwining lives was one of the great love stories of all time, and yet he was surrounded by men cynical about tender love who saw his commitment to fidelity as either naive or stupid. Their view was that there was no conflict between having a true love at home and sexual adventures abroad.

His personal and active Christian faith made him an unusual figure in the slave trade. Each day was started with an hour of prayer in his cabin—two hours if he had the time. On Sundays the entire crew were compelled to attend a church service with hymn singing and Anglican liturgy. Instead of normal leisure activities he taught himself French, read poetry, polished up his Latin, and furthered his comprehension of mathematics.

To develop his understanding of Christianity he corresponded with Dr. David Jennings, the minister who had baptized him as a child in Wapping. In one of these letters he expressed an interest in writing "a book of advices and devotions . . . adapted entirely to the business and occasions of seamen." He had already composed for his men prayers that "related entirely to our wants and views" after finding the traditional *Book of Common Prayer* "not suitable to the particular circumstances of our calling."

This was the hymn writer in embryonic form, keen to communicate Christian teachings in ordinary language. The talent with words that had made him such an inventive and lyrical blasphemer was now being considered for sacred ends. Particularly significant, in light of his future work, was his wish to be relevant. Like John Bunyan and Isaac Watts, whose writings he had been reared on, he waged war against Christian obscurantism.

Yet even as he taught his sailors how to pray he was having to slave his ship in the most economical fashion. This meant working fast to avoid unnecessary delays, developing his previous contacts, and preserving the lives of the slaves already on board his ship. His basic wage was only five pounds a month, half that of a captain in the Royal Navy, but when he returned to Liverpool this would be supplemented by a share of the profits. It was in his interest to deliver the maximum number of slaves possible in the shortest time.

The *Duke of Argyle* traded up and down the African coast for seven months between October 1750 and May 1751, during which time it collected 174 slaves. This worked out at roughly one slave for each day spent in Africa, but as they were usually bought in groups, most weeks yielded only one or two purchases, the rest of the time being spent sailing or waiting at anchor. Of these 174 slaves, 28 would die before reaching Antigua along with 7 of the crew. Newton's dividend for the fourteen-month trip would be a respectable 257 pounds, more than three times his basic wage for the same period.

The matter of how the slaves came to be in chains in the first place didn't appear to concern the traders and captains. By the time they reached the coast they had usually been bought and sold several times, mostly by their fellow countrymen, and so the captains could reassure themselves that they were merely taking advantage of a practice already in place. If slavery was acceptable to the Africans, why not to them? The slaves weren't considered as people with feelings, who had been wrenched from their families and communities, but as creatures who were little more than beasts.

The unit of exchange in the trade was "the bar"; not an actual bar of precious metal but an agreed amount of guns, gunpowder, cloth, iron, pans, kettles, beads, knives, flint, and silk handkerchiefs. Prices, as always, were determined by supply and demand. When Newton arrived on the *Duke of Argyle* the going rate on the coast was 60 bars a slave. By the next year it had increased to 90 bars, and by the time of his last voyage in 1754 it was almost 120 bars. On the other side of the Atlantic they would be sold for fifty pounds each. Bragging a little to John Bannister about the "great profit" to be made in the slave trade, Joseph Manesty wrote in 1747, "Negroes at Jamaica £50 to £55 a head, bought on the coast of Africa from £4 to £6 a head."

Newton considered most of the traders he dealt with to be "villains." The only one he respected was a mulatto named Harry Tucker, whom he referred to as "the man with whom I had the largest connection in business and by whom I was never deceived." Nicholas Owen had dealings with Tucker and described him as a fat man who lived "after the manner of the English," with silver on his table, a sideboard full of plates, and considerable wealth. So powerful was he in the region that the natives feared him, and he built an entire village and filled it with children, slaves, and seven wives. He dressed flamboyantly and had traveled to Spain, Portugal, and England. Newton liked him enough to entertain him on board.

Mr. Clow was another favorite. Newton said that he trusted Clow's advice on where to trade, and by 1750 Clow was apparently running a business with P. I. based on Plantain Island. If Newton's old master was now dead, as he implied, was this the other trader whom Newton worked for, having now amalgamated his business with P. I.'s? This would make sense of Nicholas Owen's observation three years later that Plantain Island was "inhabited by only one white trader."

Slaves could be bought onshore, or paraded for sale on deck. Those that would fetch the best prices across the Atlantic were strong young men, women capable of child bearing, and healthy children. Newton rejected more than half of the slaves he was offered, usually because they were either too old or too small. Sometimes he didn't take them because they were diseased or disabled. He reports two occasions in his journals when he turned down female slaves for being "fallen breasted."

Olaudah Equiano, an eighteenth-century slave who eventually won his freedom in America and came to England, wrote an eloquent account of the experience of capture. He was kidnapped from his village by fellow Africans when he was a child and exchanged hands several times before being sold to a ship. Like most who came from the interior, he had never seen the sea, a ship, or a white man. He was staggered by the sight of a river when he was first put on a canoe, because "I had never seen any water larger than a pond or a rivulet. . . .

"When I was carried on board I was immediately handled, and tossed up, to see if I were sound, by some of the crew; and I was now persuaded that I had gotten into a world of bad spirits, and that they were going to kill me. Their complexions too differing so much from ours, their long hair, and the language they spoke, which was very different from any I had ever heard, united to confirm me in this belief. Indeed, such were the horrors of my views and fears at that moment that, if ten thousand worlds had been my own, I would have freely parted with them all to have exchanged my condition with that of the meanest slave in my own country."

Once purchased, they were taken to the lower deck, which was five feet from top to bottom, where there were two tiers on either side of a central aisle. Here, shackled in twos, they were forced to lie side by side. It was cramped, dark, and stifling. There was a continual noise of cries, screams, and different regional languages. Vomit, urine, and feces combined to create a smell so pungent that the sailors could barely force themselves to go down. Apparently unaware of the irony, Newton complained to Mary, "I am shut up with almost as many unclean creatures as Noah was and in a much smaller ark."

Of his life on the lower deck, Equiano wrote: "There I received such a salutation in my nostrils as I had ever experienced in my life; so that with the loathsomeness of the stench, and crying together, I became so sick and low that I was not able to eat, nor had I the least desire to taste anything. I now wished for the last friend, Death, to relieve me."

Today we are astonished that Newton could blithely read his Bible and compose prayers while transporting Africans against their will into a life of servitude. How could he reconcile this with the command to follow Christ and to love his neighbor in the same way as he loved himself? He complained about the noise and smell of his human cargo but not once in his journals and letters did he betray any moral discomfort. In fact, before each journey he would request that his Christian friends in Liverpool pray for his safety.

The tenderness he showed to Mary in his letters home contrasted vividly with that shown toward the families he was in the process of breaking up. Was the love the slaves felt for their partners and children less valuable than his? How could he organize church services on deck, as part of his spiritual responsibility to his crew, while the Africans screamed in torment only feet beneath them? How could he praise God for the wonderful gift of freedom while denying it to others?

"The three greatest blessings of which human nature is capable are undoubtably, religion, liberty and love," he wrote in a letter to Mary while anchored off the coast of Sierra Leone in 1753. "In each of these, how greatly God has distinguished me! But here are whole nations around me, whose languages are entirely different from each other, yet I believe they all agree in this that they have no words among them expressive of these engaging ideas: from whence I infer that the ideas themselves have no place in their minds. And, as there is no medium between light and darkness, these poor creatures are not only strangers to the advantages which I enjoy, but are plunged in all the contrary evils."

The crude logic was that those whose language didn't embrace the grandest concepts of Western civilization didn't deserve civil treatment. At this time he never openly wondered whether the slaves had souls or whether they, like him, could receive God's grace. The theory of human rights, so prominent in ethical discussions today, had yet to be formulated, and physical cruelty didn't shock English people in the mid-eighteenth century. Whippings, beatings, and executions were an accepted part of everyday life.

When these letters were published forty years later, he felt compelled to add an explanatory footnote. "I felt the disagreeableness of the business very strongly," he wrote. "The office of a gaoler, and the restraints under which I was forced to keep my prisoners, were not suitable to my feelings, but I considered it as the line of life which God, in his providence, had allotted me and as a cross which I ought to bear with patience and thankfulness till he should be pleased to deliver me from it." Asked in 1790 whether he had any "doubts or scruples of the lawfulness of the slave trade" he answered, "I felt it very ineligible, but I had no scruple of the lawfulness of it."

Newton was later quite blunt about why he had stayed in the trade. It was because of the forces of convention—"custom, example and interest," as he put it. Slavery was as acceptable as abortion is today—it was legal, it had immediate and tangible benefits, and people predicted widespread calamity should it ever be banned. There was no social pressure for him to feel shame. Cities had been built on the fruits of slavery and the great merchants of slaves were celebrated, giving their names to buildings and streets. It was those who were opposed to slavery who were regarded as the irritants—enemies of social stability, troublemakers, idealists with no concern for progress.

The Bible, while not condemning slavery, laid down rules of behavior that ultimately and inevitably led to a decay in the practice. St. Paul knew both slaves and slave owners, some of whom were Christians. His advice to slave owners, as Newton must have known, was to avoid harsh treatment. His advice to slaves was to be obedient.

Consequently, Newton believed that his faith only required him to be a more humane trader. "I will treat them with humanity while under my power," he noted in his diary, "and not render their confinement unneccesarily grievous." He reduced the numbers on his ships to prevent the spread of disease and was thrilled on his third voyage as captain not to have had a single death. He also showed concern for improving the morals of his crew. When one of his men was caught having sex with a pregnant slave he immediately put him in chains with the threat of further punishment if anything happened to the unborn child. "I thought myself bound to treat the slaves under my care with gentleness, and so consult their ease and convenience, as far as was consistent with the safety of the whole family of whites and blacks on board my ship."

His second voyage as captain was in June 1752 on the *African*, another of Manesty's ships. A Liverpool directory for this period shows that Manesty was one of 101 local merchants trading to Africa and that he had five ships. Two of them, the *African* and the *Aldington*, were involved in the African trade while the others—the *Anson, Catherine*, and *Recovery*— were trading respectively with Jamaica, South Carolina, and Antigua.

While waiting in Liverpool for the *African* to be prepared, Newton met his old companion from the *Harwich*, Job Lewis. To his horror he found that the simple but sturdy faith that he once mocked had been re- placed by an embittered atheism. This cut Newton to the heart because he recognized his part in this transformation. In an attempt to reverse the change, he offered Lewis a job on the *African*, calculating that his best chance of influencing him was to be with him over a long period. He was later to regret the offer because Lewis showed himself to be an "exceed- ingly profane" man who tried to turn the rest of the crew against him.

In Sierra Leone, Newton purchased a ship, the *Racehorse*, which he offered to Lewis. He accepted the captaincy and sailed off, but Newton was badly let down. Lewis neglected his duties, drank too much, and be- came violent. Three weeks later, while anchored at Grande Bassa, now in the Ivory Coast, Newton saw the *Racehorse* in the distance, but as he approached it he realized that its colors were flying at half-mast. Its cap- tain was dead.

Lewis had fallen ill with a fever and had died full of anger and de- spair, sure that he was damned. He had been, said Newton, "convinced, but not changed. . . . He pronounced his own doom before he expired." In his journal Newton recorded the bare details of administering the will and appointing a new captain, but in a letter to Mary he spoke of the personal impact. "I have been much affected by this sudden stroke," he wrote. "I have known him long, and believe he had a true regard for me, and it was by my inducement that he came hither. There are other rea- sons for my concern, which I need not mention to you."

The other reasons were to do with his remorse over having attacked the man's faith when it was tender and untested. Lewis had once told him that he was the man who had introduced him to the idea of liberty.

This made Newton more aware of his wretchedness, but also more aware of grace. Why would God love someone who had encouraged others to hate him? Just as Plantain Island symbolized wretchedness, in its passive form, Newton as victim, the ignominious end of Job Lewis symbolized wretchedness in its active form, Newton as blasphemer and enemy of the faith.

When the *African* finally arrived at St. Kitts to sell her slaves, Newton had the unexpected pleasure of meeting a fellow captain who shared his faith. Alex Clunie, who lived in Wapping, was a member of a Nonconformist congregation in Stepney and a keen student of the Bible. He had arrived in St. Kitts on the *Pearl* with a crew of twelve. During the four weeks that the two men were together on the island, they met regularly to study and talk, Clunie being able to explain difficult theological concepts and to teach Newton how to pray without the use of written prayers.

Significantly he introduced Newton to the idea of grace in its fundamental Christian sense of "the free and unmerited favour of God shown towards man." Both Roman Catholics and Protestants believed in grace but Catholicism taught that grace was received and maintained through the sacraments of the Church whereas Protestantism taught that it was received by faith alone. Medieval scholasticism, in attempting to synthesize the ideas of Aristotle and St. Augustine, subdivided grace into such categories as "actual grace" and "habitual grace," whereas Protestantism viewed grace as a single continuous action. The grace that "taught my heart to fear," as Newton would later put it, was the same grace that would "lead me home." What had been started would be completed—without the need for fresh infusions of grace.

Clunie was a Calvinist and as such he would have stressed the point that although conversion, from our perspective, feels like us choosing God after testing the alternatives, the fact is that God chooses us. In our natural condition we are spiritually dead, and therefore incapable of answering the divine call. Grace begins with God giving us the spiritual life that empowers us to respond to him for the first time.

Newton said that Clunie "gave me a general view of the errors and controversies of the times." He had assumed that the same gospel was being preached in all churches but Clunie helped him distinguish between dead traditionalism, outright heresy, and what was often referred to as Gospel Christianity, the early Evangelical movement. The controversy that Clunie would have explained was the one between Calvinists and Arminians, one of the great hot potatoes of the age, typified by the disagreement between John Wesley (Arminian) and George Whitefield (Calvinist).

In broad terms this wasn't a controversy over the human problem or the divine solution but over the way in which it worked. The Arminians, named after the seventeenth-century Dutch professor, James Arminius, believed that although all were sinners the human ability to reason was not so impaired that it couldn't assess the gospel and make a cool, considered response. God would not force salvation on anyone, and, having satisfied his judgment of sin through the sacrifice of Christ, he now waited to see who would take advantage of the forgiveness available.

The Calvinist response was that sin had left us not merely short-sighted, but blind; not seriously wounded, but dead. Just as blind people can't restore their own sight and the dead can't resurrect themselves, so none of us can bring ourselves to life spiritually. It would be cruel to offer us salvation in our present state because we could only ignore or reject it. Because of this dire situation, salvation has to be a work of God from start to finish. If we made a contribution, we could claim at least part of the credit. This is the meaning of grace. One of the key supporting verses was written by the apostle Paul to the first Christians in Rome: "If by grace, then it is no more of works, otherwise grace is no more grace. But if it be of works, then it is no more grace, otherwise work is no more work."

Newton, who came to regard Calvinism as a renaissance of New Testament Christianity rather than an invention of Calvin, initially found these doctrines unpalatable. His reason was offended. What eventually convinced him was the evidence of his own life, where the operation of grace had been consistent with the Calvinistic understanding. At the point of conversion he had had no access to sacraments and was not part of any church. Rather than searching for God, he was running from his influence. Yet, despite his rebellion he felt that he had been pursued throughout the years, from London to Chatham, from Africa to the middle of the Atlantic Ocean. God had rescued him, preserved him, and drawn him.

What Newton learned from Clunie helped to solve a problem that had been bothering him. Because of the pattern of his past life—the moral resolutions followed by relapses, the asceticism followed by self-indulgence—he was afraid that his salvation would one day be lost. This was the logic of Arminianism. If through strength and conviction you could opt in, through weakness and doubt you could fall out. But Clunie assured him that as he had been saved by grace rather than willpower, it would take a failure of God's part to let him slip away. "Now I began to understand the security of the covenant of grace," he said, "and to expect to be preserved, not by my own power and holiness, but by the mighty power and promise of God, through faith in an unchangeable Saviour."

He arrived back in England in August 1753 and returned to sea in the same ship within two months, for another yearlong voyage. Although he didn't know it at the time, this was to be his last voyage. The end came suddenly and unexpectedly. He had been ready to sail, but one afternoon, while drinking tea with Mary, he had a violent seizure that left him unconscious for an hour. When the doctor arrived he was still dazed and in pain. A cause couldn't be diagnosed, and he was advised against ever sailing again. He later referred to it in a letter as having been "apoplexy," a sudden loss of consciousness caused by the rupture of a blood vessel in the brain.

This seizure had an unexpected effect on Mary. Traumatized by having seen her husband collapse on her as if dead, she had what appears to have been a total breakdown. "The blow that struck me reached her in the same instant . . . as I grew better, she was thrown into a disorder, which no physician could define, or medicines remove. Without any of the normal symptoms of a consumption, she decayed almost visibly. She became so weak that she could hardly bear anyone to walk across the room she was in. I was placed for about eleven months in what Dr. Young calls the 'dreadful post of observation, darker every hour.'" Newton would look back on this time of illness, hard to understand at the time, as further evidence of God acting in his life, this time rescuing him from a life at sea and saving him for an even greater expedition.

The poet William Cowper became Newton's closest friend.
and together they wrote hymns. ENGRAVING BY UNKNOWN ARTIST.

Olney in the eighteenth century, showing the Church of
St. Peter and St. Paul in the distance. ARTIST UNKNOWN.

Chapter 5

OLNEY HYMNS

God moves in a mysterious way
His wonders to perform;
—*William Cowper*, "GOD MOVES
IN A MYSTERIOUS WAY," 1772

I usually make a hymn weekly and sometimes it costs me so
much thought and study that I hardly do anything else.
—*John Newton*, LETTER, 1774

I hope most of these hymns, being the fruit and
expression of my own experience, will coincide with the
views of real Christians of all denominations. But I cannot
expect that every sentiment I have advanced will be
universally approved. However, I am not conscious of
having written a single line with an intention either to
flatter or to offend any party or person on earth.
—*John Newton*, "PREFACE TO OLNEY HYMNS," 1779

*J*oseph Manesty had played a crucial role in Newton's
life; offering him work in Jamaica, arranging his rescue from Africa,
establishing him as a captain in the slave trade, and finding him and
Mary with their first home in Liverpool. He had hoped that he would
command a new ship being built in the northwest of England and which
he'd invited him to name. Newton had called it the *Bee* and told Mary
that the name had significance: "I could comment a good while on the
word Bee, and talk about the sting and the honey; but I forbear. . . ."

Disappointed that Newton was leaving the sea, Manesty neverthe-less used his influence to get him an onshore job as a customs officer. Newton's conviction that his sudden collapse was further evidence of God's grace in his life was strengthened when his replacement on the *Bee*, Captain Potter, was murdered in Africa during a slave revolt. Nicholas Owen, who had sold him four slaves, recorded in his journal: "Lately we have the melancholy news of Captain Potter's being cut off by the slaves at Mano and the ship driven ashore. The captain, second mate and doctor were all killed in a barbarous manner. The slaves are all taken by the natives again and sold to other vessels."

After almost twenty years of continuous sailing, Newton was happy to be grounded. In August 1755, he became tide surveyor at the Cus-tom House in Liverpool, a job that gave him an office, sixty employ-ees, the use of a coxed six-oared rowing boat, and forty pounds a year. Although the odd job description suggested counting waves and measuring the depth of water, it was a senior position in Customs and Excise; it entailed boarding newly arrived ships to ensure duty was paid on incoming goods and that smuggled items were seized.

It was an exciting time to be an evangelical Christian and Newton gorged himself on the variety of great preaching in and around Liver-pool. A month after becoming tide surveyor he met the legendary evangelist George Whitefield through an introduction arranged by Alex Clunie's minister, Samuel Brewer, and heard him preach nine times in Liverpool. Although the message was serious he noticed that listeners seemed to be filled with joy. After a three-hour service that left many in tears, Newton wrote, "There is something extraordinary in this persecuted despised man, beyond any common attainments, beyond any other person perhaps, which the present or the former age has known."

Newton's experience of Christians broadened. It began with An-glicans but soon included Baptists, Independents, Presbyterians, Congregationalists, Methodists, and Moravians. As church leaders heard about him and his extraordinary story he was invited to preach, and the idea that he was being called to the Christian ministry began to take root.

It would have been relatively easy for him to have joined an independent church as a minister because they had their own academies and were more concerned with an individual's sense of calling and display of spiritual gifts than academic qualifications, but, surprisingly in light of his background, he felt temperamentally more suited to the Church of England.

The church's Thirty-nine Articles of Religion, drawn up in 1563, were unapologetically Calvinistic. The eleventh article said: "We are accounted righteousness before God, only for the merit of our Lord and Saviour Jesus Christ by Faith, and not for our own works or deservings. Wherefore, that we are justified by Faith only, is a most wholesome Doctrine, and very full of comfort, as more largely is expressed in the Homily of Justification." On the issue of free will it was asserted: "The condition of Man after the fall of Adam is such, that man can not turn and prepare himself, by his own natural strength and good works, to faith, and calling upon God. Wherefore we have no power to do good works pleasant and acceptable to God, without the grace of God in Christ preventing us, that we may have a good will, and working with us, when we have that good will."

In 1758 he approached the bishop of York for ordination. As expected he was rejected because he didn't have the university education required by Canon Law. The alternative was to prove that he had a knowledge of Latin and scripture and to supply testimonials from three reputable people who had known him for at least three years.

Although this law assured the church of an educated clergy, it didn't guarantee the most passionate and spiritual of leaders. Having spent all his working life with "plain people" (as they were then referred to), Newton had an invaluable common touch. He also had a broad experience of life and a compelling personal testimony. When John Wesley met Newton in 1760, he confided in his diary: "His case is very peculiar. Our church requires that clergymen be men of learning, and to this end have university education. But how many have a university education and yet no learning at all? Yet these men are ordained! Meantime one of eminent learning as well as unblamable behaviour, cannot be ordained, 'because he was not at the university'! What a mere farce is this? Who would believe that any Christian Bishop would stoop to so poor an evasion?"

Lord Dartmouth, who offered Newton the curacy
of the parish church at Olney.

COURTESY OF THE COWPER AND NEWTON MUSEUM, OLNEY.

John Fawcett, a Baptist minister, was so impressed when he heard Newton speak of his dramatic conversion that he asked him to write his story so that it could be passed around. This was done in a series of letters to Fawcett in 1762, completing the last letter with the comment, "I pray God this little sketch may animate those who shall peruse it to praise the exceeding riches of His goodness to an unworthy wretch."

A Church of England curate, Thomas Haweis, read the letters when they were circulated and contacted Newton to suggest an expanded version. Over a period of three weeks, with the aid of his journals, letters, and diaries, Newton wrote a twenty-five-thousand-word spiritual autobiography, beginning with his childhood in Wapping and ending with his crisis over ordination. His closing words were: "At present my desire to serve the Lord is not weakened, but I

am not so hasty to push myself forward as I was formerly. It is sufficient that He knows how to dispose of me, and that He both can and
will do what is best. To Him I commend myself. I trust that His will
and my true interest are inseparable. To His name be glory."

So impressed was Haweis that he showed the letters to his friend
Lord Dartmouth, who was part of a group of wealthy and powerful
evangelicals who wanted to use their influence to spread the Christian
gospel. Dartmouth was, at different times, President of the Board of
Trade and Foreign Plantations, Colonial Secretary, Lord Keeper of the
Privy Seal, and High Steward of Oxford University. Dartmouth College, the Ivy League university in Hanover, New Hampshire, would be
named after him. One of the properties he owned was a large mansion
known as the Great House in the Buckinghamshire village of Olney.
As the dominant landowner in the area, he was entitled to select the
clergy for the Parish Church of St. Peter and St. Paul.

With a population of around twenty-five hundred, Olney was a small
but plain country town, and even a century later was described as "one
long wide street, with various odds and ends of out-of-the-way places."
Its main industry, lace making, took place in the homes. Three or four
women would crowd into a room no more than six feet square and work
all day making coiffures, lappets, parasol covers, and other works. In
summer the workers would sit in the doorways singing songs known as
lace tellings. "The singing," wrote one contemporary commentator, "as-
sists them in the counting and also keeps them together in their work."

Dartmouth had recently offered the Olney benefice to Haweis because the incumbent, Moses Browne, was overstretched, with another
chaplaincy at Morden College in Blackheath southeast of London.
Haweis turned it down and then Browne, who had several children,
decided that he needed both jobs to stay solvent. As Browne was obviously going to be vicar of Olney in name only, Haweis suggested Newton as an ideal curate-in-charge running the parish in Browne's
absence. Impressed with his manuscript, Dartmouth invited Newton
to London for a meeting, and subsequently persuaded the bishop of
Lincoln to ordain him. On April 29, 1764, Newton was sworn in as a
deacon. Two months later he became a priest and moved with Mary
from Liverpool to Olney.

Dartmouth then paid for the manuscript to be published as a book in August 1764. Newton was apprehensive, concerned that it might feed his vanity, but men he respected, like Haweis and Clunie, encouraged him, agreeing that his story was: "romantic and uncommon and at the same time so interesting and instructive." It was also a commercial success and catapulted Newton to the forefront of British Evangelicalism.

This transformation in his life was a source of wonder to him. The young man with the filthy mouth who had almost withered away beneath the African sun on Plantain Island was now a Church of England priest and a friend of some of Britain's most powerful and noble people. But he never lost sight of the fact that the achievement was not due to him. When, in 1766, Lord Dartmouth arranged to have the vicarage at Olney enlarged for him, Newton wrote in his diary: "Thou hast given an apostate a name and a place among Thy children—called an infidel to the ministry of the gospel. I am a poor wretch that once wandered naked and barefoot, without a home, without a friend; and now for me who once used to be on the ground, and was treated as a dog by all around me, Thou hast prepared a house suitable to the connection Thou hast put me into."

Newton had always loved singing hymns both in corporate acts of worship and as part of his private devotions, but before Olney he had written only the occasional hymn. The earliest that can be dated were sent in a letter to Thomas Haweis in 1763. The catalyst for hymn writing as a regular practice was the arrival in the parish of a timid thirty-six-year-old unpublished poet, William Cowper, who had become a Christian two years previously while a patient in a private asylum. Although Cowper (pronounced Cooper) is now recognized as a pivotal figure in English poetry, anticipating the Romantic movement by at least a quarter of a century, when he came into Newton's life he was unacclaimed, unemployed, and better known for his behavioral oddities than for his lyrical skill.

Like Newton, he had lost his mother when young, but his background—son of a country vicar, educated at Westminister School—was far more genteel and cultured than Newton's. He had planned to become a lawyer but a series of failed suicide attempts showed him to be too unbalanced for the profession and he abandoned his studies. The truth is, he probably wanted to avoid responsibilities rather than die at his own hand. Instead of looking for employment he used a small private income to socialize in theaters and newly fashionable coffeehouses, but even in this relaxed environment he wasn't free of mental torment. He saw flashes and felt pressure on his brain. He became convinced that people were plotting against him or secretly mocking him.

Although only a nominal Christian, he knew the Bible well and theological ideas began to feed his delusions. For an unknown reason he began to think that he could never be forgiven by God. This wasn't because God was negligent or because he had never repented. In his twisted thoughts God had selected him never to be a recipient of grace. There was nothing he could do to escape this final judgment.

He latched on to a reference to "the unforgivable sin," convinced that whatever it was, he had committed it. Christians tried to explain to him that the only truly unforgivable sin was a final rejection of salvation, but this didn't alleviate Cowper's fears. He pointed to the words of Jesus, "Anyone who speaks a word against the Son of Man will be forgiven, but anyone who speaks against the Holy Spirit will not be forgiven, either in this age or in the age to come" (Matthew 12:32), and related it to an occasion when, as he interpreted it, God had given him a transcendent experience that he had wrongly thought was a result of good weather and beautiful surroundings. His bizarre conclusion was that this was the unforgivable sin—to attribute to nature what was of God. This was "speaking against the Holy Spirit."

A period of madness followed, full of visions, voices, delusions, numbness, and sweating. He expected God to vent his wrath on him at any time, comparing the feeling to being hit on the brain with a heavy hammer. "I clapped my hand to my forehead, and cried aloud through the pain it gave me. At every stroke my thoughts and expressions became more wild and incoherent. All that remained clear to me was the sense of sin, and the expectation of sin."

His clergyman brother John Cowper, although not an evangelical, tried to reassure him but nothing helped. After months of what was diagnosed as "hypochondrial melancholy" he was taken to a

The Great House at Olney, where "Amazing Grace" would have been sung for the first time.

private asylum in St. Albans run by a kindly Christian man, Dr. Nathaniel Cotton. It was here, after a further six months of despair during which he felt accused by all his past sins, that he began to accept what his brother had repeatedly told him—that salvation was as available to him as it was to anyone else. The turning point came when he picked up a Bible and read the words "Being justified freely by his grace through the redemption that is in Christ Jesus: Whom God hath set forth to be a propitiation through faith in his blood, to declare his righteousness for the remission of sins that are past, through the forbearance of God" (Rom. 3:24–25).

The verses seemed to banish his fears in an instant. "Immediately I received strength to believe it. Immediately the full beams of the sun of righteousness shone upon me. I saw the sufficiency of the atonement he had made, my pardon sealed in his blood, and all the fullness and completeness of my justification. In a moment I believed and received the gospel. . . . Unless the Almighty Arm had been under me I think I should have died with gratitude and joy. My eyes filled with tears and my voice was choked with transport. I could only look up to heaven in silence, overwhelmed with love and wonder!"

He left St. Albans in June 1765, a changed man, and went to Cambridge to be with his brother. Unable to find accommodation in the city he stayed fifteen miles away in Huntingdon, where, one morning after a church service, he met a young Cambridge student, William Unwin, who impressed him with his seriousness and breadth of education. Unwin in turn introduced Cowper to his family; his teenage sister, his mother Mary, and his father the Reverend Morley Unwin.

Cowper's friendship with the Unwins quickly deepened, and he soon moved in as a paying lodger. Here, in an undemanding atmosphere of leisure, conversation, and mild entertainment, he spent what would be some of the most blissful times of his life. On a typical day they would read the Bible together in the early morning, visit church, walk in the garden at midday, discuss religious matters and sing hymns during the afternoon, and end the day with prayer and the reading of a sermon.

An unusual closeness developed between Cowper and Mary Unwin, who was only seven years his senior. With Reverend Unwin working and the son at university, the two were alone together for much of the time. Although the relationship isn't thought to have been sexual, it was certainly intimate and loving. Despite being of a similar age she may have fulfilled the function of a mother for him, filling the gap left by the death of his own mother.

On July 2, 1767, Rev. Morley Unwin was thrown from his horse while on his way to church and died four days later from the injuries. Tongues were already wagging about the nature of the relationship between Mary Unwin and Cowper, and it now seemed prudent for them to move away from Huntingdon if they were to continue sharing a house. It was into this situation that Newton walked, a few days after Reverend Unwin's funeral, having been given an introduction by a mutual friend, Dr. Richard Conyers. Cowper asked Newton to recommend a town with a good evangelical church where he and Mrs. Unwin might move to. Newton suggested Olney.

Cowper was homeless when he arrived in Olney and so stayed with the Newtons for five months before renting Orchard Side, a tall red-brick building on Market Place. One of the attractions of Orchard Side was that its back garden led to an orchard, the other side of which was the Vicarage. Cowper and Newton paid the owner of the orchard, a Mrs. Aspray, a guinea a year for the privilege of being able to walk through it to make their various meetings. In November 1767, Mrs. Unwin joined Cowper as his housekeeper and companion.

Newton and Cowper became close friends. They both loved rambling in the countryside, reading, and conversing. Newton respected Cowper's superior learning and Cowper respected Newton's spirituality and his experience of the world. They would often read the same books at the same time so that they could discuss them together, and when at the Vicarage with Mary and Mrs. Unwin they would close off an evening of laughter and conversation with hymn singing and prayer.

To the villagers of Olney, Cowper was a lovable eccentric. Despite his long periods of inner turmoil he always had time to speak to the poor and lonely, offering them advice and consolation. He had a particular passion for plants and animals, cultivating the garden at Orchard Side and looking after a collection of hares, rabbits, guinea pigs, dogs, cats, hens, ducks, geese, and birds.

The congregation of St. Peter and St. Paul had grown so fast under Newton's ministry that there had been a demand for meetings in addition to the formal church services. There was now a time of prayer on Tuesdays attended by around forty parishioners, a lecture each Thursday, and an after-church gathering at the Vicarage on Sundays for prayer and singing. This get-together on Sundays became so well attended that Newton had to issue tickets in order "to exclude some who only come to look about them." Special meetings were innovated for children—a precursor of the Sunday School movement—and there were special sermons prepared for the young. Newton visited people at their workplaces, arranged for money to be distributed to the needy, and would sometimes preach on local, national, and international issues.

It was the popular after-church meeting that caused Lord Dartmouth to grant the use of a room in his largely unlived-in seventeenth-century Great House, starting in 1769. Its Great Room, situated at the front of the house, could hold 130 people, far more than the vicarage. It was for these occasions that Newton and Cowper began to write hymns, the move itself being marked by Newton's "O Lord, Our Languid Souls Inspire" and Cowper's "Jesus, Where'er Thy People Meet."

Jesus, where'er thy people meet,
There they behold thy mercy-seat;
Where'er they seek thee thou art found,
And ev'ry place is hallowed ground.

Vibrant hymn singing was one of the notable characteristics of the eighteenth-century evangelical revival. Songs were being composed in a more colloquial language, embracing for the first time New Testament views necessarily not included in the Psalms. Among the most prominent writers of this new style of religious song were Isaac Watts, Martin Madan, John Cennick, Philip Doddridge, and Augustus Toplady. The best known and most prolific was John Wesley's brother, Charles, who composed almost nine thousand hymns before his death in 1788.

Despite its doctrinal roots in Calvinism, the Church of England, of which Wesley and Whitefield remained members, was deeply suspicious of Evangelicalism because of its emphasis on repentance, conversion, and holy living. The term *methodist*, as applied to the followers of Wesley, was intended as an insult because they were considered to be too methodical in their approach to personal holiness. Another term of approbation used by traditionalists of evangelicals was *enthusiast*. It was considered unbecoming to show too much emotion over matters of faith.

It was still a Church of England law that nothing but metrical psalms—the Psalms as found in the King James Version of the Bible but adapted to song meters—should be sung congregationally within its buildings. According to Isaac Watts, three different meters predominated: "namely, the common metre, the metre of the old twenty-fifth Psalm, which I call the short metre, and that of the old hundredth Psalm, which I call long metre."

Martin Luther and his followers in Germany were the first to challenge this orthodoxy by introducing secular folk tunes, but the other seminal Reformer, John Calvin, who was based in Geneva, opposed this innovation, arguing that Psalms alone should be sung in church because they were the inspired word of God and therefore untainted by human error. The *Directory for the Publike Worship*, published in England in 1644 by the Westminster Assembly of Divines, took the same line. It urged that "the whole congregation join herein, everyone that can read is to have a Psalm book. . . . But for the present, where many in the congregation cannot read, it is convenient that the Minister, or some other fit person appointed by him and the other Ruling Officers, do read the Psalm, line by line, before the singing thereof." This process, later known as "lining out," was to survive into the era of hymn singing and is still practiced in some churches today.

Evangelicals in the Church of England, who felt duty bound by canon law, stuck to its letter but avoided its spirit by using the new non-Psalmic songs only in unconsecrated buildings or in the large open-air meetings that characterized the revivals of Wesley and Whitefield. The after-church meetings at the vicarage offered the same freedom of worship.

Newton's hymns were created specifically with the people of Olney in mind. Many of them were illiterate, working as laborers, carpenters, blacksmiths, lace makers, and small traders. Explaining his approach he wrote: "There is a style and manner suited to the composition of hymns, which may be more successfully, or at least more easily, attained by a versifier, than by a poet. They should be Hymns, not Odes, if designed for public worship, and for the use of plain people. Perspicuity, simplicity, and ease, should be chiefly attended to, and the imagery and colouring of poetry, if admitted at all, should be indulged very sparingly, and with great judgment."

His particular self-imposed challenge was to complete at least one fresh hymn each week for use in conjunction with a sermon. The hymn would either reinforce the main points of the preaching or itself become the topic of the sermon that followed. Several times in his letters, Newton mentions "expounding" a new hymn as though he had made its words the text for the day.

He wrote hymns with the same pastoral concerns that he showed in his letters and sermons. He would typically tease the meaning out of a Bible passage and then close with a challenge. He referred to his own experiences at times, but usually only in order to drive home the relevance of the theology. Writing words to accompany a sermon on the story of Jacob wrestling with the angel Newton began with a paraphrase of Jacob's words before introducing his own story:

Thou didst once a wretch behold,
In rebellion blindly bold,
Scorn thy grace, thy power defy,
That poor rebel, Lord, was I.

What would eventually become his best-known hymn was written without any ceremony as part of his recently established routine. He never discussed writing it and neither did he mention it by name in his correspondence. Its composition can only be dated because it accompanied 1 Chron. 17:16–17, and his notebooks reveal that he preached a sermon on these verses on January 1, 1773. This would almost certainly mean that "Amazing Grace" was written in the second half of December 1772.

Unfortunately, the diary in which he recorded 1772 has been lost, and so an exact day for the composition can't be pinned down and we can't know if any recent events affected it. When Josiah Bull wrote his biography of Newton in 1868, the diary was still in existence and he quoted from three entries for December. On December 1 he restarted a series of lectures on John Bunyan's *Pilgrim's Progress* at the Great House. Five days later he presented his hymn titled "The Burdened Sinner," again at the Great House.

A reflective frame of mind might have been produced by the fact that his entry for December 31 was the last in a three-hundred-page diary that had been started in 1756, only two years after he left the slave trade. It caused him to look back over the events of the past seventeen years and measure how far he had come and how much he had been blessed. "How many scenes have I passed through in that time! By what a way has the Lord led me! What wonders he has shown me! My book is now nearly full, and I shall provide another for the next year. O Lord, accept my praise for all that is past. Enable me to trust Thee for all that is to come, and give a blessing to all who may read these records of Thy goodness and my own vileness. Amen and Amen."

The part of 1 Chron. used as his text for January 1, 1773, tells the story of King David's determination to build a temple in Jerusalem to house the sacred ark of the covenant. The desire was good, the writer says, but God had a different plan. The prophet Nathan told David that although the temple would be built, he wouldn't be the king to do it. Just as God had cared for David, raising him from humble origins to a royal palace, he would take care of the ark and the building of a temple in his own time. Then came the promise, "I will make your name like the names of the greatest men of the earth."

Newton focused on David's response to this prophecy from Nathan. "And David the king came and sat before the Lord, and said, Who am I, O Lord God, and what is mine house, that thou hast brought me hitherto? And yet this was a small thing in mine eyes, O God; for thou hast also spoken of thy servant's house for a great while to come, and hast regarded me according to the estate of a man of high degree, O Lord God."

Although January 1, 1773, was a Friday, the church would have operated its Sunday schedule because New Year's Day services were important to Newton. He frequently made special mention of them in his journals and letters. It was a time when he would call on his congregation to assess their spiritual progress and anticipate the challenges of the year ahead. It was also a time for him to challenge those who went to church through tradition but not because of personal faith.

"I usually compose two or three for the occasion of the sermon I preach on the New year's evening," he once explained in a letter to the wife of John Thornton. "I have generally found . . . on these seasons, that the Lord has been pleased to honour me as an instrument of awakening some one poor careless sinner at least, to a desire of his salvation. And to be useful to one soul is of more importance than the temporal prosperity of a whole Nation."

He began his sermon by stressing the importance of being grateful to God for guidance: "They [David's concerns] lead us to a consideration of past mercies and future hopes and intimate the frame of mind which becomes us when we contemplate what the Lord has done for us." Having established his theme, he unpacked the passage by singling out three key phrases.

First, "Who am I? This question should be always on our minds. Who am I? What was I when the Lord began to manifest his purposes of love?" He characterized the unconverted state as miserable, rebellious, and undeserving. Miserable because "shut up under the law and unbelief," rebellious because "blinded by the god of this world," and undeserving because "it was the Lord against whom we sinned." It's not hard to detect the influence of his own story in his choice of emphasis. "His mercy came to us not only undeserved but undesired," he wrote. "Yea, few of us resisted his calls, and when he knocked at the door of our hearts endeavoured to shut him out till he overcame us by the power of grace."

Second, "That thou has brought me hitherto." This was a reminder to Christians that God was involved in their lives before their conversion, "preserving us from a thousand seen, and millions of unseen dangers," during conversion, "the never to be forgotten hour when he enabled us to hope in his mercy" and after conversion when "mercy and goodness" follow us.

Third, "A small thing in mine eyes." Was the issue of the temple a small thing for David? Only when compared to the great things that lay in the future; and in the same way, the trials of the Christian in this life are small in comparison to the glories of eternity. "We are travelling home to God. We shall soon see Jesus, and never complain of sin, sorrow, temptation or desertion any more. He has dealt with us according to the estate of a man of high degree. He found us upon the dunghill and has made us companions of princes. . . ."

He concluded with a rallying call to be grateful, trusting, and patient. Grateful for what had been done for them, trusting in the promises of God and patient during times of trial. "We are spared so far," he said, "But some, I fear, are strangers to the promises. You are entered

upon a New Year. It may be your last. You are at present barren trees in
the vineyard. O fear lest the sentence should go forth—'Cut it down'
(Luke 13:7)."

While making no reference to the verses in Chronicles, the words
of "Amazing Grace" underscore the main points of Newton's sermon.
Phrases in the notes appear to have been paraphrased: "Blinded by the
god of this world" became "was blind but now I see." "Millions of unseen dangers" became "through many dangers, toils and snares"; "the
never to be forgotten hour" became "the hour I first believed" and "yet
a little while and we shall be at home" became "grace will lead me
home." A faint trace of the idea behind the phrase "amazing grace" lies
behind the comment, "What just cause of admiration, that he should
appoint such salvation."

Like the sermon, "Amazing Grace" outlined the Christian pilgrimage from conviction of sin ("taught my heart to fear"), repentance ("a
wretch like me"), and faith ("the hour I first believed"), through the
earthly journey ("brought me safe thus far") and on to life eternal ("a
life of joy and peace"), with the focus remaining on the activity of
"grace." Grace saves, finds, brings, leads, and secures. The narrator
hears and believes. "It is impossible for the sinner to seek the Lord, for
he is so steeped in sin he is at enmity against God," he once wrote.
"Moreover, his will is depraved, probably, so he can't. Since the sinner
can't seek God, God seeks him and sheds grace upon him."

Newton wasn't the first hymn writer to refer to grace as amazing.
Isaac Watts had come close in "Alas! And Did My Saviour Bleed?" with
his lines:

> *Amazing pity! Grace unknown!*
> *And love beyond degree!*

He must also have been aware of Philip Doddridge's "Hymns
Founded on Various Texts in the Holy Scriptures" (1755) in
which hymn 99, entitled "The Humiliation and Exaltation of God's
Israel," began with the words "Amazing grace of God on high!" and
continued with a second stanza that anticipated Newton's "wretch
like me":

Weaker than worms, O Lord, are we,
And viler far then they;
Yet in these reptiles weak and vile
Dost thou thy power display.

Doddridge, who pastored an Independent church close to Olney at Northampton, also wrote in another hymn of grace having its own unique sound:

Grace, 'tis a charming sound
Harmonious to the ear . . .

Each verse of Doddridge's hymn pictured grace as a participant: "Grace first contrived a way," "Grace first inscribed my name," "Grace turned my wandering feet," "Grace taught my soul to pray," and "Grace all the work shall crown."

A misunderstanding can come from not taking into account that ("how sweet the sound") was written in parentheses. Some have wrongly assumed that Newton was implying that we could be saved by a sound ("how sweet the sound that saved a wretch . . ."). One New Age musician built a theory around the idea that there is "such a thing as a sound that would be so sweet that no one who listened to it could ever feel that there was anything wrong with them. . . . The song "Amazing Grace" has been put into the world as a way of announcing that an absolutely phenomenal thing would be happening involving that particular sound."

The less mystical explanation is that Newton was referring to the pleasure brought by the word because of the concept contained within it, just as the name of a loved one can seem to contain the characteristics of the person if repeated over and over. There is often a close relationship between people and their names in the Bible, so that "at the name of Jesus every knee shall bow" is the same as saying "every knee will bow before Jesus." Newton seems to have been aware of this relationship, because it is the thought behind his other well-known hymn:

How sweet the name of Jesus sounds
In a believer's ear.

Newton embroidered Biblical phrases and allusions into all his writing. The image of being lost and found alludes to the parable of the Prodigal Son, where the father is quoted as saying, in Luke 15:24: "For this my son was dead, and is alive again; he was lost, and is found." His confession of wretchedness may have been drawn from Paul's exclamation in Rom. 7:24, "O wretched man that I am! who shall deliver me from the body of this death?" The contrast of blindness and sight refers directly to John 9:25, when a man healed by Jesus says: "One thing I know, that, whereas I was blind, now I see." Newton had used this phrase in his diary during his seafaring days when he wrote (August 9, 1752), "The reason [for God's mercy] is unknown to me, but one thing I know, that whereas I was blind, now I see."

Every word in "Amazing Grace" appears to have been carefully chosen. The phrase "dangers, toils and snares," for example, can seem to be the repetition of three synonyms for "trouble," used for effect, but in biblical usage "dangers" referred to physical uncertainties, "toils" to natural hardships, and "snares" to spiritual temptations. Although the "rule of three" is an acknowledged poetic technique, in Newton's case he was aiming for spiritual veracity, only secondarily for lyrical impact.

The "shield" of the fourth verse is the "shield of faith" (Eph. 6:16) also referred to in the Psalms as the "shield of salvation." A "portion" is an inheritance. "The veil" (or 'vail' in the original) refers to the curtain separating the Holy of Holies from the public part of the tabernacle or temple through which only the High Priest could pass into the presence of God. At the crucifixion "the veil of the temple was rent in twain" (Matt. 27:51) symbolizing the open access now available to all believers. The phrase Newton picked comes from the verse "Which hope we have as an anchor of the soul, both sure and steadfast, and which entereth into that within the veil" (Heb. 6:19). The image of the earth "dissolving like snow" comes from Peter's description of the end of the age when "the heavens shall pass away with a great noise, and the elements shall melt with a fervent heat, the earth also and the works that are therein shall be burned up" (2 Pet. 3:11–12).

There almost certainly wouldn't have been musical accompaniment when "Amazing Grace" made its debut because Newton wasn't a

musician and his church didn't have an organ at that time, organs having been among Calvin's forbidden instruments. It might have been
sung, but to a tune already in use with the metrical psalms. Newton
wasn't concerned with aesthetic impact but with leaving his congregation with meaningful words that would remind them of the essence of
his sermon. With all his hymns his wish was to promote "the faith and
comfort of sincere Christians."

Amazing grace! (how sweet the sound)
That saved a wretch like me!
I once was lost, but now am found,
Was blind, but now I see.

'Twas grace that taught my heart to fear,
And grace my fears relieved;
How precious did that grace appear,
The hour I first believed!

Through many dangers, toils and snares,
I have already come;
'Tis grace has brought me safe thus far,
And grace will lead me home.

The Lord has promised good to me,
His word my hope secures;
He will my shield and portion be,
As long as life endures.

Yes, when this flesh and heart shall fail,
And mortal life shall cease;
I shall possess, within the vail,
A life of joy and peace.

The earth shall soon dissolve like snow,
The sun forbear to shine;

But GOD, who called me here below,
Will be for ever mine.

Could Newton have had Cowper on his mind when writing? Was he thinking of his friend's recent decline when he wrote his lines of stirring assurance? It seems quite remarkable that the day Newton presented the hymn for the first time was also the day that Cowper attended church for the last time. Preaching Cowper's funeral sermon in May 1800 Newton said: "The last sermon he ever heard preached was on New Year's Day, 1773. He drank tea with me in the afternoon. The next morning a violent storm overtook him which caused a very great shyness. I used to visit him often but no argument could prevail with him to see me. He used to point with his finger to the church and say, 'you know the comfort I have had there and how I have seen the glory of the Lord in his house and until I can go there I'll not go anywhere else.' "

Two years previously, Cowper's madness had showed signs of returning. The doubts that he thought he had defeated were rising again. "My soul is among lions," he told Newton in March. Three months later, in a letter to the wife of the hymn writer Martin Madan, he wrote: "I have temptations that are almost ever present with me, and shed a thick gloom over all my prospect. Sin is my burden, a sure token that I shall be delivered from its remaining power, but while it remains it will oppress me. The Lord, who chose me in the furnace of affliction is pleased to afford that tempter a large permission to try me. I think I may say I am tried to the utmost."

Cowper composed many of his most enduring hymns while in this state, so they were tinged with a melancholy that was unusual in Christian worship. His opening lines were often foreboding rather than triumphal: "Oh! for a closer walk with God," "My former hopes are fled," "The billows swell, the winds are high," "My soul is sad and much dismay'd," "When darkness long has veil'd my mind," "The Saviour hides his face!" This admission that the Christian pilgrimage could be fraught with doubts, disappointments, and temptations would later win him wide appreciation. In admitting his own vulnerability, he brought consolation to others.

Fierce passions discompose the mind,
As tempests vex the sea;
But calm content and peace we find,
When, Lord, we turn to thee

Newton didn't ignore this tension between the work of grace in his life and the opposing work of sin, but appeared confident that grace would get the upper hand, whereas Cowper was not so sure. Newton wrote:

Strange and mysterious is my life,
What opposites I feel within!
A stable peace, a constant strife!
The rule of grace, the power of sin:
Too often I am captive led,
Yet daily triumph in my head.

Although varying in intensity, Cowper's second period of despair was to be permanent. He never renounced his fundamental beliefs, arguing forcefully against anyone who challenged them and continuing to write religious poetry, but he was also convinced that he was excluded from the kingdom of God. He was called, but not chosen.

No appeal to reason or Scripture had any long-term effect on the suffering poet. Cowper's assurance of his damnation was as firm and unshakable as Newton's was in his salvation. The two men remained close, Newton once commenting that in the twelve years that they were together at Olney there was barely half a day that passed when they weren't together. "The first six [years] I passed in daily admiring and trying to imitate him. During the second six I walked pensively with him in the valley of the shadow of death."

Hymn writing was Newton's way of cementing the bond between them as well as usefully occupying Cowper's fragile mind, but after the breakdown of 1773, Cowper could write no more hymns. "Ask not hymns from a man suffering despair as I do," he wrote to one correspondent. "I could not sing the Lord's song were it to save my life, ban-

ished as I am, not to a strange land, but to a remoteness from his presence, in comparison with which the distance from east to west is no
distance."

Newton continued composing alone and was encouraged to think
of compiling a hymnal after his work began appearing in magazines,
sometimes attributed to others. With an annual salary of thirty pounds
(three quarters of what he earned as tide surveyor), he couldn't consider funding a first print run of a hymnbook himself, but help came
from John Thornton, a wealthy Christian friend of Lord Dartmouth,
who was director of the Bank of England. Thornton agreed to pay for a
thousand copies to be printed and distributed, and Newton arranged
for the profits to be used to benefit Olney's poor.

Olney Hymns, which had work by both Newton and Cowper, went to
press in February 1779 and was ready for distribution by July. The published book, measuring six and a half inches by four inches, was 428
pages long and arranged in three themed sections: "On select texts of
scripture," "On occasional subjects," and "On the progress and
changes of the spiritual life." There was a preface by Newton and the
hymns composed by Cowper (roughly 20 percent of the whole) were
prefixed by the letter *C*.

"Amazing Grace," hymn 41 in "On select texts of scripture," began
at the bottom of a right-hand page (53) and continued overleaf. Under
the heading "I CHRONICLES" it was given the title "Faith's Review and
Expectation" with the citation (Chap. xvii. 16, 17).

Its publication coincided with the end of Newton's tenure at Olney.
John Thornton was enticing him to London, where he thought he
would have a greater national influence and offered him the living of
St. Mary Woolnoth in Lombard Street close to the Bank of England.
Newton was reluctant to leave the countryside, saying that "London
was the last place I should have chosen for myself," but he realized that
the time was right for change. There were divisions at Olney between
those who only attended the church and those who went to the Great
House, and Newton felt less welcome in the town than he had when he
first moved there.

His reputation, enhanced first by his autobiography, then by his hymns, had outgrown his role as a curate-in-charge of a small country parish. He was ready for a tougher challenge on a more public stage. He knew that in London he would not only be able to influence but to influence the influential. He had started life in Wapping and now he was almost going back home.

*The politician William Wilberforce was inspired
by Newton and went on to be the leading figure in
the British campaign to abolish slavery.*

Chapter 6

ABOLITION

I hope it will always be a subject of humiliating reflection
to me, that I was once an active instrument in a business
at which my heart now shudders.
—*John Newton*, THOUGHTS UPON THE
AFRICAN SLAVE TRADE, 1788

Some men excel in one virtue more than another. But
Newton's character was beautiful in its entireness. It
rested on a solid foundation—the initial Christian grace of
humility, and of this grace he was a most striking
example. He never for a moment forgot that by the grace
of God he was what he was.
—*Josiah Bull*, JOHN NEWTON OF OLNEY, 1868

How wonderful must be the moment after death!
—*John Newton*, LETTERS TO A WIFE, 1793

*I*t's difficult to pinpoint exactly when and why Newton's
attitude toward the slave trade changed. In his autobiography he confessed to having felt uneasy during his captaincy and praying that
he might be given a "more humane calling" but, paradoxically, he continued to believe that it was God who had provided him with the work.

That he felt it necessary to defend his participation when the book
was written in 1763 shows that his conscience was becoming exercised
over the issue. Six years later, in his history of the Christian church, *A
Review of Ecclesiastical History,* he briefly attacked British colonialism

in these words: "We are taught from our infancy to admire those who, in the language of the world, are styled great captains and conquerors, because they burned with a desire to carry slaughter and terror into every part of the globe, and to aggrandise their names, by the depopulation of countries, and the destruction of their species, while [the] generous spirit of St. Paul is almost totally overlooked." Yet his sermons, letters, and diaries don't betray any signs of an inner struggle over the issue. Very conscious of his moral infirmities he didn't yet count slave trading among his past sins, and neither did he refer to it in his sermons on the state of the nation.

Whatever thoughts he had about the legitimacy of the slave trade, he kept them to himself during his years at Olney, possibly erring on the side of caution because he knew that any public pronouncement would go on record and he would have to be sufficiently convinced to be able to defend it. It would be against his interests to sermonize on provisional judgments.

He must have been aware of the debate about slavery, particularly as some of the trade's most vociferous opponents were Christians. In 1757, the Member of Parliament for Hull, David Hartley, introduced a debate in the House of Commons as to whether the slave trade was "contrary to the laws of God and the rights of men." In 1769, Granville Sharp, who was to become one of the most prominent abolitionists, published *A Representation of the Injustice and Dangerous Tendency of Tolerating Slavery in England.* Sharp was from good Anglican stock, his father being an archdeacon and his grandfather a bishop. In 1774, John Wesley, who had read Newton's autobiography several times, produced his polemic *Thoughts on Slavery.*

Newton was also aware of Selina Hastings, Countess of Huntingdon, an evangelical aristocrat devoted to spiritual and moral reformation. She had become a Christian after hearing Whitefield and was then herself responsible for the conversion of Lord Dartmouth. Well bred and wealthy, she was passionate about using her influence and money to spread the gospel, educate Christian ministers, and relieve suffering and injustice. Her best-known contribution, Lady Huntingdon's Connexion, was a network of independent chapels that she financed.

An underlying belief of the age was that everyone had his or her place in a divinely ordained hierarchy. Some were born to lead and some were born to serve. As Samuel Johnson put it: "Subordination tends greatly to human happiness." This was why the suggestion of freedom for slaves or education for the poor was so contentious. If Africans were released from slavery, might they not rebel? If the illiterate began to read and learn, might they not begin to challenge their superiors and destroy the "Great Chain of Being"? Order in society depended on people knowing where they belonged and staying in place.

Inspired by her Christian faith, Countess Huntingdon was more concerned about individual dignity and national justice than the dangers of crossing barriers of class and race. In 1765 when it was common for an educated English person to describe Native Americans as "savages," she sponsored a tour of Britain by Samson Occum, a converted Mohegan from Connecticut involved in land rights issues and raising money for charity schools. He came to Olney and preached at St. Peter's and St. Paul's.

Newton was impressed with Occum, and what particularly struck him was that despite their racial and cultural differences their experience of conversion was identical. "In describing to me the state of his heart when he was a blind idolater [he] gave me, in general, a striking picture of what my own was, in the early part of my life," he wrote in a letter. "His subsequent views of the gospel corresponded with mine as face answers to face in a glass, though I dare say, when he received them, he had never heard of Calvin's name."

In 1773, Countess Huntingdon financed the printing of *Poems on Various Subjects*, by the former slave Phillis Wheatley, the first book by an African American to be published. This was a potentially subversive act because if Africans could be seen to have the same spiritual and intellectual capacity as whites, then slavery would be impossible to justify. One of Wheatley's poems was pointedly dedicated to Lord Dartmouth, now secretary of state for North America, whom she had met on a visit to London. The poem appealed to him to remove: "the iron chain / Which wanton Tyranny with lawless hand / Has made."

By 1781, Newton's old friend Cowper was writing poetry that criticized the slave trade. Wasn't everyone, regardless of skin color, a sinner before God and yet capable of being redeemed? In one poem, "Charity," he wrote:

Canst thou, and honour'd with a Christian name,
Buy what is woman-born, and feel no shame?
Trade in the blood of innocence, and plead
Expedience as a warrant for the deed?

Newton must have read this poem, because it was included in Cowper's first collection of poems, published in 1782, for which he wrote the preface.

Yet, despite these influences, Newton didn't publicly commit himself to the abolition movement until the mid-1780s, and this shift appears to have been prompted by a renewed relationship with the son of a family friend rather than through the force of a particular argument.

Hannah Wilberforce was the half sister of John Thornton and was in charge of her eight-year-old nephew, William, whose father had died, leaving him a fortune. They lived in London, and Newton would visit the family home to give talks on Bunyan's *Pilgrim's Progress* and she and William would in turn visit the Newtons in Olney. William Wilberforce was particularly taken by this curate, who although only in his forties seemed like an old man to him, and they enjoyed a good relationship. Unusual for a churchman of his time, Newton paid particular attention to children and wrote special songs for them.

The extent of his concern can be shown by a letter he later wrote to Hannah: "I hope your nephew engages good bodily health, and his soul nourished and refreshed. And though he lives in a [spiritually] barren land, I trust he finds that the Lord can open springs and fountains in the wilderness. The word of grace and the throne of grace afford wells of salvation, from which he cannot be debarred."

Wilberforce was an exceptionally gifted child, going to Cambridge University at the age of fourteen. Newton followed his progress, but they no longer saw each other. At twenty-one Wilberforce had become the Member of Parliament for Yorkshire, and from then on his progress was charted in the newspapers and fashionable magazines. He was a topic of conversation in society not only because he was talented, wealthy, and powerful but because he was part of the fast set of the day: a member of five exclusive London clubs, a singer known as "the nightingale of the House of Commons," a witty conversationalist, a great dancer, an expert card player, a convincing mimic, and a friend of royalty.

When Newton had known him in Olney he had seemed a Christian, but as the years passed, and the influence of his aunt Hannah weakened, there was less and less evidence of any heartfelt faith. Around the time that he entered Parliament, Newton used him as an example of what can happen to the spiritual convictions of children. "The strongest and most promising views of this sort I ever met with, were in the case of Mr. Wilberforce when he was a boy" he said in a letter to Cowper. "But they now seem entirely worn off, not a trace left behind, except a deportment comparatively decent and moral in a young man of a large fortune."

After five years as an MP, with his star still rising, Wilberforce found himself challenged by the beliefs of his childhood. Matters came to a head when reading the New Testament in Greek and hymn writer Philip Doddridge's book *The Rise and Progress of Religion* while traveling in Europe with the brilliant scientist and Christian Isaac Milner. Discussing these books with Milner led to a slow conversion similar in detail to Newton's. He started a journal, recording his spiritual progress, and became aware of an increased moral sensitivity. It awakened a desire to get back in touch with his old friend John Newton, who he knew was living in Charles Square, Hoxton, a district of London close to the City.

On November 28, 1785, in words that echoed "Amazing Grace," Wilberforce wrote in his journal, "True Lord, I am wretched, and miserable, and blind, and naked. What infinite love, that Christ should die to save such a sinner, and how necessary it is He should save us altogether, that we may appear before God with nothing of our own." Five days later he added: "Resolved again about Mr. Newton. It may do me good; he will pray for me; his experience may enable him to direct me

*St. Mary Woolnoth, in London, where Newton spent the final years
of his ministry and in whose crypt he was originally buried.*

ARTIST UNKNOWN.

to new ground of humiliation, and it is only that which I can perceive
God's spirit to employ to any effect. It can do me no harm, for that it is
a scandalous objection which keeps occurring to me, that if ever my
sentiments change I shall be ashamed of having done it."

For someone as prominent as Wilberforce to associate with a man
like Newton, who although an Anglican was often derided as an *enthu-*

siast or even a *methodist,* could have affected his standing as a politician by inviting ridicule. For this reason he proceeded cautiously by dropping a note off at the vestry of St. Mary Woolnoth on December 4, 1785, requesting a meeting and making it clear that discretion on Newton's part was paramount. "I have had ten thousand doubts within myself whether or not I should discover myself to you but every argument against doing it has its foundation in pride. I am sure you will hold yourself bound to let no-one living know of this application, and of my visit, till I release you from the obligation."

On Wednesday, December 7, he walked several times around the tree-lined Charles Square, postponing the moment of knocking on Newton's door, because he sensed that it would be a momentous meeting. His questions were about the direction of his life. Now he was a Christian, should he still associate with his high-living friends, or was he in danger of becoming frivolous? Should he remain in politics or use his gifts of intellect and oratory to spread the gospel? Was his wealth something to enjoy or to give away?

Wilberforce did eventually knock on the door and was welcomed warmly by Newton, who listened intently to the flood of questions. Possibly Wilberforce thought that he would be advised to let go of his privileges and his position. After all, Newton had abandoned a career in Customs and Excise to take Holy Orders. If this was what he was expecting to hear, he would have been shocked by Newton's response. Newton told him that he should keep the friends he already had and that he would be a far more effective worker for God if he used his obvious talents in the field of politics than if he stood down.

A letter written by Newton shortly afterward gives an indication of the nature of Newton's advice: "My heart is with you, my dear sir. I see, though from a distance, the importance and difficulties of your situation. May the wisdom that influenced Joseph and Moses, and Daniel rest upon you. Not only to guide and animate you in the line of political duty but especially to keep you in the habit of dependence upon God, and communion with him, in the midst of all the changes and bustle around you." Wilberforce left Charles Square "much comforted" and commented in his journal: "I found my mind in a calm, tranquil state, more humbled, and looking more devoutly up to God."

The two men stayed in touch, and each time they met, Wilberforce was refreshed by Newton's wisdom and encouragement. "Very unhappy," he wrote in his journal on one such day. "Called at Newton's, and bitterly moved: comforted me." Half a century later his son Samuel Wilberforce commented: "It was a happy choice that sent [my father] so calm an advisor. There were many then who would have tried to turn him from the public life which was his true vocation. Newton, though no man of genius, had in his stormy experience of life matured a calm judgment, and he urged now upon the young statesman that he should not hastily form new connections, nor widely separate himself from his former friends."

Over the next year, Wilberforce considered how to integrate his Christian concerns with his political duty. Alarmed by what he saw as moral decay in British life he embarked on a campaign to improve the "religion and morals of the people," canvassing the support of fellow MPs as well as church leaders. As a direct result, a Royal Proclamation against Vice and Immorality was issued in 1787, and out of this grew the Proclamation Society, an organization dedicated to Sabbath observance and the suppression of prostitution, blasphemy, and indecent publications.

At the same time a movement against slavery was cohering, organized largely by men and women of Christian conviction. Individual Church of England communicants had attacked the slave trade from as far back as 1680, but the church itself had not passed a resolution. The Quakers, though, opposed it in 1727 and almost fifty years later vowed to excommunicate any member who had dealings with the trade. In July 1786 a small group of dedicated opponents gathered at the vicarage of Rev. James Ramsay in Teston, Kent, not too many miles from Chatham, where Newton had been forced into service on the *Harwich* forty-two years earlier. Those present included some Quaker merchants from the City, Beilby Porteous (bishop of Chester), Benjamin La Trobe of the Moravian Brethren, clergyman Thomas Clarkson, who had recently published his *Essay on the Slavery and Commerce of the Human Species*, the evangelical Lady Middleton and her husband, Sir Charles Middleton, MP, and the Anglican Granville Sharp, who in 1772 had fought and won a case to prove that as English law didn't recognize slavery, any slave landing on British soil was automatically a free person. It was Sharp who, in May 1787, would become the first chairman of the newly formed Committee for the Abolition of the Slave Trade.

The ambitions of these dedicated campaigners were held back by lack of access to those in power. Although Sir Charles Middleton was an MP, he didn't have a high profile and rarely spoke in the Commons. He admitted himself that he was not the right person to make it a political issue. The members of this group could debate and produce pamphlets, but it couldn't hope to abolish such a large and profitable industry by sniping from the sidelines. How could they hope to persuade the country that morality was more important than prosperity? To succeed they needed an advocate in high places, someone already well connected, who could give prominence to the cause.

Wilberforce was an obvious choice. He was young, dynamic, and Christian, and had shown himself to be capable of effecting change. He was unafraid of controversy yet exhibited self-control, he was committed to high moral standards yet wasn't unbearably pious, he was a passionate speaker on behalf of the causes he believed in and yet was well respected even by those who vigorously opposed him. In addition, he had the ear of his close friend, Prime Minister Pitt.

Newton knew that Wilberforce's initial impact would be among his social class. There was a lot of religion in the higher echelons of society, but very little true Christian discipleship. Years later, when Wilberforce published a book on the subject of the difference between the "prevailing Christian system" and "real Christianity," Newton excitedly wrote: "[Wilberforce's] situation is such that this book must and will be read by many in high circles, to whom we little folks can get no access. If we preach they will not hear us. If we write they will not read. May the Lord make it useful to the great men both in Church and state."

Wilberforce was under pressure from several sources to become the advocate for abolition. In later life he wrote that there were "many impulses" in his life at that time that combined in "giving to my mind the same direction"; Lady Middleton wrote to him in 1786 suggesting the idea, and he replied saying that the issue was so serious that he would take his time considering it. As part of his consideration he began researching the trade. The following year Thomas Clarkson also approached him and then, that spring, while visiting the prime minister's country estate in Kent, Pitt confronted him directly saying: "Wilberforce, why don't you give notice of a motion on the subject of the Slave Trade? You have already taken great pains to collect evidence, and are therefore fully entitled to the credit which doing so will ensure you. Do not lose time, or the ground may be occupied by another."

This cause perfectly matched the aspirations and talents of the man. It fitted in with his aim to reform the moral life of Britain and he had both the passion and the intellectual capability to take it all the way. In his journal on Sunday, October 28, 1787, he made a statement that would crystalize his political and spiritual mission: "God Almighty has set before me two great objects, the suppression of the Slave Trade and the Reformation of Manners."

Whereas it is an established fact that Newton helped Wilberforce in his decision to apply Christian principles to politics, we can only surmise that it was Wilberforce's stand as an abolitionist that stirred Newton to make his first public denouncement of the slave trade. In 1788 Newton published a ten-thousand-word essay, *Thoughts upon the African Slave Trade*, which was unambiguous in its condemnation. He had finally and irrevocably nailed his colors to the mast. He called the trade "iniquitous," "cruel," "oppressive," "destructive," "disgraceful," "unlawful," and "wrong," declaring that he was "bound in conscience to take shame to myself by a public confession, which, however sincere, comes too late to prevent or repair the misery and mischief to which I have, formerly, been accessory."

He didn't build a theological case, as he did in his sermons, and no Bible verses were quoted in support of his position. His appeal was to what he hoped was the consensus view of humane treatment. What made his approach different to most others was that he showed concern for the captors as well as the captives, arguing that those who were brutal were in turn brutalized by the experience. Everyone involved in the trade, from agents to slave ship captains, slaves to merchants, was debased. He offered evidence from his own experience of ordinary Englishmen changed into callous barbarians: crew members raping girls, captains torturing disobedient slaves, and one sailor who threw a baby overboard because he was upset by its crying. The slave trade, he concluded, "robbed the heart of every gentle and humane disposition."

At the same time William Cowper, who had moved from Olney to a mansion in nearby Weston Underwood in July 1786, added his talent to the cause. His second book, *The Task*, which consisted of more than five thousand lines of blank verse, had been well received by both the critics and the public. John Thornton's daughter had contacted him through Newton, asking him if he would write a song that could be used by the Society for the Abolition of the Slave Trade to promote its case. Cowper obliged by composing a ballad, "The Negro's Complaint," which was to be sung to the tune of "Admiral Hosier's Ghost." It was printed in newspapers and as a broadsheet and became a popular antislavery song.

> Forc'd from home and all its pleasures,
> Af'ric's coast I left forlorn;
> To increase a stranger's treasures,
> O'er the raging billows borne;
> Men from England bought and sold me,
> Paid my price in paltry gold;
> But, though theirs they have enroll'd me,
> Minds are never to be sold.

Cowper wrote more songs and poems condemning the slave trade, using blistering satire, as in "Sweet Meat has Sour Sauce," also known as "The Slave-Trader in the Dumps," and adding warnings of God's judgment. But he soon came to doubt the value of such propaganda. The ballads were being sung, he thought, only because people liked the tunes and, besides, the common people among whom they were popular were not those who had the power to change things. Writing to Newton he said, "General censure of the iniquity of the practice will avail nothing, the world has been overwhelmed with such remarks already, and to particularise all the horrors of it were an employment for the mind both of the poet and his readers of which they would necessarily soon grow weary."

As Wilberforce and the committee began to compile evidence of what went on in the slave trade, the Trade Committee of the Privy Council interviewed those who had firsthand experience so that it could determine "the conditions of British commercial intercourse in West Africa." One of the witnesses called in 1788 was the Reverend John Newton, Rector of Saint Mary Woolnoth. He was asked to describe his involvement, provide background details on West African society, and explain precisely how slaves were collected and transported.

"Are wars entered into for the purpose of making slaves?"

"I cannot exactly say. The people are like European travellers and tell such wonderful stories there is no depending on them."

"Do the slaves show great apprehension on being sold?"

"They are often under great apprehension at the sight of the sea. They imagine they are being bought to be eat."

"Is the condition of the slaves that are not sold worse than that of the slaves in our islands?"

"I was never any length of time in our islands, but I believe that the situation of slaves at home is bad. It's worse on board ships and worst of all on our islands."

The central argument of those who supported slavery was that abolition would destroy the economy and ruin major cities like Bristol, Liverpool, and London. Without slave labor Britain would lose its colonies to less scrupulous nations. The very discussion of abolition would imply that Westminster was weakening and this would lead to slave revolts.

Most defensive of all were the merchants, who of course stood to lose the most if abolition came into force. To the accusation that conditions on their ships were inhumane they countered that it would defeat the object of their business to lose or harm slaves in transit. Lord Heathfield claimed that slaves had more space, in terms of cubic feet, than soldiers on maneuvers had in their tents. When told that slaves working on plantations in the British colonies were far happier than they would be if they were in Africa, Wilberforce wittily responded: "Be it so. But we have no right to make people happy against their will."

In April 1789, the Privy Council Report containing the evidence of Newton and others was published, and a month later Wilberforce presented his Bill for the Abolition of Slavery. Like Newton, he didn't buttress his argument with explicit theology. Slavery was wrong, he said, because it destroyed the harmony of West African culture and violated the individual captives. If slavery was essential to support our living standards, was it right that our contentment was dependent on the misery of people in another part of the world? The important issue for Britain was not what was expedient, but what was right.

Newton eagerly followed these events and no longer hesitated to speak out against the slave trade from the pulpit. He refrained from naming it a national sin because, as he said in one sermon: "I hope, and believe, a very great majority of the nation earnestly long for its suppression, But, hitherto, petty and partial interests prevail against the voice of justice, humanity, and truth." At the end of 1788 he thanked Wilberforce for drawing him into his confidence at such an early stage in the campaign. "It is hoped and believed," he wrote, "that the Lord has raised you up for the good of His church and for the good of the nation."

There was a wonderful symmetry in that Wilberforce helped establish Sierra Leone, the scene of Newton's exile, as a haven in Africa for freed slaves. Along with Thomas Clarkson, Henry Thornton (son of Newton's patron John), and ten others, Wilberforce became a director of the Sierra Leone Company, which was authorized by an act of Parliament to allow equality of citizens regardless of color; free education for children; and the protection of English common law. Wilberforce also saw it as an opportunity of making the locals "acquainted with the great truths of Christianity" so that within a relatively short time Christian missionaries were visiting the Sherbro region and Plantain Island, and churches of Lady Huntingdon's Connexion were established in the country. One missionary who visited Sherbro in the early nineteenth century was amazed to find a copy of Newton's sermons in the home of an African Christian.

As the abolition campaign accelerated, Mary Newton was being diagnosed with breast cancer. She had been unwell for more than a year, gradually losing her strength, and on December 15, 1790, she died. For Newton this presented the supreme test of the faith he had preached for so long, because his love for Mary had played such a vital role in his conversion. During his time on the *Harwich*, the thought of her had saved him from suicide and murder. On Plantain Island his longing to be reunited with her had given him the will to survive. When he was spotted by the *Greyhound*, it was only the promise of seeing her that had deterred him from carrying on his life as a trader on the Kittam.

Despite her importance to Newton she remains a shadowy figure

The landing place at Plantain Island in the 1930s.

because we know so little about her character and her side of the story. From her extant letters and the references made to her in the letters of others she appears to have been a vibrant, fun-loving woman who, although not the intellectual equal of her husband, provided a necessary balance. Whereas he was studious and given to serious statements, she liked to laugh, and this made it easier for many people to visit the Newton household. She enjoyed reading and listening to sermons but could be caustic if she found something boring or overbearing. She enjoyed gardening and would spend many hours talking to Cowper about geraniums, melons, and glazed frames.

From the first letter Newton wrote as a teenage sailor through to those written on the slave ships and the notes he penned in his old age whenever they were separated, there was a constant yearning for her presence. When he wasn't with her he repeated her name aloud, imagined her daily routine, and reconstructed past conversations. The sin he felt most vulnerable to was idolatry, and even close friends, such as Richard Cecil, "wished this violent attachment had been cast more in the shade." After having been married for twenty-two years he wrote to her, "Every room where you are not present, looks unfurnished."

His friends worried about how he would react to her death. His views were well known. What he had taught was that even though a Christian might suffer "he cannot be properly unhappy" and times of trial were an opportunity to show "the power of divine grace." But it was only in the absence of Mary that he would have to live this out and he was conscious that he had to be a good example to those who looked to him for leadership. He had hoped, in his heart of hearts, that he would be the first to die.

What he discovered was that, when he needed it most, he had access to a supply of strength he never knew existed. The day of her death he preached at St. Mary Woolnoth. The next day he visited parishioners, and when it came to her funeral, he delivered the sermon. "The Bank of England is too poor to compensate for such a loss as mine," he later wrote. "But the Lord, the all-sufficient God, speaks, and it is done. Let those who know him, and trust him, be of good courage. He can give them strength according to their day."

Ten years later, on April 25, 1800, his most intimate friend, William Cowper, died in East Dereham, Norfolk. At the time Cowper was working on a revision of his translation of Homer's *Iliad*, and his earlier work was having an influence on a new generation of English writers, including William Wordsworth and Samuel Coleridge, who admired his evocations of nature, use of plain language, and concern for ordinary working people. William Blake, the visionary poet and engraver, was fascinated by the combination of religion and madness in his life, because he believed that as society moved toward scientific explanations for everything, religious people would increasingly appear insane. Years later he claimed that Cowper had appeared to him in a vision and told him that his one regret was that he hadn't allowed himself to be as mad as he could have been.

Newton delivered the sermon at Cowper's funeral, referring to his mental problems but stressing the comfort that he gave to others and the security of his salvation. Although Newton never fully understood the doubts that Cowper battled with, he had a very enlightened attitude toward it, believing that it was physical rather than spiritual in origin—what we today would refer to as brain chemistry. "He suffered much here for twenty-seven years, but eternity is long enough to make amends for all. For what is all he endured in this life, when compared with that rest which remaineth for the children of God?"

The Abolition of Slavery bill continued to face tough opposition in both the Commons and the Lords. It had been defeated more than once, amended, delayed, and because it had been around so long became a topic of indifference even for those who had supported it. In March 1797 it had faced its narrowest defeat so far, not because the size of the opposition vote had increased but because Wilberforce's supporters were becoming apathetic. The date of the vote coincided with the opening night of a new opera in Covent Garden, and many of the abolitionists opted for a night out rather than overtime in the House of Commons.

After it had suffered two further defeats, Wilberforce agreed not to raise the bill for five years but when he did, in May 1804, it passed the first of its three readings in the Commons with a majority of seventy-five, and three years later it was passed by the Lords. On March 25, 1807, the king gave his assent and the Bill for the Abolition of Slavery became law.

It had been Newton's prayer that he would live to see the law passed. Three years earlier he had told Wilberforce that "the hopeful prospect of its accomplishment will, I trust, give me daily satisfaction so long as my declining faculties are preserved." Wilberforce replied with a tender letter of thanks in which he said: "O my dear sir, it is refreshing for me to turn away my eye from the vanities with which it is surrounded, and to fix it on you, who appear in some sort to be already enlightened with the beams of that blessed day which is beginning to rise on you, as you approach to the very boundaries of this world's horizon. May you soon enjoy it in its meridian lustre."

By now old age was telling on him. He could hardly see to read and would lose track of his theme while preaching. It was gently suggested to him that he should retire, but he wouldn't listen. To the question, "How are you today, sir?" he would invariably reply, "I am just as God would have me." When one friend reminded him that he was now over eighty and might consider that his work was done, he cried: "What! Shall the old African blasphemer stop while he can speak?"

He didn't stop speaking until October 1806. He preached his last sermon at a service to raise money for those who had suffered the previous year in the Battle of Trafalgar, where the British fleet, under Horatio Nelson, had defeated the French and Spanish off the southwest coast of Spain. It was easier for him to accept death than retirement. Even as he protested against stepping down from the pulpit his diaries and letters were increasingly focusing on his hope of heaven. In 1802 he had written, "The day of opportunity wears away, and the night is approaching." Two years later, after signing a letter, he added: "Time, how short! Eternity, how long." To a friend he now said that he was "packed and sealed and waiting for the post."

He died on December 21, 1807, after a year of rapidly declining powers during which he was confined to his home. His legs were swollen, his sight was failing, and he found it hard both to hear and to speak. To one of his final visitors he said, "My memory is nearly gone, but I remember two things—that I am a great sinner, and that Christ is a great Saviour." His last recorded words were "I am satisfied with the Lord's will," which were said to someone who asked him if he was comfortable. This brief phrase, not intended as a sermon, nevertheless encapsulated his theology.

He had requested that his funeral be "performed with as little expense as possible, consistent with decency." The sermon on the wise and faithful steward recorded in Luke 12 was preached by Richard Cecil, later to become his first biographer. The *Times* of December 23, 1807, reported his death and remarked that "his unblemished life, his amiable character, both as a man and as a minister, and his able writings are too well known to need any comment." According to his wishes he was buried in the vault of St. Mary Woolnoth alongside his beloved Mary. He left instructions for an epitaph to be carved on a plain marble tablet and to be fixed to the inner wall of the church. It remains there to this day, although the bodies were reburied in Olney in January 1893 after work on the new underground train tunnels meant that the vault had to go.

JOHN NEWTON
    CLERK,
once an Infidel and Libertine,
a servant of slaves in Africa,
was, by the rich mercy of our Lord and Saviour
    JESUS CHRIST,
preserved, restored, pardoned,
and appointed to preach the faith,
he had long laboured to destroy.
He ministered near 16 years as curate and vicar,
Of Olney in Bucks
and 28 years as rector of these united parishes.

On Feb. 1, 1750, he married
    MARY,

daughter of the late George Catlett,
    of Chatham, Kent,
whom he resigned to the Lord who gave her,
    on December the 15th, 1790.

Once when asked to tell his story he said that it could be summarized in the words of Deut. 32:10: "He [God] found him in a desert land, and in the waste howling wilderness; he led him about, he instructed him, he kept him as the apple of his eye." He added: "He found me in a howling wilderness indeed! He has led me about into a variety of situations, and in them all He watched over me, and kept me as the apple of His eye."

His influence has been disproportionate to his separate abilities as a preacher and hymn writer. Perhaps because he was self-educated he never developed a "body of divinity," nor did he break any new ground in Protestant theology. He stayed within the Calvinism that he discovered early in his Christian life and was more keen to promote the fundamentals of doctrine that Christians agreed on than he was to explore the issues that divided. Even John Wesley, with whom he disagreed over predestination and perfectionism, once wrote to him, "You appear to be designed by divine providence for a healer of breaches, a reconciler of honest but prejudiced men, and a uniter (happy work!) of the children of God."

What distinguished him was a unique insight into the human heart and the mercy of God and this had come not through his learning, although that played an important part, but through his personal experience. This meant that his ministry wasn't characterized by spellbinding oratory but by love and affection for individuals, and the power of his sermons and letters lay not in academic research but in his memorable illustrations, well crafted aphorisms, and his ability to relate the things of heaven to life on earth. For this reason, his writing can still move people, whereas the work of eighteenth-century theologians can seem as dry as dust. He was not interested in theology as a subject but in God as a living person. It seemed impossible for him to write about sin or forgiveness or judgment without writing about his own experience. "So much forgiven, so little little love," he wrote to one correspondent in November 1772, just a few weeks before composing "Amazing Grace." "So many mercies, so few returns. Such great privileges, and a life so sadly below them."

PART TWO

Dissemination

*"Amazing Grace" as it appeared for
the first time with its now familiar tune.*

THE SOUTHERN HARMONY (1835).

William Walker, editor and compiler of The Southern Harmony.

PHOTOGRAPHER UNKNOWN.

Chapter 7

MEETING THE MUSIC

The poem is by Newton. The tune's source is unknown to
the southern compilers.
—*George Pullen Jackson*, SPIRITUAL FOLK-SONGS
OF EARLY AMERICA, 1937

There are, it is true, many music books circulating, but it is
generally admitted that no one of them is in all respects
adapted, either for the wants of the church in her triumphal
march, or to the demands of the rising genius of our country.
—*Benjamin Shaw and Charles Spilman*,
COLUMBIAN HARMONY, 1829

Those who are partial to ancient music will find here some
good old acquaintances, which will cause them to
remember with pleasure the scenes of life that are past and
gone, while my more youthful companions, who are more
fond of modern music, I hope will find a sufficient number of
new tunes to satisfy them, as I have spared no pains in trying
to select such tunes as would meet the wishes of the public.
—*William Walker*, THE SOUTHERN HARMONY, 1835

*D*uring *the twenty-seven years between the publication of
Olney Hymns* and Newton's death, "Amazing Grace" appeared four
times in other collections. In 1780 it was chosen for a hymnal used in
the chapels of Lady Huntingdon's Connexion, and in 1789 it appeared
in *Psalms of David with Hymns and Spiritual Songs*, printed in New York

for the Reformed Dutch Church. In the first book, the stanzas were run together without a break. In the second, five stanzas were taken and sandwiched into another, longer hymn. In neither case was Newton credited. It then appeared in *Hymns and Spiritual Songs* by the Baptist preacher Eleazar Clay (Virginia, 1793) and *The Hartford Selection* (Connecticut, 1799) by Congregationalist Nathan Strong.

The fact that it had already been selected for three American collections of different denominations but only one British was significant, because it was in America that "Amazing Grace" would take root and grow. *Olney Hymns* was first published in New York in 1790 and then in Philadelphia in 1791. Americans took the song into their hearts, and every subsequent development of it, from the selection of its now familiar tune to the editing of its stanzas, took place in America. It wasn't that the British didn't know it—*Olney Hymns* went through forty reprints in Britain during the nineteenth century—it was just that they never warmed to it in quite the same way.

When, in 1885, the Reverend James King surveyed fifty-two hymnals then used in the Church of England, Newton was the eighth most represented hymn writer, yet "Amazing Grace" was in none of the books. His most published hymns were "Glorious Things of Thee Are Spoken" and "How Sweet the Name of Jesus Sounds." The only others that had made the transition from *Olney Hymns* were "May the Grace of Christ Our Savior," "Approach My Soul the Mercy Seat," "Day of Judgment, Day of Wonders," "Come, My Soul, Thy Suit Prepare," "While with Ceaseless Course the Sun," and "As When the Weary Traveler Gains."

The British indifference is captured in John Julian's classic *Dictionary of Hymnology* (1892), where he says of "Amazing Grace": "In Great Britain it is unknown to modern collections, but in America its use is extensive. It is far from being a good example of Newton's work." Over half a century later, when Englishman Bernard Martin published his comprehensive biography of Newton, the situation was unchanged. "Amazing Grace" wasn't mentioned, and only two of 365 pages were devoted to his hymn writing. Again, "How Sweet the Name of Jesus Sounds" and "Glorious Things of Thee Are Spoken" were cited as his best-known works.

Glorious things of thee are spoken,
Zion, city of our God!
He, whose word cannot be broken,
Formed thee for His own abode.
On the rock of Ages founded,
What can shake thy sure repose?
With salvation's walls surrounded,
Thou may'st smile at all thy foes.

This indifference might have been because the tune that now seems so essential to the attractiveness and memorability of "Amazing Grace" wasn't used, or because if the British took to religion it was usually of a restrained and unemotional type. Christianity in America emphasized the experience of conversion: the remorse over past sin and the commitment to a new way of life. The words of "Amazing Grace" were an articulate expression of this.

At the time of Newton's death the religious revival later known as the Second Great Awakening was in progress. Initially centered on the border of Tennessee and Kentucky, it was characterized by a huge emotional outpouring resulting in members of church congregations dancing, wailing, hopping, jumping, weeping, laughing, and even collapsing. There had been no campaign designed to produce these results, but once the revival started, it spread like wildfire.

The extraordinary happenings attracted crowds of the inquisitive, and soon the church-based meetings were moved to fields, where the preachers set up platforms and the congregations stuck candles in the bark of the trees when night fell. Few people had ever seen such large gatherings. At Stanley Creek there were 8,000 people, and more than 250 were "struck down." At Cane Ridge, in August 1801, at a meeting that lasted for five days, there were 12,000, and more than 300 were "struck down."

The new style of "camp meeting" demanded a new style of worship. The number of people to be reached meant that everything, including the preaching, had to be louder, simpler, and more repetitive. The songs had to be interdenominational, because there were Baptists and Methodists, Congregationalists and Presbyterians. The songs also had to be memorable, because out in the fields, in the half light, there could be no hymnals.

The songs of Wesley, Watts, and Newton were trimmed for the occasion. The most used technique was to take the best-known stanza—the first stanza in the case of "Amazing Grace"—and attach to it a refrain that could be repeated many times. This refrain could be built from bits of the remaining stanzas or borrowed from another hymn. A camp-meeting version of "Amazing Grace" from a later date illustrates the process:

> Amazing Grace! How sweet the sound
> That saved a wretch like me.
> I once was lost, but now am found,
> Was blind but now I see.
>
> Shout, shout for glory,
> Shout, shout aloud for glory;
> Brother, sister, mourner,
> All shout glory hallelujah.

As this religious revolution intensified, a parallel musical revolution was under way. Neither was directly responsible for the other, but because they both started at the same time and in the same region, they became mutual influences. Ordinary working people liked to sing, yet almost none of them could read music, and most churches didn't have musical instruments. This meant that congregations were entirely dependent on song leaders to strike up tunes and to carry them.

To make music more accessible, a different notation had been developed that was relatively easy to learn. This was known as the "shape-note system," so called because the key to recognition was the shape of the note head rather than its position on the lines. It wasn't totally new. The fasola system had existed in England for three hundred years. But it had recently been refined in America and presented in two influential books: The Easy Instructor by William Little and William Smith (circa 1800) and The Musical Primer by Andrew Law (1803).

The method was to use only four syllables in singing the basic scale;

singing *fa* for the first note, *sol* for the second, *la* for the third, *fa* for the forth, *sol* for the fifth, *la* for the sixth, *mi* for the seventh, and *fa* for the octave. The whole scale would be *fa-sol-la-fa-sol-la-mi-fa*. Shapes of the note heads were varied according to their position on the staff to make sight-reading easy. Because it was a four-syllable system, only four shapes were needed: a triangle for *fa*, a circle for *sol*, a square for *la*, and a diamond for *mi*.

The shape-note system still needed to be taught, and for this purpose singing schools were established. These were not held in dedicated buildings. Peripatetic singing instructors would visit a town for two or three weeks, setting up evening classes in available spaces. The natural outcome was a surge of interest in communal singing and then a growing body of ordinary Americans who had not only mastered the rudiments of music but who had trained voices. Out of this enthusiasm and confidence came the gatherings known as "sings" or "singings," where the newly taught could practice their skills.

The singing, which could last for an entire day, was a new phenomenon in America. Although most of the songs used would be religious, it was not a worship service. Although participants were there to enjoy themselves, it was not purely for entertainment. In the South at this time there was no partition between secular and sacred. The songs sung at family gatherings were the songs people learned at church. The language of the newspaper was close to the language of the King James Version of the Bible.

An obvious legacy of European Calvinism was the absence of any musical instruments. As in a church service, there was an air of reverence, and songs were concluded with a murmur of appreciation rather than a round of applause. In true democratic spirit, the participants would sit around a hollowed square or circle so that no individual or group was more important than any other. Everyone was simultaneously performer and audience, watcher and watched. Anyone was free to announce the next song.

Exactly how these songs sounded we can only guess at from the earliest field recordings. A typical performance begins with a rehearsal of the first verse using the shape-note names rather than the words. Then the song itself is taken up. The only sound other than the ranks of tenors, sopranos, and basses rising and swelling in a ragged form of harmony is a foot beating out time on a floorboard. The notes have barely died away before someone announces the next song. After recording shape-note singing in northern Alabama in 1959, folk archivist Alan Lomax commented, "Here, I thought, is a choral style ready-made for a nation of individualists."

Shape-note singers used tune books rather than hymnals. Hymnals were pocket-size books with texts only. Tune books were large oblong-shaped books with hard covers (nine inches by six inches was a typical size), often running to over four hundred pages. They included both music and text and were introduced by an extended essay on the rudiments of singing. Each song was known by the name given to its tune rather than by a title drawn from the text.

It was in one such tune book that the music we now use with "Amazing Grace" was first published. For many years it was believed that the source of the tune was *Virginia Harmony*, an 1831 shape-note collection published in Winchester, Virginia, and put together by Methodist lay preacher James P. Carrell and Presbyterian elder David L. Clayton. As recently as 1986 *The New Grove Dictionary of American Music* claimed: "*Virginia Harmony* . . . has the distinction of including the earliest known printing of the anonymous pentatonic folk melody 'Harmony Grove,' now associated with 'Amazing Grace.' "

In *Virginia Harmony* the melody wasn't used with "Amazing Grace" but with an Isaac Watts hymn, "There Is a Land of Pure Delight," which was written to the same meter. Carrell and Clayton named the tune "Harmony Grove."

> *There is a land of pure delight,*
> *Where saints immortal reign;*
> *Infinite day excludes the night,*
> *And pleasures banish pain.*

Virginia Harmony remained the accepted source until 1990, when the American hymnologist Marion Hatchett, who had a special interest in shape-note music, discovered a previously unheard-of tune book in the Special Collections Library of the University of Tennessee at Knoxville. *Columbian Harmony* by Charles H. Spilman and Benjamin Shaw, published in Cincinnati in 1829, didn't appear in any checklists of shape-note tune books, and Spilman and Shaw were unknown as compilers. Because of the book's obvious rarity Hatchett paid it particular attention, singing over to himself the melody lines of each tune that appeared unfamiliar. Two of the tunes, "Gallaher" and "St. Mary's," proved to be not so unfamiliar. They both shared striking similarities to the tune we now associate with "Amazing Grace." "St. Mary's" accompanied the text of another Isaac Watts hymn, "Arise, My Soul, My Gentle Powers," and "Gallaher" accompanied the Charles Wesley hymn "Come Let Us Join Our Friends Above."

Neither tune was credited and no biographical details were supplied for Spilman and Shaw. When Hatchett published his findings in *The Hymn* (January 1991) he hazarded a guess that Spilman was Dr. Charles Harvey Spilman of Garrard County, Kentucky. Because the book was published in Cincinnati and yet almost all the retail outlets listed on the flyleaf were in Kentucky, Hatchett inferred that its authors were almost certainly from Kentucky. He then turned to a nineteenth-century biographical encyclopedia for the state that listed a Dr. Spilman. His life span (1805–92) made him a likely candidate. "However," concluded Hatchett, "no direct evidence has been found linking this Charles H. Spilman with the *Columbian Harmony.*"

But direct evidence exists. Dr. Charles Harvey Spilman studied medicine at Transylvania University in Lexington, Kentucky, and in the archives of the university's special collections there is a thirty-one-page handwritten autobiography of Dr. Spilman titled "Record of facts and events, and reminiscences of early life. Also a sketch of the most profound incidents of my riper years, together with some moral reflections."

The manuscript opens with information about his parents, who were both from Virginia; describes his childhood on farms in Kentucky and Illinois; and then covers his patchy education and subsequent work as a farm laborer. At the age of twenty he became a teacher and developed a love for books. In order to improve himself he went to a high school in Vincennes, Indiana, where in return for teaching he received lessons.

Here he met a wealthy older man from England named Stephen Webb, who appears to have taken an unusually affectionate interest in him.

In his notes Spilman refers to Webb simply as an "old bachelor" but tells how Webb would shower him with gifts, offer him money, and continually visit him in his room. "From some cause he achieved a very strong attachment for me," he wrote. "But he was an old gentleman and to me rather repulsive and I did not appreciate his kindness, nor did I manifest any reciprocity, but rather avoided him."

In 1826 the old man made Spilman an offer. He told him that rather than split his time between being a teacher and a student he should devote all his time to study, and that he, Webb, would pay the college fees. Spilman, for obvious reasons, was reluctant to accept, but Webb insisted and said that there were no strings attached. "He urged it as a duty, saying it was a pleasure to him and he hoped I would gratify him. He further added that he had no near relations in the country and he wished to make an heir of some one who would devote a life to usefulness after he was gone. I accepted, and soon after went to Centre College, Danville, Kentucky."

Centre College had been founded six years earlier by Presbyterians who wanted to train educated people who would in turn be qualified to teach their children. It provided a classical curriculum of Latin, Greek, rhetoric, and logic. Spilman arrived in January 1827, attacking the course with relish, but after only a few months received disturbing news from Indiana. "My friend and patron, who was very fleshy, had fallen from the upper to lower floor of his business house and was instantly killed." He didn't speculate about whether this was suicide.

There was no mention of shape-note music in the manuscript up to this point although there were passing references to God that suggested a Christian commitment. Then, on the fourth page, with no preamble came the statement: "Whilst at college I had devoted all my leisure, and perhaps time that ought to have been appropriated to sleep and bodily exercise, to the compilation of a selection of music suitable for churches and concerts. To this enterprise, in which I was aided by Ben Shaw, my room and classmate, I addressed myself through the solicitation of the Rev. David Nelson, then pastor of the Presbyterian Church at Danville. The winter of 1829–30 I spent in Cincinnati for the double purpose of recreating my health and superintending the publication of our book under the title of Columbian Harmony."

In the preface to *Columbian Harmomy*, Spilman and Shaw said that they had made the collection because they thought that no other music book then available had taken into consideration what they called "the wants of the Church in her triumphal march." "Some [music books] are too voluminous and costly, others too small and barren, and in most if not all of them, some of the best pieces of music have been admitted with such barbarous alterations and distortions, as to destroy that happy effect, which sacred music is designed to produce. To remedy these evils, and to give the Church a book in which is contained a large collection of the most substantial tunes, suitable for public worship, together with many devotional pieces most suitable for revivals, and a number of the most approved odes and anthems, has been our humble endeavour."

There is no other mention of *Columbian Harmony* in Spilman's autobiography. The archives of Centre College have no records for Ben Shaw other than that he enrolled in 1825 but didn't graduate. A little is known about David Nelson, the clergyman whom Spilman cites as having initiated the project. He was born near Jonesborough, Tennessee, in 1793, served as an army surgeon in Kentucky and Alabama, and became pastor of the Presbyterian church in Danville and one of the trustees of Centre College in 1828.

A passionate advocate of emancipation, Nelson led an eventful life. He left Danville in 1830 and started a college in Marion County, Missouri, where he was found to be in possession of antislavery literature. (He lived close to Hannibal and founded its Presbyterian church, which was attended by Mark Twain's family.) He was offered the choice of being hanged or leaving the state. He chose the safer option, but only after being shot at while preaching. He then opened a similar school, the Mission Institute, a few miles north in Quincy, Illinois. Ostensibly this school was to train missionaries to evangelize the Indians, but in fact it helped fugitive slaves cross the Mississippi and then housed them before setting them on their way to Chicago or Canada on the Underground Railroad. The Mission Institute was eventually burned down by proslavery enemies from Missouri.

In the only book he ever wrote, *The Cause and Cure of Infidelity* (1837), Nelson made a reference to Mary Newton indicating that he must have read Newton's *Letters to a Wife* (1793), in which Newton added an appendix describing her death. Nelson said that anyone reading about "the death of the wife of the celebrated John Newton, will find a very plain and very interesting instance where the Saviour seemed to meet with a smiling countenance his dying servant."

Spilman and Shaw found most of the tunes in *Columbian Harmony* in other tune books. Marion Hatchett has been able to establish the origins of all but 12 of the 159 tunes, the majority coming from shape-note collections published during the previous sixteen years. Unfortunately for researchers of "Amazing Grace," "Gallaher" and "St. Mary's" were two of the 12 that couldn't be sourced.

The fact that such a high proportion of the tunes were from other books suggests that neither Spilman nor Shaw was a composer. There is no mention of writing or playing an instrument in Spilman's autobiography. This leaves two main possibilities. The two tunes could have been lifted from a book, all copies of which have since vanished. Or they could have been variations on a single tune that was popular as a folk melody but that had never previously been transcribed.

The tune of "Amazing Grace" is pentatonic, meaning that the fourth and seventh notes aren't used. This is a characteristic of folk music in general, so it doesn't narrow the search down to a particular country or region. The titles "Gallaher" and "St. Mary's" could be seen as clues, the one being an Irish name originating in county Donegal and the other a Roman Catholic saint, but titles can be deceptive. They were sometimes tributes to friends ("Nelson" in *Columbia Harmony* obviously refers to Spilman's minister), and at other times referred to a place where the tune was either written or discovered.

"Amazing Grace" is often assumed to have Scottish origins, but this assumption might be based simply on its popularity as a bagpipe tune over the past thirty years. It wasn't thought of as a traditional Scottish tune before this. However, it could have seemed so natural as a bagpipe tune because in fact it was originally Scottish, the Royal Scots Dragoon Guards merely having returned it to its rightful home. Peter Van der Merwe, author of *Origins of the Popular Style*, argues that "Amazing

Grace" is an "overwhelmingly Scottish tune." He is convinced of this not merely because it uses the pentatonic scale but because it is "pentatonic in a specifically Scottish way."

What does it mean to say that music is specifically Scottish? This is impossible to discuss without introducing musical terms, but it's a worthwhile detour. Van der Merwe quotes the *Oxford Companion to Music,* by Percy A. Scholes, which says that Scottish song is "equally remarkable for pathos and vigour" and adds that it is especially Scottish to combine both in the same tune.

Vigor, Van der Merwe suggests, comes from foursquare phrasing (simple, repetitive, often rather martial rhythm), major modes (greater emphasis on tonic and dominant notes), craggy melodic contour (steep rises, especially from the low G to the G an octave above), and the use of pentatonic scale. The pathos is contributed by emphasis on A and E (minor-mode color), steep rises balanced by deep descents (usually in the first third of the tune), and falling pentatonic cadence (D-C-A-G).

Van der Merwe believes that "almost all these features, as well as some typically Scottish graces" are to be found in the tune of "Amazing Grace" ("New Britain"), and that in this it shares characteristics with genuine Lowland Scots tunes that have achieved worldwide popularity, such as "Loch Lomond," "Auld Lang Syne," and "Ye Bank and Braes o' Bonny Doon."

If this is true, how did the tune come to America? The most obvious possibility is through immigration. Kentucky, where Spilman was living when *Columbia Harmony* was published, had a high proportion of immigrants from Scotland. Another possibility is that it was an American tune with strong Scottish derivatives.

Virginia Harmony was the next tune book to feature the melody, followed by Robert Willis's *Lexington Cabinet* (1831), Samuel Wakefield's *The Christian's Harp* (1832), where it was used with "When God Revealed His Gracious Name," and Joseph Funk's *Genuine Church Music* (1832), with Cowper's "There Is a Fountain Filled with Blood."

The marriage with Newton's words took place three years later, in William Walker's celebrated tune book *The Southern Harmony,* an event that makes Walker second only to Newton himself in the story of "Amazing Grace." Today it is hard to hear the tune without imagining the words, and hard to read the words without hearing the tune, yet until Walker saw their compatibility both elements of the song were leading independent lives.

Walker, born in 1809, was a singing instructor from Spartanburg, South Carolina. At his local Baptist church he had met Benjamin Franklin White, who was also a singing instructor. The two men formed a deep friendship, Walker even marrying a sister of White's wife, and started to collect music together. Their experience of singing schools taught them what songs were popular and also made them aware of what was lacking in currently available tune books. Like Spilman and Shaw before them, they decided to publish the fruits of their research.

By the time they were ready to submit a collection they had amassed a solid body of old favorites taken from half a dozen popular tune books, almost a hundred unpublished tunes either from contemporary authors or from the folk tradition, and twenty-five new songs composed by Walker. Among the tunes that had already been published was the same one that had been collected in two early forms by Spilman and Shaw, then shortly afterward named "Harmony Grove" by Carrell and Clayton. Walker polished it up, named it "New Britain," and paired it with the words of "Amazing Grace."

Until this time "Amazing Grace" had been sung to a variety of tunes. Its "common meter" form—stanzas of four lines where the first and third lines have eight syllables, and the second and fourth six syllables—made it adaptable. When Walker put it with "New Britain" he was merely continuing the practice, but he displayed real genius, because not only did the words fit snugly into the required musical space but the music enhanced the meaning. It was a marriage made in heaven.

It was as though the tune had been written with these words in mind. The music behind "amazing" had a sense of awe to it. The music behind "grace" sounded graceful. There was a rise at the point of confession, as though the author was stepping out into the open and making a bold declaration, but a corresponding fall when admitting his blindness. There were places where Walker appeared to have made changes to the melody, because it differed slightly from both "St. Mary's" and "Gallaher."

Walker didn't record the reasons behind his choice, but he assembled his collections with fastidious care, always searching for new tunes or trying out new relationships between familiar music and texts. The late Glenn C. Wilcox, author of the introduction to the fourth edition of *The Southern Harmony* (1987), estimated that Walker would have searched through ten thousand pages of available music before making his final selection.

His major sources for tunes were other tune books, folk tunes, and contemporary composers. Walker always traveled with music-writing materials so that he could record tunes he hadn't heard before, and it was a strong selling point if a tune book could boast new material. In a later tune book featuring "Amazing Grace" Walker noted: "Where the authors of the tunes were positively known, they have been given; but where several persons claimed the same tune, we have dropped all names, fearing we might not do justice to some of the parties. Many of the tunes appear without any name as author; but we hope no author will think hard of us on this account, for we would have given names with pleasure had they been known."

Walker found the words of "Amazing Grace" in Staunton S. Burdett's *Baptist Harmony*, a hymnal published in Philadelphia in 1832. Other hymns in *The Southern Harmony* were taken from the same book. The title he gave the tune is puzzling. The only New Britain in America is a parish outside Hartford, Connecticut, named in honor of Great Britain by Revolutionary War veteran Colonel Isaac Lee, but Walker had no known connections with this area. It might have been suggested by the book's publisher, who was from Connecticut.

The Southern Harmony and Musical Companion was published in New Haven by Nathan Whiting, a twenty-seven-year-old printer who had recently produced a three-volume set of *The Works of John Bunyan*. For an unknown reason, Benjamin White was not mentioned as one of the book's authors. The preface, written by Walker in September 1835, didn't refer to a collaborator, and he spoke of himself in the third person as "the compiler of this work."

This might have been because he didn't believe that White's contribution warranted acknowledgment. However, White's story, as passed down to his children and then repeated by Joe S. James in *A*

Brief History of the Sacred Harp (1904), was that Walker had cheated him. The disagreement led to a breakdown in their relationship, and eventually White moved with his family to Harris County, Georgia, from where he planned his musical revenge.

The Southern Harmony, with its 209 pieces of music spread over 216 pages, proved to be an enormously successful tune book that sold in general stores as well as in bookshops. It was revised four times during Walker's life and sold an estimated 600,000 copies in a country where the population in 1850 was only just over 23 million. It was the bible of many singing schools. A writer in the tune book magazine *Musical Million* commented in 1880, "Thousands and thousands have blessed the name of William Walker who has sent *The Southern Harmony* into almost every home in the southern land, breaking up the ground and creating [a thirst] for sacred music in the masses."

The tune book also played a vital role in establishing "Amazing Grace" in America. The words corresponded to the American experience in a unique way, not only by delineating the archetypal evangelical conversion but by articulating the groans of a people who frequently had to struggle with poverty, sickness, and the elements in order to survive. No other nation was made up of so many pioneers and immediate descendants of pioneers. The reference to "dangers, toils and snares" had particular resonance for those who'd suffered for their adventure, as did the promise that grace would "lead me home."

A further fillip to the fortunes of "Amazing Grace" came from an unlikely quarter. Benjamin Franklin White, along with a new friend, Elisha J. King, had compiled another tune book to rival *The Southern Harmony*. This time his name would be included. The collection was sent to a printer in Philadelphia in the spring of 1844 and was published as *The Sacred Harp*. One of its songs was "Amazing Grace," set to "New Britain" as it had been in *The Southern Harmony*, but now in four-part rather than three-part harmony. This was to become the most influential tune book of the shape-note movement. Today "Sacred Harp singing" is used as a synonym for "shape-note singing."

The Civil War interfered with the publication of tune books but didn't stop the spread of "Amazing Grace," which was now a vital part of many American lives. Hymnals such as *Hymns for the Camp* (1862) and *The Soldier's Hymn Book* (1864), both of which included "Amazing Grace," were distributed along with New Testaments to troops. The prospect of death created a mood of seriousness, and there was a dramatic increase in Bible studies and informal church services among the new recruits.

The Civil War was sobering for the country as a whole. It caused Americans to fear that their great experiment in nation building could implode, that the light on a hill was about to be blown out. Why had God allowed things to come to this in such a God-fearing land? Was it a punishment, or a trial? Most important, whose side was God on?

The response of Charles Spilman, now a doctor in Harrodsburg, Kentucky, was typical. On February 12, 1863, he added these thoughts to his autobiography: "The political horizon is dark; the clouds lower, the heavens are black with conflicting elements. He alone who rides upon the whirlwind and directs the storm can guide the ship of state safely through the breakers. My trust is in Him, and my petitions hourly directed towards his mercy seat. Can it be that the best government on earth, for the happiest people on earth, with the richest natural resources on earth, is destined to perish in the midst of the development of its prosperity, wealth and power? I trust in God, such a calamity is not in store for us."

A month later, President Abraham Lincoln signed a resolution introduced by Senator James Harlan of Iowa calling for a national day of "humiliation, fasting and prayer." The proclamation acknowledged that the war might have come as a chastisement, to bring America back to God:

> We have been the recipients of the choicest bounties of Heaven. We have been preserved, these many years, in peace and prosperity. We have grown in numbers, wealth and power, as no other nation has ever grown. But we have forgotten God. We have forgotten the gracious hand which preserved us in peace, and multiplied and enriched and strengthened us; and we have vainly imagined, in the deceitfulness of our hearts, that all these blessings were produced by some superior wisdom and virtue of our own. Intoxicated with unbroken success, we have

become too self-sufficient to feel the necessity of redeeming and preserving grace, too proud to pray to the God who made us. . . .

James Booker, a twenty-three-year-old soldier in the Thirty-eighth Virginia Regiment, was affected by the resurgence of Christian faith among his colleagues. Writing to his cousin, Chloe Blair, on New Year's Day, 1864, from a Confederate camp near Kinston, North Carolina, he expressed the hope of "coming home, if I live" after three years of continuous service. On the back of the last page, almost as a postscript, he wrote:

Through many dangers toils and snares
I have already come
Tis grace that brought me safe thus far
And grace will lead me home.

This knowing reference not only illustrates how far "Amazing Grace" had penetrated the fabric of American culture but shows how its material application was being taken alongside the spiritual. Booker hoped to literally come home to Virginia, but was equally content to go home to heaven. Three months later he wrote to Chloe: "If it is the will of [my] maker for me to be cut down in this war I don't ask to be spared for I believe that he will do what is the best for me, there is but few things that I would ask to stay in this troublesome world for."

The shape-note movement was never quite the same after the Civil War. William Walker believed that its life could be extended through seven-note as opposed to four-note singing and produced *Christian Harmony* in 1866, with "Amazing Grace" again set to "New Britain." The book sold well, and Walker announced that the combined sales of his tune books was 750,000. However, *The Southern Harmony* was now being eclipsed by *The Sacred Harp,* and one rumor suggested that this was because fans of shape-note music had shifted their allegiance after learning of the shabby way that Walker had treated White.

The truth is that White's success was due to his skills as an entrepreneur. He knew not only how to put a book together but how to put people together with the book. He founded the Southern Musical Convention in 1847, and this led to the formation of singing groups exclusively devoted to *The Sacred Harp*. Their performances became known as "Sacred Harp singings" and eventually superseded all other singings.

Walker died in 1875 and White in 1879. The *Carolina Spartan* (September 29, 1875) said of Walker, "He was no ordinary man. His life, origin, birth, resources and character will ascribe to him a higher position than our notes will afford. His whole life in fact is illustrative of his devotion and energy to the good of mankind at large." During his final hours White compiled an inventory of his sins toward God and God's blessings to him before announcing: "The end has come and I am ready." He then sang an Isaac Watts song that he had used in *The Sacred Harp*:

> *Behold, the morning sun*
> *Begins his glorious way;*
> *His beams through all the nations run,*
> *And life and light convey.*

Charles Spilman continued to practice medicine in Harrodsburg, Kentucky, into his eighties, by which time his wife, three of his sons, and one of his daughters had died. By 1887 he was one of the oldest residents in Mercer County and much respected. That year it was reported that "though he has long passed the allotted limitation of life of which the Psalmist sung, he is still well preserved in the possession of all his faculties and mentally alert and active." He died on December 15, 1892.

Between them Spilman, Walker, and White had helped transform John Newton's text into a compelling song that was starting to spread and to become a recognizable part of southern culture.

*Edwin Othello Excell produced the standard version of
"Amazing Grace" in 1909.*

COURTESY OF ROSE LAWN MUSEUM,
CARTERSVILLE, GEORGIA.

Chapter 8

SPREAD BY REVIVAL

Mr Sankey literally 'sings the Gospel' just as truly and not
less powerfully than his friend Mr Moody preaches it.
—*Rufus W. Clark*, AUTHOR AND JOURNALIST, 1875

I am going to take, tonight, a subject rather than a text.
I was to talk to you about free grace. I say free grace;
perhaps I had better drop the word "free" and say just
"grace." There is a sermon just in the meaning of the word.
It is one of these words that are very little
understood at the present time, like the word gospel.
—*Dwight L. Moody*, 1876

If I cannot entertain a man, I won't detain him.
—*Evangelist Sam Jones*, 1889

*O*ne *of the most important transitions for "Amazing*
Grace" in its journey from a frequently collected *Olney* hymn to America's spiritual national anthem was the one made in the late nineteenth
century. In the twenty-five years following William Walker's death it
retained its popularity in the rural South, the natural home of *The
Southern Harmony* and *The Sacred Harp*, and then spread into the major
cities of the North. It also firmed up its relationship with the tune "New
Britain," so that by the early years of the twentieth century they were
virtually inseparable.

These two advances helped "Amazing Grace" avoid the fate of many
other songs written in the eighteenth century, which were dropped

from the hymnals to make way for the work of new writers. If it hadn't been taken up by northern city dwellers, the tastemakers of postbellum America, it could well have been regarded as merely a quaint example of what country folk used to sing before the war. If Newton's words hadn't become permanently wedded to one tune, "Amazing Grace" would have lacked the distinction necessary for greatness.

Even though it had been set to "New Britain" in shape-note books since 1835, this combination wasn't used in a hymnbook until 1888, when F. T. Shore used *The Sacred Harp* harmonization in *Baptist Chorals*, published in Tipton, Missouri. Before this, hymnbook compilers had set it to more than twenty tunes, one called "Arlington" being the most popular. Before the end of the century three other hymnbooks used "New Britain," but it was still just one tune among many.

The song's spread to the North was helped by a new style of urban evangelism that gave great prominence to vocal music. The best-known practitioners were preacher Dwight L. Moody, a Congregationalist from Massachusetts, and his musical assistant, Ira D. Sankey, an Episcopalian Methodist from Pennsylvania. As choir leader, performer, composer, and hymnbook compiler, Sankey became a role model in religious music as well as one of the best-known musical figures in late-nineteenth-century America.

Moody and Sankey had met in 1870 at a YMCA convention in Indianapolis. After Sankey sang Cowper's "There Is a Fountain Filled with Blood" at a prayer meeting, Moody, already a seasoned evangelist, invited him to be his musical director. Arminian rather than Calvinist in his theology, Moody believed that music could play a vital role in changing minds. Used before his sermons, it could help create a more receptive mood. Used immediately afterward, it could tip the balance of emotions in favor of making a decision. Consequently, Sankey's most popular songs were those directed at the undecided, in which music and words combined to produce a final, hopefully irresistible, tug.

"Almost persuaded," now to believe;
"Almost persuaded," Christ to receive;

Seems now some soul to say,
"Go, Spirit, go thy way,
Some more convenient day
On thee I'll call."

Moody and Sankey were the first evangelistic team to exploit the modern breakthroughs in transport and communication. They traveled by steamship and rail, news of their campaigns abroad was telegraphed back to America via the newly laid transatlantic cable, their photographs were published in magazines, and they even experimented with recorded sound. Their missions were held in large arenas in cities such as Chicago, Boston, New York, Philadelphia, London, Liverpool, and Dublin, and to ensure maximum publicity, newspaper reporters were always given seats with lighted desks close to the platform.

The team initially became famous in America through reports of a two-year tour of Britain that started in June 1873. The British were notoriously impervious to religion, especially religion imported from America, and yet turned out in droves to see and hear these two men. In Edinburgh, where the evangelists stayed for almost two months, an estimated 1,500 people claimed conversion. In Dundee they appeared in the open air for a week and attracted crowds of up to 16,000 every day. By the time they got to Scotland, in February 1874, there were no buildings large enough to hold the number of people who wanted to hear them. During one meeting in Glasgow, Moody went outside and preached to 20,000 people unable to gain admission.

The same pattern was repeated in other Scottish cities and then in Belfast, Dublin, Manchester, and Sheffield. In Birmingham, a city of 400,000, they appeared before 156,000 people in twelve days. In Liverpool they hired the newly built Victoria Hall, capacity 8,000, but had to supplement it with meetings in a concert hall and circus arena. The climax of the visit was four months spent in London, where they held 285 meetings and appeared before 1.5 million people. British prime minister William Gladstone came to see them at the Agricultural Hall in North London, and Queen Victoria at Her Majesty's Theatre.

Moody's extraordinary success as a preacher perplexed contemporary observers. His message, though spiced with anecdotes, was the same one preached in thousands of churches every week. He wasn't a great orator—his thoughts at times seemed disconnected, and his language was folksy rather than refined. What he was able to achieve though was an atmosphere of intimacy, regardless of audience size, and the conviction among his listeners that he was passionate about what he preached. "He is in downright earnest," observed one critic. "He believes in what he says; he says it as if he believed it, and he expects his audience to believe it. He gets wonderfully near to his hearers, without any apparent effort. Whatever size the audience may be, he is at home with them at once, and he makes them feel that they are at home with him."

In a similar way, Sankey's talent as a vocalist was seemingly modest, but he could move people through the sincerity of his emotions. Accompanied by only a harmonium, Sankey had an approach that was nevertheless startlingly new to the British. "He has introduced amongst us a style of music which to a great extent is new in public worship," wrote one reviewer in Edinburgh. "In Scotland, our service of praise has been hitherto chiefly confined to the use of psalms. In many of our churches hymns have been used to a considerable extent, and gradually this style of music is finding its way among all denominations. Mr. Sankey has given us a clearer understanding of what is meant under the third division of the apostle's classifications, *viz.*, spiritual songs."

Although at times Sankey used familiar hymns, his reputation was built on promoting songs he'd coauthored or those written by contemporaries such as Philip Bliss, who wrote "Almost Persuaded." The new songs had lively or haunting melodies, repeated refrains that imitated the hooks of popular songs, and sentiments that reflected common experience. As one reviewer commented, "Our hymn books are too stiff and cold. People want to sing, not what they *think*, but what they *feel.*"

Religious music performed on such a scale and with such conviction was a new experience for many. Hymns in the past had seemed ethereal, full of heavenly descriptions and finely wrought language, but the songs that Sankey chose were dramatic and down to earth. Religious poems by amateur writers were often used as texts. The words of "A Shelter in the Time of Storm" and "The Ninety and Nine," two of his most requested songs, were found in newspapers. "I Am Praying for You" was the text of a pamphlet.

In Sunderland in 1873, the Reverend Arthur A. Rees, a local vicar involved in promoting a forthcoming appearance of Moody and Sankey, described what Sankey did as "singing the Gospel." It was a coinage that would attach itself to Sankey for the rest of his life. The songs he specialized in would become known as "gospel songs" to differentiate them from psalms and hymns, and this would eventually give rise to the term "gospel music." "It is [Moody's] belief that the gospel may be presented in song as well as in speech," said the *Daily Review.* "And that while the song has a marvelously attractive power, it is also fitted to express better than plain speech the emotion suitable to the truths of the gospel."

People grew eager to get copies of the words and music Sankey used. A publisher, R. C. Morgan, in Sunderland to review the meetings for a religious newspaper, suggested that the company he part-owned, Morgan & Scott of London, publish some of the most popular songs. Sankey had been working from a small scrapbook and offered this as the basis of his first book. "I cut from my scrapbook twenty-three pieces," he later said. "I rolled them up, and wrote on them the words 'Sacred Songs and Solos sung by Ira D. Sankey at the meetings of Mr. Moody of Chicago.' "

The finished product was a small pamphlet priced at two pence. During the first six months of 1875 it sold 3.5 million copies, appealing particularly to the newly emerging middle class, whose latest home entertainment was the upright piano. On his return to America he published *Gospel Hymns 1* with Philip Bliss and then, to coincide with a series of meetings starting in Boston in January 1877, *Gospel Hymns 2,* where for the first time he included "Amazing Grace," setting it to the popular tune "Warwick." Two years later, when increasing the number of hymns in *Sacred Songs and Solos* to 271, he added "Amazing Grace," although with a different tune. This time he used "Claremont," a tune written by the English composer John Foster.

Sacred Songs and Solos was the defining hymn collection of late-nineteenth-century Evangelicalism. It was updated every few years until what had started as a pamphlet had grown into a massive tome. In 1906 Sankey could say: "This book, together with the edition of words only, has now grown into a volume of twelve hundred pieces, and up to the present time has had possibly the largest sale of any book except the Bible."

For "Amazing Grace," the significance of being included in

Ira Sankey's songbooks introduced "Amazing Grace"
to the urban, middle-class audience.

COURTESY OF THE BRITISH LIBRARY, LONDON.

Sankey's publications was not just the introduction to a wider audience but the fresh context. Sankey was at the cutting edge of religious music, and his decision to include it alongside such recent hymns as "Jesus of Nazareth Passeth By" and "Hold the Fort" added to its credibility. It was reinvigorated through association.

Sankey was the first to identify the hymn by the title "Amazing Grace" rather than by the name of its music or a number. Prior to this it was often referred to informally as "Amazing grace, how sweet the sound," the first line becoming the title. Sankey used Newton's first three stanzas, then ended with the fifth ("Yes, when this flesh and heart shall fail"). Above the music he printed the verse "That the abundant grace might, through the thanksgiving of many, resound to the glory of God" (2 Cor. 4:15). In later editions of *Sacred Songs and Solos* this verse was replaced with "The grace of God that bringeth salvation" (Titus 2:11).

The fact that Sankey used three different tunes for "Amazing Grace" (in *Gospel Hymns 4* he tried William Gardiner's 1812 tune "Belmont") illustrates the state of flux the song was in a century after appearing in *Olney Hymns*. It still didn't have a tune that it could call its own, and even the vast popularity of the shape-note tune books hadn't resulted in the automatic acceptance of it with "New Britain" in the churches of America.

This state of flux lasted until 1900, when the grandly named Edwin Othello Excell, a hymn writer, publisher, singer, and song leader based in Chicago, took "Amazing Grace" with "New Britain" and developed a slightly different arrangement for a hymnal he was publishing. The impact of this publication was significant. From 1900 to 1910 Excell's arrangement of "New Britain" was chosen by fourteen collections featuring "Amazing Grace," with its closest competitor, "Arlington," being used by only four. From 1911 to 1920 it became even more popular; eleven out of fifteen collections used it, with "Arlington" now reduced to a single usage.

Excell's achievement was in making "Amazing Grace" sound more contemporary by adding harmonies and ironing out some of the awkward transitions in William Walker's version. This made it more acceptable to the newly enfranchised middle classes, who wished to appear cultivated and to throw off the primitive associations of the shape-note tradition. The churches of the North were also more likely to use musical instruments and therefore to want printed music with round note heads to read from.

Born in 1851 in Stark County, Ohio, to a German Reformed pastor and his wife, Excell had worked as a bricklayer and plasterer on the Pacific Coast before becoming a full-time musician. He had a powerful singing voice, which could range from bass to tenor, and in 1877 he came to Chicago to study under George Root, the former assistant to the celebrated composer and arranger Lowell Mason.

Root and Mason had a profound effect on Excell's music. Both men were anxious that American music should be as sophisticated as the music of Italy, Germany, Austria, and France. They reacted against the music of the musically illiterate, believing that it was crude and inferior, and devoted their lives to educating Americans in musical theory and musical appreciation.

Mason, who died in 1872, was a prolific writer, composing over 1,200 religious songs, including the hymn "Nearer, My God, to Thee." But he made his lasting mark in musical education: pioneering the teaching of music in the public school system, setting up programs to train music teachers, serving as president of the Handel and Haydn Society, and cofounding the Boston Academy of Music. He believed that an improved church music would automatically be more refined technically and more devotional in atmosphere. To this end he encouraged round notation rather than shape notes, and European-style four-part harmony with the melody in soprano.

In 1852 he took an extended tour of Europe, attending every concert recital, music festival, and church service that he could. The congregational singing in England disappointed him. Organists had a habit of stopping abruptly at the end of each stanza, and many of the hymn tunes were inappropriate for massed voices. After attending a Baptist church in London's Devonshire Square, he wrote: "The tunes were too difficult, and the effect of the singing was wretched. We are more and more satisfied that tunes must be made more simple in time, and limited in compass of melody, to insure success in this form of church song."

He was more pleased with the music at St. Mary Woolnoth, where he worshiped on September 29. "Attended a service in the church where John Newton used to preach. Here we heard an excellent and faithful sermon. The spirit of Newton, or rather the spirit of the Gospel, is yet manifested within these walls. The singing was led by about a dozen charity children; the girls being dressed as the old ladies of New England used to dress half a century ago, each having a square handkerchief folded about the neck, a high white muslin cap, and a white apron. The chants were plain, and tolerably well done, and so were the tunes—all the people singing."

George Root was of a similar mind. Like Mason he had written hymns—"She Only Touched the Hem of His Garment" and "Come to the Savior" being the most popular—and had traveled to Europe (he studied singing in Paris). With Mason he organized the first Normal Musical Institute in New York, where teachers were instructed in how to teach music.

Excell obviously imbibed the values of Root and Mason, and he set about composing music that was simple yet sophisticated while building a reputation as a singer and choir leader. Moody's use of Sankey had become the role model for contemporary mass evangelism, and in May 1886 Excell was invited to be musical director for the flamboyant Methodist evangelist Sam Jones, a reformed drunkard who prided himself on not having studied theology. He was bluntly colloquial in his sermons, and his pithy sayings were avidly collected. "The road to hell is paved with good intentions" is one that has survived and entered our language.

While on the campaign trail with Jones, Excell acquired the skill of building mass choirs out of singers recruited from different churches who had never worked together before. "He is the biggest choir singer that ever struck Dallas," commented the *Dallas Morning News* in 1893, "and he knows how to pull a melody out of a choir just like a dentist knows how to pull a tooth." He also knew how to choose songs that complemented the mood that Jones was setting in his sermons and that would cross denominational and cultural boundaries.

Yet it isn't as a singer and musical director that Excell is now remembered but as a publisher, composer, and arranger. He wrote more than two thousand gospel hymns, some of which—"Count Your Blessings," "Jesus Bids Us Shine," "He Needs Me Every Hour," and "Jesus

Wants Me for a Sunbeam"—are still sung today, and became the single most important publisher of religious music in America by the turn of the twentieth century. He compiled fifty hymnbooks under his own name that together sold over a million copies a year, and helped compile thirty-eight for other people and organizations.

Excell first used "Amazing Grace" in *Make His Praise Glorious*, a collection "for the Sunday School and Church" published in Chicago in 1900. As with most of his collections, two-thirds of the songs were contemporary, either written by himself or owned by him as publisher, and a third were from the public domain. It was in this third, contained at the back of the book under the heading "Favorite Hymns," that "Amazing Grace" was printed. Six other contemporaries of Newton were represented in the same section: Wesley, Watts, Cennick, Toplady, Doddridge, and Cowper.

The choice of songs had been made in conjunction with a group of almost fifty "leaders of the Christian church in America" who were listed on the acknowledgments page. The names themselves mean nothing today; what stands out are the attached qualifications and the cities that the leaders came from. The list shows a clear bias toward educated middle-class northerners, and this inevitably affected the preferences in music. All but three of them held doctorates in divinity, while only three (not the same three) came from the South.

Like Sankey, Excell used only four of Newton's stanzas, but whereas Sankey dropped stanzas four and six, Excell dropped stanzas five and six. The reason he didn't publish the full version as it appeared in *Olney Hymns* might simply have been the lack of space. No song in the book exceeded four stanzas. Newton was identified as the author and E. O. E. (Edwin Othello Excell) as the arranger.

In arranging the melody Excell took it a long way from its origins in the shape-note singing of the South. He wrote it in standard European harmony, the type of harmony acceptable to contemporary choirs, and the melody was in the soprano. Decorations were added, and there was a different ending to the second line.

Nine years later Excell further embellished the tune for R. A. Torrey's collection *World Renowned Hymns*. Different chord changes were introduced, which altered the melody on the third line (changing on the upbeat rather than on the downbeat as he had done previously), and this helped bring out the phrase "but now am found." The whole song now sounded smoother, more solid. This arrangement, which was then published in Excell's own collection *Coronation Hymns* (1910), was picked up by other collectors, and the use of alternatives to "New Britain" such as "Harp," "Arlington," and "Warwick" diminished year by year.

Torrey was a Congregational evangelist who had been invited to Chicago by Moody in 1889. He compiled and edited *World Renowned Hymns* because he wanted a hymnal "that combined the classic hymns of the church with the masterpieces of hymnology which appeared in connection with Mr. Moody's campaign, and also with the best recent Gospel hymns." Although it was published by the Montrose Christian Literature Society in Montrose, Pennsylvania, Excell was a shaping influence. Torrey said of him in the introduction that "he could hardly have spent more time on the book, in giving me counsel and helping me in other ways, if he had been the editor or publisher of the book."

One obvious trace of his counsel is the choice of the hymn printed directly above "Amazing Grace." Written by Excell with words by J. E. Ramsay and titled "The Song My Mother Sang," it was a sentimental song of someone remembering his mother singing "Amazing Grace" to him as a child. The gimmick was that after each stanza the congregation was to sing the corresponding stanza from "Amazing Grace."

Sing me the old, old melody,
In accents hushed and low,
The song my mother sang to me,
In childhood long ago.
Methinks I hear her voice again,
And see her smiling face,
As when she sang that sweet refrain,
Of God's Amazing Grace.

Amazing grace (how sweet the sound) . . .

Because this version of "Amazing Grace" was intended to be incorporated into the other song, Excell printed each stanza inside quotation marks. When he used the same plate for future hymnbooks he forgot to remove the punctuation. This was of no concern to the ordinary person in the pew but later caused puzzlement among hymnologists, who wondered why only one hymn had received this unusual treatment.

The other major change that Excell made to "Amazing Grace" in *World Renowned Hymns* was the inclusion of a new fourth stanza, four lines not written by Newton:

When we've been there ten thousand years,
Bright shining as the sun,
We've no less days to sing God's praise
Than when we first begun.

These lines had never appeared with "Amazing Grace" in a hymnbook, but they had appeared together in a book: Harriet Beecher Stowe's influential antislavery novel *Uncle Tom's Cabin,* published in 1852. In one compelling scene the dejected slave Tom, who has been ridiculed by his owner for having such a childlike faith in God, lies beside the embers of a fire and has a vision of the suffering Christ. As he gazes at the vision, the thorns turn into rays of light, and he hears a voice telling him that one day he too will be clothed in this glory.

How long Tom lay there, he knew not. When he came to himself, the fire was gone out, his clothes were wet with the chill and drenching dews; but the dread soul-crisis was past, and, in the joy that filled him, he no longer felt hunger, cold, degradation, disappointment, wretchedness. From his deepest soul, he that hour loosed and parted from every hope in the life that now is, and offered his own will an unquestioning sacrifice to the Infinite. Tom looked up to the silent, ever-living stars, types of the angelic hosts who ever look down on man; and the solitude of the night rang with the triumphant words of a hymn, which he had sung often in happier days, but never with such feeling as now—

The earth shall be dissolved like snow,
The sun shall cease to shine;

But God, who called me here below,
Shall be forever mine.

And when this mortal life shall fail,
And flesh and sense shall cease,
I shall possess within the veil
A life of joy and peace.

When we've been there ten thousand years,
Bright shining like the sun,
We've no less days to sing God's praise
Than when we first begun.

As a lifelong Congregationalist and sister to a hymn writer and preacher, Harriet Beecher Stowe would have known what she was doing to "Amazing Grace." She would have known that this was not the version printed in hymnbooks and tune books. The most obvious explanation is that she did it to add authenticity, the same reason that led her to jumble the order of the stanzas to reflect Tom's confusion or his reliance on oral transmission. It seems likely that she had heard slaves singing "Amazing Grace" in this way, slotting in stanzas from other sources if they appeared to be appropriate. Excell could have taken the idea from reading *Uncle Tom's Cabin,* or possibly he too had heard the adaptation from former slaves.

These four lines originated in the hymn "Jerusalem, My Happy Home" as it appeared in *A Collection of Sacred Ballads,* published in Virginia in 1790. The hymn itself dates back at least a further two hundred years and has been published in so many different versions that there are at least fifty stanzas that have at one time or another been a part of it.

Using stanzas interchangeably was a common practice in folk music. The concept of a definitive version only arose with the emergence of print, recording, and copyright laws. Although the slaves lived in an age of literacy, they were forced by law to live in a preliterate culture in which stories and music were passed on by word of mouth, and creativity manifested itself in trying out new combinations of old material.

Some stanzas were particularly adaptable and were constantly used in new contexts. Hymnologists called them "wandering stanzas." In the case of "Amazing Grace" the switch in authorship is obvious. Suddenly the narrative alters from singular ("me") to plural ("we"), and the focus abruptly shifts from the operation of grace in this life to the singing of praises in heaven. This is because "Jerusalem, My Happy Home" is not about grace but about the "new heaven and a new earth"; the "new Jerusalem" predicted for the end of the age in the Book of Revelation. The image of light was probably based on the verse "And there shall be no light there; and they need no candle, neither light of the sun; for the Lord God giveth them light: and they shall reign for ever and ever" (Rv. 22:5); the figure of ten thousand is used in the Bible to mean countless or eternal, as when the number of angels is described as "ten thousand times ten thousand" (Rv. 5:11).

"New Britain" is a compelling and memorable tune, but it didn't win in the competition to become the standard tune through merit alone. It triumphed because of Excell's influence in the world of Christian music at the turn of the twentieth century. When churches and parachurch organizations came to him to publish a collection for them, he played a significant role in the choice of material, offering them not only a first-class range of contemporary songs but a library of printer's plates containing the classic hymns of the Christian church. Whenever a client took his suggestion to include "Amazing Grace," the version he or she got was naturally the one arranged by Edwin Othello Excell to the tune "New Britain" with the "ten thousand years" stanza.

Between its appearance in *World Renowned Hymns* and Excell's death in 1921, this arrangement of "Amazing Grace" appeared in fourteen major American hymnals; significantly, ten of them were published by Excell. One of his most regular clients during this period was Robert H. Coleman, a Baptist layman from Dallas, Texas, who was to become one of the most prolific hymnbook compilers of the first half of the century and a music leader for the Southern Baptist Convention's annual meetings. He used "Amazing Grace" in his hymnbooks from 1909 onward and played a pivotal role in establishing Excell's arrangement as standard among Southern Baptists.

Excell's treatment of "Amazing Grace" was to become the standard version of the song. It is because of him that half of Newton's original text is rarely sung. It is because of him that we finish our renditions with a rousing stanza about the new Jerusalem. The harmonies he wrote out in 1909 are the ones we use today.

*The Happyland Jubilee Singers became The Blind Boys
of Alabama and recorded "Amazing Grace" three times
in a fifty-year career.*

Chapter 9

THE GOSPEL SOUND

"Amazing Grace" has an effect on everybody. The guy that
wrote that song, he really put that one together. He really did.
The song has never died down. They sing it in every church.
—*Ira Tucker*, DIXIE HUMMINGBIRDS

There is a lot of meaning in that song. The grace of God is
something that we don't deserve but which is given to us
anyhow. That's what makes it so amazing! It says "saved a
wretch like me." It's about being *trans*formed rather
than just *re*formed.
—*Maceo Woods*, GOSPEL ORGANIST AND PREACHER

I already know what the words of "Amazing Grace" mean
and I know that it's a fact of life that if God takes his hand
off you—man! You're done! When you just put that
together alone, you know whether he's with you or not. One
thing God says is, "I will never leave you nor forsake you."
He told the preachers that and that goes for everybody else if
he said it. He didn't say it and I didn't say it. God said it.
Whether you agree with it or not makes no difference.
It'll come out his way anyway. We can't change nothing.
—*Clarence Fountain*, BLIND BOYS OF ALABAMA

$\mathcal{H}$arriet Beecher Stowe's description of the old slave
Tom singing pointed to something that was happening to "Amazing
Grace" away from the gaze of professional musicians. Its growth as a
white song had been clearly recorded in tune books and hymnals but

not so its parallel development as a black song. Enforced illiteracy prevented the slaves and their immediate descendants from keeping a detailed record of cultural changes, and the majority culture wasn't interested enough to do it on their behalf. Additionally, the African American musical tradition didn't require songs to be written down to be preserved. If a song wasn't good enough to be committed to memory, it probably wasn't good enough to sing.

The slaves took warmly to eighteenth-century English hymns. A particular fondness for Isaac Watts led to them referring to all these hymns, whether they were written by Watts, Wesley, Newton, or Doddridge, as "Dr. Watts hymns." They responded to the primal imagery of blood and flowers, scars and crowns. Above all they connected with the acknowledgment that life on Earth could be a struggle but that whatever your present status, however you were being treated, if you trusted in Christ you would one day be given the privileges of royalty. The hope expressed by these words made life bearable.

It's easy to see why "Amazing Grace" would emerge as the most loved of these hymns. It appeared to tell their story. The very fact of their survival was, in their eyes, evidence that God had looked after them so far. They might be downtrodden, but there were still victories to be gained, problems to overcome, temptations to resist, diseases to be freed from. Like Paul and Silas when they were imprisoned in Philippi, they were able to sing in their chains.

Slaves first learned "Amazing Grace" at the churches of their white masters and mistresses, where they were taken to ensure that they learned how to be worthy, obedient servants; yet contained within its words was the secret of inner release. From the lyrics, the slaves gained assurance that it was possible to be physically enslaved and yet spiritually free. It was possible to be materially impoverished and yet have an overflowing account of righteousness in heaven.

In his definitive history of gospel music, *The Gospel Sound,* Anthony Heilbut says that "no song so moves black congregations" as "Amazing Grace." He isolates Newton's third stanza ("Through many dangers, toils and snares . . .") as "*the* universal testimony" of gospel churches because they are lines that can resonate with specific experience. These people knew about hardship and risk. They knew about traps and temptations.

"You gotta be in God to have these things happen to you," said Clarence Fountain, who has recorded three versions with the Blind Boys of Alabama since the 1950s. "If you've never been through these things then you don't know what God can do. I am a witness because I know what he can do. I'm not speaking about what I've heard. I'm talking about what I know he can do."

The first slaves to sing "Amazing Grace" wouldn't have known the story of John Newton and would therefore have been unaware of the irony involved in expressing their hopes through the words of a man who had helped capture their ancestors in Africa and transport them across the Atlantic. By the time of emancipation there would have been more than fourteen thousand direct descendants of the slaves brought to Charleston on the *Brownlow* and around forty thousand descendants of those brought to the Caribbean on the two ships Newton commanded.

But Newton had also experienced the other side of slavery, and that had empowered him to write many of these words. He had been "a servant of slaves in Africa," and Plantain Island had been the school where he had learned the meaning of wretchedness and fear. Now his voice was traveling down the years and speaking to other enslaved people.

The changes that happened to "Amazing Grace" in the white community were text-led. They were announced by new publications, and the consistent aim of the compilers and singing instructors was to encourage fidelity to words and music as printed on the page. In the black community, where books were rare, fidelity was to emotional truth. You sang the song correctly if you tapped a corresponding seam of personal experience.

For this reason the most telling contributions of the slaves came when they departed from the page and added personal commentary through interjections, moans, shouts, improvised stanzas, and repeated refrains. The "long-meter" style (a term that, confusingly, doesn't refer to the meter of the text) meant that the song was slowed down to such a degree that all comprehensible notions of melody and harmony disappeared. All that remained was a colorful swell of vocal sound among which the old familiar words could occasionally be heard.

"It seems perfectly simple and easy for the singers but the listening white person is utterly confused, cannot make musical head or tail out of what he hears," wrote music collector George Pullen Jackson after hearing "Amazing Grace" still being sung in this way in the 1930s. "His concepts of melody, rhythm, music, fail to help him through the maze. He cannot even check the trends by the words he has heard lined out, for the singing surges on with so many graces and strings of graces (entwined about longer notes which he feels must be parts of an unfolding melody), that all words, syllables even, lose their identity and evade recognition."

One of the rare glimpses of how "Amazing Grace" was used during the days of slavery comes from an interview carried out by a worker for the Federal Writers Project in the 1930s with Charles Butlington, a former slave by then in his nineties. He described attending camp meetings in the Missouri countryside in the days before emancipation:

Preachers in that day conducted the services in the following manner. He would word out the song two lines at a time, the congregation committing this to memory would sing these two lines, then two more lines were worded out and so on until that song was ended.

Then the preacher would get up and call on someone to pray. Some could gather up something to say; others expected the Lord to do it all by using such expressions as "Lord, help!", "Lord, make me what I oughta be," "I wants to be a Christian," "Lord I believe," "Lord, pour down the Holy Ghost." Then we'd sing some more such as "Amazing Grace, how sweet the sound, that saved a wretch like me." Then pray again, using the same expressions and others such as "Lord, don't you know me? I'm your follower," "Yes Lord, we adore thee," "Come, Gabriel, any time. We'se all ready to go." Had very little preaching. Mostly praying and singing.

A similar interview with Nick Waller, who was described simply as a "Negro" from Athens, Georgia, provides another glimpse, this time of "Amazing Grace" in church:

> When us went to church, it was in old home-made clothes that our mothers made. But bless the Lord she didn't stop us from having meeting. Folks had religion then and from the time the pastor read out the song and the brother in the corner started it off, everybody would 'gin to git happy and when that old song "Amazing Grace, How Sweet the Sound" was sung, the shouting could be heard for a mighty ways off 'cause didn't nobody stay home 'cause they didn't have no clothes to wear. Everybody was there shouting.

No one at the time could have anticipated that this "shouting" and "singing," this wild, apparently uncivilized behavior, would one day transform the style and substance of American music. Out of the abandon of the camp meetings and country churches would come the foundations of jazz and gospel, blues and rock, funk and soul. It was from music such as this that passion would begin to take precedence over control, commitment to sense over enunciation of language.

One of the first indications of change came with the publication, in 1867, of *Slave Songs of the United States* by three white collectors: William Francis Allen, Charles Pickard Ware, and Lucy McKim Garrison. It was an anthology of words and music that included such spirituals as "Roll, Jordan, Roll," "Blow Your Trumpet, Gabriel," "Lord, Remember Me," and "Rock o' My Soul." Four years later a group of black singers from Fisk University in Nashville, Tennessee, the Fisk Jubilee Singers, began a tour that would eventually take them to Europe, where they would sing these spirituals in front of white audiences to raise money for new university buildings.

In Edinburgh they appeared on the platform with Ira Sankey to sing "Steal Away to Jesus," "The Angels Are Hovering Over Us," and "Depths of Mercy." In his account of the campaign Rufus Clark wrote: "Their and Mr. Sankey's deep sympathy with the sentiments they utter so melodiously, will elevate the conception of Christian song among us, as not a hallowed amusement merely, but elevated and elevating worship. Mr. Moody pronounced the benediction, and Mr. Sankey and the sweet Jubilee Singers burst out from supercharged hearts into joyous, triumphant praise, the likes of which have never been heard."

The biggest change was ushered in by the introduction of recorded sound. It had been possible to record since the invention of the phonograph in 1877, but the switch from wax cylinders to flat discs took a further ten years, and it wasn't until 1894 that these discs were available commercially for the entertainment market. There was an initial burst of activity between then and the early part of the twentieth century, during which time both the Jubilee Singers and Ira Sankey made records, but disagreements over standardization halted progress until the early 1920s.

The gospel music industry began not with groups or choirs but with men known as "shouting preachers." Their style was to tell folksy tales with arresting titles such as "Death's Black Train Is Coming" or "The Dying Mother and Her Child" and then break into a song supported by a small congregation assembled in the studio. The restrictions imposed by one side of a 78 rpm record meant that content had to make way for drama.

In this way the first gospel recordings of "Amazing Grace" were made in New York City in 1926, first by Rev. H. R. Tomlin and a month later by Rev. J. M. Gates. Both men had been talent-spotted in Atlanta by New York record companies looking for material for the "race" market, and Gates was rapidly becoming the star of the genre. His second record had advance orders of 34,025, an impressive figure at the time.

These two releases provide the earliest accurate record of how "Amazing Grace" was being sung in black southern churches of the period. What we hear are versions without any of the changes introduced by Edwin Othello Excell. There are no four-part harmonies, the melody is slightly different in places, and the "ten thousand years" stanza isn't used. They are direct descendants of *The Southern Harmony*, using William Walker's arrangement of "New Britain" and lining out twice during each stanza.

Tomlin's version was clearly derived from the camp meeting style.

After singing Newton's words and using a different melody, he broke into a refrain of "I will trust in the Lord / I will trust in the Lord / I will trust in the Lord till I die." Gates's version used a "moaned-out" stanza where the melody was held but deep moans were used in place of the words. According to Heilbut, this nonverbal expression is the essence of the gospel style and has become the style "from which all Afro-American music derives." In jazz it became the wail of the saxophone. In blues it was the bent notes of the guitar.

The "shouting preachers" represented the transition from congregational hymn singing, camp meeting songs, and spirituals to the blues- and jazz-inspired music of gospel that grew in the 1930s and entered its golden age during the 1940s and 1950s. "Amazing Grace" was one of the few songs to live through the changes. All the great gospel artists recorded "Amazing Grace": Sister Rosetta Tharpe, Mahalia Jackson, James Cleveland, the Five Blind Boys of Mississippi, the Soul Stirrers, the Golden Gate Quartet, the Pilgrim Travelers, the Dixie Hummingbirds, the Fairfield Four, the Swan Silvertones, Albertina Walker, the Mighty Clouds of Joy, the Blind Boys of Alabama, Marion Williams, Shirley Caesar, Jessy Dixon.

As gospel singers continue to testify, "Amazing Grace" has a unique ability to calm and unite. Joe Ligon of the Mighty Clouds of Joy said: "It's a song that reaches way down. Anybody that's got any kind of religion can feel the sincerity of that song." To Shirley Caesar, it was "one of the greatest hymns in the world. You become a part of that song. It becomes like an old friend." Anthony Heilbut called it simply "the most beloved gospel hymn of all."

Most of the gospel singers used "New Britain" as the tune, although the vocal arrangements were often so complex that it was difficult to detect, hardly any of them sang the "ten thousand years" stanza, and all of them performed the song in a unique way. Because "Amazing Grace" was so well known, it was important for gospel singers to stamp it with something original so that their version stood out.

The vintage of the song suggested an idealized past when society was more Christian and Christians were more solid in their faith. Rev. J. M. Gates had introduced it on his record as "one of the good old familiar hymns," and in the age of the Charleston, rising hemlines, the

Scopes trial, and Josephine Baker he clearly saw it as a reminder of a more stable era. It was as if through the singing of "Amazing Grace" the piety of times gone by could be re-created.

"We ought to sing more," Gates urged his listeners. "We're living in a scientific age now where people are trying to lay aside the old hymns and keep up with style. We're living in a time where Atlanta gets her style from New York and New York gets her style from Paris and Paris is getting her style from hell. Except we sing more of these old familiar hymns, we'll find ourselves in the same city."

In 1938 the Reverend J. C. Burnett announced the song in a similar way as "one of old Dr. Watts' hymns that my mother used to sing years ago." In 1960, recording a live version with the Mighty Clouds of Joy, Joe Ligon said: "This reminds me of a long time ago, of a time back when people really knew the power of prayer. You know they've gotten away from it and they don't sing the old songs like they used to sing them."

"Amazing Grace" was frequently associated with parents and grandparents as representatives of past godliness. Even the great blues guitarist Blind Willie McTell, recording in a hotel room in Atlanta in 1940, introduced his instrumental version by speaking about country churches, his early life in rural Georgia, and his "old folk parents." "Amazing Grace," he said, was a song that "our mothers and fathers used to hum back in the days when they would be pickin' cotton and pullin' corn." The plaintive slide notes from his guitar imitated the sound of that humming.

In 1938, Roberta Martin, then one of the most powerful figures in gospel music, published a song called "God's Amazing Grace," which, like Edwin Othello Excell and J. E. Ramsay's "The Song My Mother Sang," was about a godly mother singing "Amazing Grace" to her child and incorporated Newton's words. This was later recorded by top gospel stars the Blind Boys of Alabama, the Pilgrim Travelers, the Harmonizing Four, the Caravans, and Marion Williams.

I was young but I recall singing songs was mother's joy.
As the shadows gathered at the close of day
And I'd sit upon her knee

In those days that used to be
As she sang of God's amazing grace.

Amazing grace. How sweet the sound . . .

"Amazing Grace," as one of the "old, familiar hymns," reminded gospel singers of family roots and the fundamentals of the faith. When storms hit their lives, when they seemed bereft of inspiration, they would turn to this classic to revive and reassure them. If they wanted to honor their parents or mourn for their sins they would sing the songs they had first heard in revivals when they were children.

"As a little boy I grew up in Alabama watching my daddy sing those songs and my grandfather sang 'Swing Low, Sweet Chariot,' 'Amazing Grace,' and 'Precious Lord,'" remembered Joe Ligon. "All of those songs were part of my growing up. So when I sang 'Amazing Grace' I sang it from experience. This was something I had watched, something I had listened to. I was in those revivals back home. I put it on record the way that I heard it."

Early quartet recordings, like most early church performances, had no musical accompaniment. Groups such as the Golden Gate Quartet and the Fairfield Four dazzled with a latticework of vocal sound. Later solo vocal recordings, influenced by the popular music of the day, introduced instruments. Ernestine Washington, who recorded "God's Amazing Grace," performed it Dixieland-style backed up by veteran New Orleans trumpet player Bunk Johnson and his band. The Highway QCs used acoustic guitar, the Caravans a vibraphone, and the Soul Stirrers electric guitars and bass. One of the most unusual arrangements ever was recorded in 1952 by Aunt Martha Wiltz, who wailed the vocal against a background of a solitary African drum.

The Soul Stirrers were one of the few gospel groups not to use "New Britain." Sam Cooke, who later became a leading soul star, wrote a completely new arrangement and altered the lyrics so that each stanza was made up of Newton's first line repeated three times plus his fourth line. When Arthur Crume joined the group in 1965 he added something else. In the way it had been arranged by Cooke it had no bridge, so he created one out of a stanza taken from the nineteenth-century hymn "I Heard the Voice of Jesus Say," written by the Scottish minister and hymn writer Horatio Bonar:

> *I came to Jesus as I was*
> *I was weary, worn and sad.*
> *I found in him a resting place*
> *And he has made me glad.*

A different stanza from the same hymn had been used in "Amazing Grace" in 1958 by the Five Blind Boys of Mississippi. All of these groups were carrying on the tradition identified by Harriet Beecher Stowe a century before and endorsed in the hymnbooks by Edwin Othello Excell. "Gospel writers and gospel singers quote a lot," said Crume. "They take excerpts from things that they've heard and incorporate it into a song."

As a rule, gospel singers tended to omit from rather than add to stanzas from "Amazing Grace." Newton's final three stanzas were almost never used, and the most popular recordings either used the first stanza alone or the first and third. This reduction was made on artistic rather than theological grounds. A pared-down lyric provided the opportunity to stretch out and improvise. Gospel artists, like jazz musicians, liked to play with themes, to tease apart and reconstruct so that what might previously have been taken for granted was transformed into something new and memorable.

A favorite technique, particularly with quartets, was to use only the first stanza but to repeat it using different inflections and harmonies. The Dixie Hummingbirds recorded a version in 1946 in which the rhythm accelerated with every stanza. "When I was going to church with my mother and father at Golden Street Baptist Church in Spartanburg, South Carolina, we would sing it like it was in the book," said vocalist Ira Tucker. "But when I got with the group I changed it for four voices, and on the record we started it up and then after the first verse we started it up again. It was a very unique arrangement at the time."

The best-known gospel recording of "Amazing Grace" was by Mahalia Jackson, the Queen of Gospel Music, who taped two alternative versions in October 1947 for the Apollo label. Raised in New Orleans,

Jackson had moved to Chicago, where she became part of a gospel group at the Greater Salem Baptist Church. Two of her favorite hymns at the time were "The Day Is Past and Gone" and "Amazing Grace." "Those songs come out of conviction and suffering," she said. "The worst voices can get through singing them, 'cause they're telling their experiences."

Mahalia's style was pure southern. Although raised Baptist, she took much of her musical influence from the less restrained Sanctified or Holiness Church, whose preachers worked their congregations into paroxysms of ecstasy and where speaking in tongues and falling out were commonplace. She played with the notes like an experimental jazz musician, moved her hips sensuously, and uttered spontaneous praise whenever she felt "led by the spirit." She was as influenced by the emotional delivery of the preachers she saw as she was by the singers.

When Mahalia first came to Chicago there was suspicion of her style because it seemed so raw and primitive during an age and in a region where modernity was being celebrated. Nevertheless, she built a reputation in the city's churches and then, in 1946, signed a deal with Apollo. Her third release, "Move On Up a Little Higher," recorded in September 1947, sold over a million copies, becoming the best-selling gospel record ever. It changed the perception of gospel music overnight. No longer was gospel merely a quaint and interesting tributary of American music—it was part of the mainstream. The song also made Mahalia Jackson the best-known gospel singer ever, a subject for magazine covers, a recipient of awards, a guest on television programs. In postwar America she was, as Anthony Heilbut has said, "the vocal, physical, spiritual symbol of gospel music."

It was during her next session after "Move On Up a Little Higher" that Mahalia recorded "Amazing Grace," producing the template for the soulful female version with the haunting gospel organ behind the lingering, stretched-out vocal. Mahalia spent so much time savoring each word and exploring the layers of possible meaning that it took her over two minutes to get through the first stanza. The first word took her thirteen seconds to enunciate. On the second version she sang the first stanza twice, but between them she "moaned out" a verse in exactly the same way that Reverend Gates had done just more than twenty years earlier.

For Mahalia, "Amazing Grace" was more Baptist than Sanctified because it was slow and moving, dependent on subtle emotional inflections rather than energetic twists and turns, and it took her back to her roots in New Orleans. "I believe the blues and jazz and even the rock-and-roll stuff got their beat from the Sanctified Church," she said. "We Baptists sang sweet, and we had the long and short meter on beautiful songs like 'Amazing Grace, How Sweet It Sounds' [sic], but when those Holiness people tore into 'I'm So Glad That Jesus Lifted Me Up,' they came out with real jubilation."

After Mahalia left Apollo and began recording in New York under producer George Avakian for Columbia in November 1954 with the Falls-Jones Ensemble, "Amazing Grace" was among the first songs she recorded. In one day she covered fourteen songs, among them "Didn't It Rain," "When the Saints Go Marching In," "Jesus Met the Woman at the Well," "You'll Never Walk Alone," and "I'm Going to Live the Life I Sing About in My Song." There were no rehearsals or even any talk about arrangements. She was so familiar with the material that she performed in the studio as though it were another concert. "She recorded 'Amazing Grace' for us because contractually she was free to do so and it was a great song," said Avakian. "With Mahalia it was never a case of me telling her what to do. She recorded whatever she wanted to and I was all for having 'Amazing Grace' by Mahalia Jackson as part of our catalog."

The same year the first instrumental version ever to be released was put out by Vee-Jay Records in Chicago. Label owner Vivian Carter had asked the house keyboard player, Maceo Woods, to come up with theme music for a radio show she was hosting in Gary, Indiana. Woods responded by sketching a version of "Amazing Grace" on the Hammond organ, intending to work on it later. But unknown to him, an engineer had recorded it. Carter was so pleased with this rough idea that she not only used it for her show but had it released as a single. It became the largest-selling gospel instrumental ever.

One unintended result of this recording was the adoption of "Amazing Grace" as funeral music. At the time of its release a national convention for funeral directors was taking place in Chicago, and an enterprising record plugger from Vee-Jay paid a visit and sold the idea of Maceo Woods's version of "Amazing Grace" as the ideal mood-setting music for times of grief. Since then it has become one of the most popular choices of music for funerals and memorial services.

The recording of "Amazing Grace" introduced new elements that would profoundly affect its direction throughout the rest of the century. The first was the element of originality in performance. Hymn-book compilers aimed at a level of conformity so that everyone was literally "singing from the same hymn sheet." In contrast, each artist who recorded "Amazing Grace" in sound was looking to do something unique so that his or her innovations would stand out.

The second was the element of secularization. "Amazing Grace" was now being sold as entertainment in return for financial reward and listened to outside of the context of prayer, worship, and teaching. The words Newton had intended to promote "the faith and comfort of sincere Christians" were now being listened to by people who were not necessarily Christian and who wanted musical value more than faith and comfort.

This undoubtedly affected the way the song was received. The context in which a song is heard contributes to its meaning. "Amazing Grace" heard in a revival meeting in Alabama where everything surrounding it endorses the message is very different from "Amazing Grace" heard on a car radio while driving down the Santa Monica Freeway, or in the kitchen while preparing lunch.

This was recognized by the writer and poet Langston Hughes, who said of an early Mahalia Jackson recording: "Its slow syncopated rhythms caught the fancy of jazz fans, who bought it, not for religious reasons, but as a fine example of a new kind of rhythmical Negro singing. The gospel song began to reach a public for whom it was not intended at all, and its vogue has been mounting ever since."

The Weavers: Lee Hays (left front) taught "Amazing Grace" to Pete Seeger (right front) in the 1940s. Seeger has been singing it ever since.

Chapter 10

IN THE FOLK TRADITION

I've been singing "Amazing Grace" for a long time
now and the reason I've been singing it so long is because
I love the story of the man who wrote this song.
—Arlo Guthrie, 1981

I thought of the song and thought that it would be a good
thing to use one of the old gospel songs that fitted into the
frame of the so-called folk revival and to let people hear it.
I didn't have any idea that Miss Judy Collins would record
it and that it would one day be on all the juke boxes.
I did it because I wanted to do it.
—Doc Watson, 2001

I see "Amazing Grace" as a song of very definite hope.
—Pete Seeger, 2001

*T*hrough gospel music "Amazing Grace" had been able
to reach an audience outside the church, but it was still instantly recognizable as a religious song. Few would have doubted that when she sang it Mahalia Jackson identified with every word. Through folk music it moved even further away from the church, into the clubs, halls, and bars of the city. It was now being performed by nonbelievers and being heard by people who had no idea that it had come from a hymnal. "I never thought of it as a Christian song," said Joan Baez, who helped popularize it in her concerts during the 1960s. "It was a song that was associated with civil rights and with the Movement. I don't think that

anyone at the time thought of it as a religious song. Like 'Swing Low, Sweet Chariot,' it had developed a life of its own."

Considered a folk song because of its longevity and its rural origins, "Amazing Grace" was not in the strict sense folk. In 1954 the International Folk Music Council adopted a definition of folk that excluded songs with a known authorship passed to the community as a completed work. Thirty years later, in *A Folk Song History of America*, Samuel L. Forucci came up with eight generalizations: Folk music was the expression of the common people. It wasn't the work of a skilled musician. The author was unknown. It was written in colloquial language. It was highly singable. It was simply structured. It could be sung without music. It was indigenous to a particular region.

If all eight requirements had to be fulfilled, "Amazing Grace" was clearly excluded. It expressed the feelings of common people, but as a Church of England cleric, John Newton was part of the establishment of his day. No one knew if the composer of "New Britain" was skilled. The author of the text was known. The language was biblical rather than colloquial. It was highly singable and simply structured, and could be sung a cappella. Musically it was indigenous to the American South or, possibly, Scotland.

Postwar folk revivalism was part of a revolt against conformity. When assembly-line pop was reducing emotion to clichés and people to consumers, this music, which was rough around the edges, spoke of authentic human experience and dared to question authority. Folk musicians were associated with an urban bohemia where intellectuals and authors rubbed shoulders with painters, poets, dropouts, and political revolutionaries. "There was no money in folk music," said Bob Dylan. "It was a way of life. And it was an identity which the three-buttoned-suit postwar generation of America really wasn't offering to kids my age."

Folk musicians accepted that many spirituals, gospel songs, and hymns came from the same fount of inspiration as ballads, laments, and work songs. Despite using the same language as bishops and kings they were often politically subversive. The folkies also found it wasn't necessary to share the belief of the writers to create a good performance. It was possible to sing "Michael Row the Boat Ashore" without believing in archangels; "When the Stars Begin to Fall" without any fear of a literal apocalypse; and "Sinner Man" without accepting the doctrine of original sin. It was possible to sing "Amazing Grace" without agreeing that divine intervention was essential for personal salvation.

The first folk-style recordings of "Amazing Grace" were made in the 1920s. The same companies that went to Atlanta and signed the Reverend H. R. Tomlin and the Reverend J. M. Gates for the race market had signed the Wisdom Sisters and Fiddlin' John Carson for the "hillbilly" market. The Wisdom Sisters, a female vocal trio, made the first such recording of "Amazing Grace" on April 23, 1926, for Columbia, and Carson made the second, on December 9, 1930, for OKeh.

The Wisdom Sisters sang a slow a cappella version to "New Britain," but Carson, a sixty-year-old fiddle player who recorded with his daughter, Moonshine Kate, on guitar and an unidentified third person on banjo, was responsible for the first version ever with musical backing. He began by singing "At the Cross" and continued with the same tune for "Amazing Grace." This four-line refrain, usually attached to Isaac Watts's hymn "Would He Devote That Sacred Head," was then repeated after each stanza.

At the cross, at the cross, where I first saw the light,
And the burden of my heart rolled away (rolled away),
It was there by faith I received my sight
And now I am happy all the day.

Carson's style was a precursor of bluegrass music. His choice of "Amazing Grace" made sense in the context of his regional background but not in the context of his previous output. His songs were usually frankly secular, often with humorous titles such as "Who Bit the Wart Off Grandma's Nose?" and "Whatcha Gonna Do When Your Licker Gives Out?" Critics have speculated that it was a tongue-in-cheek recording because at the time a hymn set to such worldly accompaniment was so incongruous that it could have been taken only as blasphemy or a joke. Supporting this theory is the fact that the track wasn't released.

The foundation of the urban folk revival, however, lay not in these early commercial recordings but in fieldwork carried out in the 1920s and 1930s by folklorists concerned that organic American music was being threatened first by gramophones, then by radio and film. As entertainment was homogenized the fear arose that the songs that had survived by oral transmission would soon be forgotten. It was possible that the vast musical memory of a culture would be wiped out within a generation.

The most important of these folklorists were John and Alan Lomax, father and son, who traveled down the highways and byways to find the authentic music of America. Alan Lomax wrote: "By making it possible to record and play back music in remote areas, away from electrical

John Lomax, whose field recordings became the basis of the Archive of American Folksong.

COURTESY OF THE LOMAX ARCHIVES.

sources, it gave a voice to the voiceless. It documented music, such as the complex polyphony of the blacks, which notation couldn't represent. Thus the portable recorder put neglected cultures and silenced people into the communication chain." Their field recordings provided the basis of the Archive of American Folksong at the Library of Congress in Washington, D.C., and would later provide source material for the folk revolution of the 1950s and 1960s.

In 1932, when John was sixty-five and Alan was seventeen, they set out with a crude 350-pound recording machine powered by two 75-pound batteries that cut directly onto aluminum discs, and traveled around the South in the family Ford. They covered sixteen thousand miles in four months, collecting songs for a book later published as *American Ballads and Folk Songs*. Wherever they could find people willing to sing the songs that they had inherited, the Lomaxes would record.

As the southern culture of the time was so pervasively affected by Protestant religion, many of the songs that ordinary people treasured were expressions of Christian faith. They understood the world in a basic biblical way, and therefore spirituals and hymns were not seen as an escape but as a facing up to facts.

The earliest Lomax recording of "Amazing Grace" was made in 1935 by Alan with assistant Mary Elizabeth Barnicle. The performer was Aunt Molly Jackson, a fifty-five-year-old white labor activist from the Appalachian Mountains of Kentucky. Over the next five years they recorded at least eleven more versions of "Amazing Grace" by a variety of people black and white, young and old, solo and in groups.

In 1939, for example, John and his wife, Ruby, drove 6,502 miles through the South in their Plymouth on a ten-week song search and collected two versions. The first was in Medina, Texas, by an elderly white couple, a Mr. and Mrs. Braley, who sang a brisk version in their living room. The only significant difference from the *Olney Hymns* version was that they sang only the first, second, and fourth of Newton's stanzas, an unusual combination, and "He will my shield and portion be" had mutated into "He will my friend and portion be." Three weeks later, in Livingston, Alabama, they recorded two black cousins, Doc

Reed and Vera Hill, who sang it long metre style using Newton's first and second stanzas with Doc lining it out. Lomax noted one variation in the text—"'Tis grace hath brought me safe thus far" had become "This grace hath brought me safely far," another example of mutation.

Lomax's field notes for the Reed and Hall recording gave this background: "They are good singers of the old style spirituals, are perfect in 'seconding'—'following after' they call it—and they know many songs. Not having book learning they store in the backs of their heads innumerable tunes and stanzas. Vera Hall is particularly quick to 'catch up' a new tune and if they do not understand completely the text, they are ingenious in supplying substitutes, either from other spirituals or from their own feelings of the moment."

Most of the singers of "Amazing Grace" recorded by the Lomaxes—people like Bill and Pauline Garland, Lucy McKeever, and Rev. J. R. Gipson—remained unknown. The exception was a blind street singer from Atlanta spotted by Ruby Lomax and invited back to their hotel room to record. His name was William McTell, known to history as Blind Willie McTell, and he played "Amazing Grace" on his twelve-string guitar, chipping in Newton's words only to remind himself of where he was in the tune.

The collector with the keenest interest in religious music was George Pullen Jackson, a professor of German at Vanderbilt University in Nashville and music columnist for the *Nashville Banner*, who in 1933 published the definitive study of shape-note singing, *White Spirituals in the Southern Uplands*. When he began writing about shape-note music in the 1920s, the tradition was close to extinction and yet had never been the subject of academic research. The stories of William Walker, Benjamin White, and other compilers were in danger of being lost as the last of those with first-hand memories of them were now old. Fastidiously and single-handedly Jackson documented the history of this great form of American music.

For *White Spirituals in the Southern Uplands*, he pursued copies of every shape-note tune book that he could find and then learned whatever he could about their compilation. He found James P. Carrell and David S. Clayton's "Virginia Harmony" in a secondhand-book store in Nashville and in their tune "Harmony Grove" he thought that he had

found the earliest printing of "New Britain." Out of curiosity he traveled to Carrell's hometown of Lebanon, Virginia, where he discovered
his grave on a hillside overlooking the town (he had died in 1854), saw
his portrait hanging in the local Methodist church, and learned some
brief biographical details from the older residents.

He also went on the trail of William Walker. In Spartanburg he saw
a first edition of *Southern Harmony* in the main library, donated by
Walker's wife after his death, and was allowed to take it home to
Nashville to have it photographed. Excited by his find, Jackson explained its rarity to his photographer, George Douglas, and noticed
that "the cameraman's thoughts were far away, that they were occupied
with something he was about to reveal."

Douglas was able to tell Jackson that *Southern Harmony* was still at
the center of a living tradition back in the town where he'd been raised;
Benton, Kentucky. In this small town annual singings had been taking
place in the local courthouse on the fourth Sunday in May since 1884.
Families came from miles around to spend the day and either ate their
lunches under the trees in the square outside or were invited into the
homes of Benton residents. At least thirty of the regular participants
were still using original copies of the 1854 edition and one of them was
the proud owner of William Walker's original tuning fork.

Geography rather than human effort had preserved the tradition.
Benton was bounded by rivers that successfully protected it from the
penetration of modern culture. The locals had just kept to ordinary
things the way they had always done them, unaware that their way of
life was becoming unique. When they sang "Amazing Grace" they were
singing it the way it was sung in Walker's day, without the influence of
Sankey and Excell, hymnals or gospel discs.

Jackson visited Benton in 1931 and his account of taking part in the
singing was a pivotal point in *White Spirituals in the Southern Uplands.*
He had been enabled to go back to the past he was so anxious to preserve. His conclusion was a compound of relief that the event was taking place at all and anxiety that he was witnessing its death rattle. It
was, he said, "a unique survival in cultural tradition," but with an ag-
ing group of participants, he feared that the tradition would be buried
with them.

"The *Southern Harmony* singings at Benton are probably the last of their kind anywhere and dissolution stares them in the face. The only thing that can lengthen their life is a new supply of song books with which the tradition is bound up. Will some worshipper at the shrine of 'old time songs' provide that supply? I heard rumors in Benton that one of the faithful was about to undertake that labor of love."

The rumors were right. In 1939 the Young Men's Progress Club of Benton issued a photoreproduction of the 1854 edition, and the tradition was kept alive and has continued into the twenty-first century with CDs issued of each year's singing. The Benton singing is now a local tourist attraction.

Enthusiasts like the Lomaxes, Jackson, and others not only created a channel for the urban folk revival but provided raw material for musicians who were for the most part neither poor nor downtrodden but university-educated liberals who wanted not only to explore the musical heritage of America but to write their own songs in the same spirit. These musicians viewed the promotion of music by the oppressed as a statement of solidarity.

To Alan Lomax the true "renaissance of American folk song" began in 1940 in New York when Pete Seeger, a Harvard drop-out, was introduced to Lomax discovery Woody Guthrie. Guthrie was just the sort of singer that the intellectuals idealized; he was poor and lacked any formal education but possessed a vitality that poured out in songs, drawings, stories, and philosophical meditations. He was from Oklahoma, stole rides on railroad trains, lived like a hobo, and wrote songs that celebrated the lives of ordinary working people while pointing out the injustices they suffered.

Seeger and Guthrie traveled America playing for workers rallies and political action groups, and when Seeger returned home to New York he formed the Almanac Singers with Millard Lampell and Lee Hays. Rather than a fixed group it was a pool of musicians any combination of which was entitled to perform as the Almanac Singers. Besides Seeger, Guthrie, Lampell, and Hays it would at various times include Josh White, Sonny Terry, Brownie McGhee, Agnes "Sis" Cunningham, and Cisco Houston.

It was Hays who taught Pete Seeger "Amazing Grace" in the 1940s and through the Weavers, a group they later formed, it reached a young, white audience. Hays had heard it growing up in Little Rock, Arkansas, where his father was a Methodist minister. He'd come across it not only in his home church but in the black churches where they sang it long-meter style. Seeger, raised as an agnostic and with no church experience, had never heard it before but liked it enough to add it to his repertoire of old American songs.

Hays sang lead vocal on "Amazing Grace" with the Weavers. Usually he used only the first stanza, but the version he had taught Seeger had an additional stanza that Seeger later discovered was adapted from Isaac Watts's hymn "Am I a Soldier of the Cross?"

Must I be wafted to the skies
On flowery beds of ease,
While others strive to win the prize
And sail through bloody seas?

At the time Seeger seemed an unlikely user of "Amazing Grace." Not only was he not a Christian, but at a time when the most feared en-

Doc Watson (far right) with Fred Price, Clarence Ashley, and Clint Howard
singing "Amazing Grace" in New York, 1961.

emy of "Christian America" was "Godless Russia," he was a member of
the American Communist Party and a supporter of various left-wing
causes. The words that to the Christian suggested repentance and conversion suggested justice and freedom to the man who wrote "If I Had
a Hammer" and "Where Have All the Flowers Gone?" "I tell the story
of the man who wrote it," Seeger said. "I say that if he could turn his
life around like that it gives us all hope that we can turn this world
around."

In Seeger's case the loss of most of Newton's stanzas subdued the
Christian statement and the added stanza invited a political interpretation. Understood against the background of Newton's life, the lines
of Watts appeared to compare the privilege of the captain's cabin
("beds of ease") to the fate of his slaves below deck ("bloody seas").
"Am I a Soldier of the Cross?" had no such intention. It was a call to
Christians to be bold in expressing their faith and to expect persecution. The opening stanza set the tone:

Am I a soldier of the cross,
a follower of the Lamb,
and shall I fear to own his cause,
or blush to speak his name?

There had been an obvious sociopolitical dimension to some early
spirituals, the urge to escape repression being cloaked in the language
of the Bible. These interpretations of such classics as "Run to Jesus,"
"Steal Away," and "Go Down Moses" were ballast to the folk movement. Seeger sang "Get Thee Behind Me (Satan)," "Joshua Fit the Battle of Jericho," and the Sankey favorite (written by Philip Bliss) "Hold
the Fort," with new meanings emerging from the new context.

They became a vital part of the culture around the civil rights
movement. Spirituals and hymns were used to bolster spirits on the
Freedom Marches, with blacks likening themselves to the wandering
Israelites in search of a promised land where justice would reign. The
best-known speeches of Martin Luther King rang with the words of
spirituals and he personally invited gospel artists such as Mahalia
Jackson to sing at rallies. "By singing the folk songs black activists

could tap into the legacy of their ancestors' suffering," wrote civil rights historian Kerran Sanger. "They could also add another chapter to that struggle."

Such songs united people across the divides of culture, background, denomination, color, and age. Some activists believed that hymns and spirituals created a symbolic shield that offered protection from the missiles and blows of those who hated them. Some believed they could soften the hearts of white Christians who sang the same hymns on Sundays.

The songs were usually selected according to their popularity in the region. "Amazing Grace," for example, was sung most widely in Georgia, Alabama, and Mississippi. Bernice Cordell Reagon, who formed the Freedom Singers in 1962, was on some of these marches and remembers leaders lining out hymns as ministers had done in churches. She said, " 'Amazing Grace' by John Newton and 'A Charge to Keep I Have' by Charles Wesley were among the hymns I heard the most."

A charge to keep I have,
　A God to glorify,
A never-dying soul to save,
　And fit it for the sky:

To serve the present age,
　My calling to fulfil;
O may it all my powers engage
　to do my Master's will!

John Cohen of the New Lost City Ramblers believes that the popularity of "Amazing Grace" with East Coast folksingers of the 1960s can be dated back to a performance that the guitarist and singer Doc Watson gave in New York in 1961 as part of Clarence Ashley's band. The concert, organized by Cohen, Ralph Rinzler of the Greenbriar Boys (who had discovered Watson at the age of thirty-seven in Deep Gap, North Carolina), and Izzy Young of the Folklore Center, was held at PS 41 on West Eleventh Street in Greenwich Village. The audience was made up of New York's most influential folkies.

"There were about four hundred of us there, mostly musicians, and we were really moved," said Cohen. "The experience was heightened because it was a blind man singing it and it made us realize that this was a personal statement of the course of someone's life. We had no experience of something like this and it was happening right in front of us. It was an interesting thing. We were mostly non-religious people, we didn't go to church or synagogue, but this song cut through."

Watson was appreciated because he was unaffected by commercial trends in music. He played for pleasure, was rooted in the community he was born into, and sang songs that had been passed down the generations. For him "Amazing Grace," which he had first heard in the 1920s at the Free Will Baptist Church, where his father was the singing leader, was a personal testimony rather than a cultural heirloom. He didn't perform it for purely aesthetic reasons but because he thought it would be good for people "to think of the real meaning of it."

The real meaning for Watson was that "when Jesus went to that cross it took more than what old-timers called 'biting the bullet.' It was him showing that he loved us all enough that by the grace of God he would pay the sin debt for us on the cross and his grace showed me the way to go. The amazing grace of God is what the song is about."

The Newport Folk Festival, which had resumed in 1963 after a three-year break, helped set the agenda for the folk revival; introducing newly discovered old-timers, launching new talent, and suggesting the parameters of folk music. Spiritual songs received a warm welcome at Newport, and there was every encouragement to accept gospel music as a form of folk music.

At the 1964 festival, "Amazing Grace" was performed together by Clarence Ashley, Clint Howard, Fred Price, Doc Watson, and Jean Ritchie. The following year, on the same day that Bob Dylan created controversy by electrifying his music, there was a "Concert of Religious Music," featuring the Chambers Brothers, the blind gospel-blues musician Rev. Gary Davis, Maybelle Carter of the celebrated Carter Family, and Jean Ritchie. Alan Lomax was part of a panel discussion titled "Talking About Music."

Headlining on another night was the twenty-three-year-old Joan Baez, who'd been converted to folk music after seeing Pete Seeger in concert ten years before. In the summer of 1962, she had played at four black colleges in the South and attended a black Baptist church meeting, experiences that gave her a new perspective on hymns, gospel songs, and spirituals. "Amazing Grace" became part of her set the following year, and although she didn't record it until the 1970s, it was included along with songs such as "Kumbaya," "Twelve Gates to the City," and "We Shall Overcome" in *The Joan Baez Songbook,* which was published in October 1964.

It became one of her most requested songs, yet she cannot recall exactly where she first heard it. "It has beautifully arranged notes and beautiful words," she said. "There are all the possibilities for many harmonies. But I don't know where the magical effect starts. I don't know whether it's there the first time you hear it or whether it's something that starts as the song gathers momentum and begins to collect memories. It's a natural song for me because it's spiritual, yet non-denominational."

By the mid-sixties "Amazing Grace" had become a folk standard, not widely recorded (although between 1960 and 1966 it was recorded by Jesse Fuller, Horton Barker, Chet Atkins, Stanley Brothers, the Limeliters, Burl Ives, and "Mississippi" Fred McDowell) but frequently used as a participatory closing number. So much of a staple did it become that Jay Ungar of the Putnam String County Band developed an irreverent parody, which began

> *Amazing grass! (how sweet the smell)*
> *That stoned a wreck like me.*
> *I once was straight, but now I'm stoned,*
> *Could see but now I'm blind.*

Arlo Guthrie, son of Woody, was one such mid-sixties performer of "Amazing Grace." Initially unaware of its origins, he read a biography of John Newton in 1965 while at a Methodist college in Montana and felt that he was reading about someone who would have felt at home among counterculture kids. To Guthrie, Newton was someone who valued moral integrity more than social acceptance, spiritual transcendence more than material wealth. He was also someone courageous enough to confront the dominant ethics of his day.

"I used to think, what's this 'saved a wretch like me'? Was it the same old Puritanical 'we hate everything including ourselves' stuff?" said Guthrie. "In Newton's case, he really was a wretched character and he really did feel like he had been saved. In his case it wasn't keeping the world safe from weirdos and he ends up being a countercultural figure. He went against the grain of the times. He gave up a well paid job and there are people today for whom the money is everything and justifies everything and they would never do that."

"Amazing Grace" was heavily featured in Guthrie's movie, *Alice's Restaurant*, which was directed by Arthur Penn and released in 1969. The story, based on one of Guthrie's songs, which in turn was based on incidents in his life, is centered on a white clapboard church building in Stockbridge, Massachusetts, where the local would-be hippies take refuge under the watchful eye of owners Alice and Ray. In real life they would all sing together, and one of the songs they would sing was "Amazing Grace."

The song proved to be a useful device to explore the generation gap. In one scene Guthrie and his hippie friends sing it and in another a re-vivalist preacher, appropriately played by Lee Hays, is at a tent meeting leading the congregation in singing it, raising the question of which gathering was closer to the true spirit of "Amazing Grace." Was the Christian way to be neat and clean and support the war in Vietnam or to be pleasantly untidy and refuse to fight? Was God's grace at work defeating evil through war or promoting health and harmony through peace?

"It provided a juxtaposition of sixties culture and 'Kill! Kill! Kill' militarism," said Guthrie. "There is a wonderful moment in the film when you hear the song playing and you sweep past all these beautiful, empty, New England churches and come to this one ragged church and as the song gets louder the camera goes inside and here are all these hippies singing this song which is traditionally associated with people who are a little bit more serious. It showed a sensitivity to heartfelt truth and at the same time played on the different cultural transitions going on at the time."

In August 1969 Guthrie performed at the opening night of the Woodstock Music Festival on a bill that included Melanie, Ravi

Shankar, Ritchie Havens, the Incredible String Band, and Joan Baez. No one at the time realized that this three-day event held on a farm in Upstate New York would one day be seen as the high point of 1960s countercultural optimism, the epitome of the idea that all you needed was love, peace, drugs, and music. He performed three songs: "Coming into Los Angeles," "Walking Down the Line," and "Amazing Grace."

"Amazing Grace" was to become a highlight of his live show and lengthened over the years as he broke between stanzas to recount a fanciful version of Newton's life story and to tell his listeners that "no matter what your story is, how bad you've been, if you believe something is right and worth doing, then don't quit trying. If you don't quit, someday you will succeed."

The folk revival hadn't turned "Amazing Grace" into a pop standard, but it had introduced the idea of it being a song rather than a hymn, a story of self-determination rather than divine rescue—two modifications that were necessary for the next stage in its march forward.

The version of "Amazing Grace" performed by Judy Collins hit the charts and brought about its recent mass popularity.

Chapter 11

INTO THE CHARTS

"Amazing Grace" certainly had an enormous impact. Far
beyond sales. George McGovern, when he was running for
president against Nixon, came up to me and said, "I want to
thank you for Amazing Grace. It meant so much to me." It
was Judy's recording that made that song an anthem for
so many people.
—*Mark Abramson*, RECORD PRODUCER, 1998

It's always a magical moment when I play "Amazing Grace."
I can't tell you how interesting that is. That song always
does the trick. I have a friend who says it changes the
electromagnetic field; that it has the ability to
transform the room into something different and better.
It really is powerful.
—*Judy Collins*, 2001

I think that "Amazing Grace" was a watershed
in military music. No doubt about that.
—*Captain Mel Jameson*, ROYAL SCOTS
DRAGOON GUARDS, 2001

*I*t's difficult to calculate the number of recordings that
have been made of "Amazing Grace" because even the best collections
are incomplete. The performing rights organizations ASCAP and BMI
together list 972 separate arrangements. There are more than eleven
hundred currently available albums featuring versions. Whatever the

actual total, the essential story of the song on record is that before 1971 it was recorded infrequently, mostly by gospel or folk artists, but that after 1971 it started to be covered by musicians from almost every genre. Of the 457 commercially released recordings held by the Library of Congress, 97 percent were made in the years between 1971 and 2001.

The watershed event was the a cappella single released by Judy Collins in December 1970, which climbed into the best-seller charts in both Britain and America early in 1971. Although "Amazing Grace" was a pop hit, Judy Collins was not a pop singer. She was a folksinger who had never disguised her roots. Her recording of "Amazing Grace" owed nothing to either rock or pop and in fact flouted the conventional wisdom of both. There were no drums or guitars, the vocal was controlled and clearly enunciated, and there was no repeated refrain or middle eight.

Yet Collins had the advantage of being considered part of the "rock culture" that was documented by magazines such as *Rolling Stone.* She operated in the same milieu as Bob Dylan, Leonard Cohen, and Joni Mitchell and the purity of her voice, which might have suggested conservativism and wholesomeness, was offset by her commitment to radical politics. She may have sounded sweet but she didn't flinch from conflict with authority.

Prior to her release of "Amazing Grace" three rock recordings had been made but only one had been released. Janis Joplin had been taped singing it with Big Brother and the Holding Company at San Francisco's Matrix club in January 1967 but this didn't make it onto an album until 1982. She had learned the song from records of Jean Ritchie, the Kentucky born singer of traditional American songs, and it was already part of the Big Brother repertoire, founding member Peter Albin having learned it while working the Bay Area folk club scene in the early sixties.

Albin had tackled it with psychedelic humor, introducing it with a rambling story of someone replacing the bread and wine of the Eucharist with tabs of LSD. In this context, the lines "I once was lost but now am found / Was blind but now I see" were about a powerful hallucinogenic revelation, and "When we've been there 10,000 years" was about the drug taker's experience of suspended time.

The Byrds used it as a closing number for their shows in 1969 and in June 1970 cut a studio version for their album *Untitled* but again it remained unreleased, in this case for thirty years. That the Byrds would perform it wasn't surprising given the folk backgrounds of the members and the spiritual curiosity of founding member Roger McGuinn. The Byrds had been one of the first rock bands to record religious songs. They had a number one hit with "Turn! Turn! Turn!" Pete Seeger's adaptation of Ecclesiastes 3:1–9, and there were album versions of "I Am a Pilgrim," "The Christian Life," and "Oil in My Lamp."

The only rock recording of "Amazing Grace" to be released during the 1960s was a 1969 instrumental by The Great Awakening, which although it didn't sell in America achieved cult status in Britain after being played by two of the hippest deejays of the time, Jeff Dexter (live shows) and John Peel (BBC Radio 1). Dexter was given a prerelease "white label" and made it his signature tune as he took his Light and Sound Show on the road.

As the mainstage deejay at the 1969 Isle of Wight Festival he introduced the record to an audience of two hundred thousand, for whom it soon became as inextricably linked to the event as the music of such headline acts as Bob Dylan, The Who, and Joe Cocker. He used it again the following year (Jimi Hendrix, the Doors, Miles Davis), and when Sony released a video of the festival twenty-six years later, it was included on the soundtrack.

Although the record was popular no one knew who The Great Awakening were. No group of that name appeared at the festival, or at any subsequent rock festival. There was no photograph, no album, and no follow-up single. Although obviously alluding to the eighteenth-century religious revival, the name also sounded very West Coast '67. Rumors were rife that it was a secret project cooked up by guitarists Jeff Beck and Eric Clapton. Others assumed that the David Cohen credited as arranger was the David Cohen who played keyboards with the San Francisco band Country Joe and the Fish.

The Great Awakening was actually not a working band at all but a concept of David Cohen, an L.A.-based session guitarist, who'd recorded the song to disprove a friend's argument that American hymn tunes were "uninteresting." Cohen had studied folk music at

UCLA under D. K. Wilgus (author of *Anglo-American Folksong Scholarship Since 1895*) and, like Peter Albin, had first heard "Amazing Grace" on a record by Doc Watson. He thought it had "a beautiful melody" and enlisted Joe Osborn (bass) and Jimmy Gordon (drums) to record it "as if someone was singing alone in the fields, almost unrhythmically, and gradually other people started singing and joining in."

The single, released on the independent Amos label in America and on London in Britain, sounded like a group of electric guitarists imitating a bagpiper (although at this time there had been no pipe recording of "Amazing Grace"). A short intro on acoustic guitar glided into the multitracked sound of a fuzz-tone lead guitar underpinned with a heavy bass riff and drums. "I had always been impressed with the fierce intensity of shape-note singing," said Cohen. "I didn't know if it had originally been a shape-note piece, but I thought it would be interesting to treat it that way."

In 1970, Judy Collins was a seasoned thirty-one-year-old singer who had been performing since the beginning of the sixties folk revival and recording for Jac Holzman's Elektra Records. She had started with purely traditional material and then added songs by new writers such as Bob Dylan, Phil Ochs, Randy Newman, Tom Paxton, and Leonard Cohen. Sensitive to social issues she had marched for civil rights and against the war in Vietnam. She helped publicize the formation of the Yippie movement in 1968, and because of her plans to perform on behalf of Jerry Rubin, Abbie Hoffman, and Rennie Davis in Chicago during the Democratic National Convention that year, she was called to appear as a witness at the trial of the Chicago Seven.

When asked in court to reiterate comments she had made when the Yippie movement was launched she said: "I want to see a celebration of life, not of destruction. I said that my soul and my profession and my life has become a part of a movement toward hopefully removing the causes for death, the causes for war, the causes for the prevalence of violence in our society, and in order to make my voice heard, I said that I would indeed come to Chicago and that I would sing. That is what I do. That's my profession. I said that I was there because life was the force that I wished my songs and my life to be known for."

Her biggest success to date had been in 1968 with the album *Wild-*

flowers, which included some of her own songs beside those of Jacques Brel, Leonard Cohen, and Joni Mitchell. "Both Sides Now," a Joni Mitchell song from the album, became her first hit single, earning her a Grammy for Best Folk Performance of 1968, and *Wildflowers* stayed in the charts for over twelve months. The following year she branched into theater, taking a role in Ibsen's *Peer Gynt* in New York, and while she was acting her next album began to take shape in her mind. A couple who had just returned from making the first sound recordings of humpback whales off Bermuda visited her backstage and left her a reel-to-reel tape of their favorite whale "songs" and this proved to be a significant stimulus.

Listening to this haunting music she began to improvise the lyrics of a song buried in her memory, the nineteenth-century Scottish sailing song "Farewell to Tarwathie." It seemed to work. She had also written a song called "Nightingale" and wanted to attempt an adaptation of the Shaker song "Simple Gifts," written by Elder Joseph Brackett, Jr., in 1848. By then she knew that the album that was growing in her imagination would be called *Whales and Nightingales* and that the keynote would be purity, simplicity, naturalness.

She craved simplicity at this point because, like many others at the close of such a tumultuous decade, her life was "in a muddle." The demands of touring strained intimate relationships and deprived her of a still center to things. Admired by audiences, she began to feel a fraud, a messenger with no message. "I traveled all over the world, and most of the time I felt out of kilter—in the wrong movie, in the wrong script, on the wrong road. From airport to airport and from town to town, I tried not to think about the chaos in my life, holding back the madness like a monster I knew was out there somewhere."

She tried to bring a bit of sanity to her life by staying put in her adopted home of New York. She joined an encounter group, built up a circle of close friends, and in 1970 began to record *Whales and Nightingales* with engineer John Haeny and producer Mark Abramson. In keeping with the theme of simplicity it was decided to record the tracks in uncluttered rooms that would lend their ambience to the performance. Accordingly, "Simple Gifts" was recorded in a Greenwich Village loft, "Prothalamium" on the empty stage at Carnegie Hall, and Jacques

Brel's "Marieke" in a ballroom previously used for recording Broadway cast albums.

"Amazing Grace" was a song that she felt she had always known. It had come down to her from rural Tennessee, where her mother's family had produced missionaries and ministers, and from Idaho, where her father's family had farmed. It was sung in the Methodist church in Denver where she was part of the choir as a child, and when she came to New York in the early sixties she heard it being performed in the folk clubs. In the civil rights movement she heard "Amazing Grace" in yet another context, sung by the marchers as well as by gospel singers brought in to boost morale. With activist Fannie Lou Hamer, she attended voter registration marches in Mississippi, where they would join to sing the song for the crowds. "During those days," she later wrote, "I sang 'Amazing Grace' as a rune to give magical protection—a charm to ward off danger, an incantation to the angels of heaven to descend. I had left the choir of the Methodists and was not sure magic worked outside of church walls—whether wine would be turned to blood and bread to flesh in the open air in Mississippi. But I wasn't taking any chances."

She sang "Amazing Grace" in her concerts because it was one of the few songs that everyone knew at least one verse of. "It made a wonderful encore," she said, "because it's very bonding, very unifying and tells an inspirational story." When the singer and author Richard Farina, brother-in-law to Joan Baez and running buddy of Bob Dylan, died in April 1966 after crashing his motorcycle on a road outside Carmel, California, she broke off from her tour to sing an a cappella version of it at his graveside.

"The reason I recorded it is kind of odd," she said. "I was part of an encounter group on the Upper West Side and one night, after a particularly disruptive session during which people were viciously honest with each other, I asked everyone to pause for a moment while we sang 'Amazing Grace.' My producer, Mark Abramson, was there that night with his wife and the next morning he called me and said, 'You know what? You should record that song.' That's really how it happened."

Whales and Nightingales was the perfect record on which to include it, and to retain its simplicity she chose to perform it a cappella with a group of close friends as background vocalists, none of whom was a professional singer. Abramson was a former Columbia University student and suggested St. Paul's Chapel, a domed church on the campus, as an ideal venue. Declared a New York City Landmark in 1966, it had been designed at the turn of the twentieth century in Italian Renaissance style with stalls built in Florence of Italian walnut and a floor paved totally with marble terrazzo, including small fragments taken from a razed early Christian church in Rome. Using a portable eight-track recording van, engineer John Haeney miked the chapel to ensure a full sound—a vocal mike for Judy, close mikes, mikes sixty feet away, and then other mikes at the back of the chapel and even up inside the dome.

The result was startling for its clarity and for the resonance of the vocals. Although no musical instruments were played, the humming of the informal choir on the second stanza had the effect of chords gently played on an organ and the ambience of the chapel produced a quality of sustain and echo that could never have been created in a studio. Emphasizing purity and harmony, it wasn't the only way to sing "Amazing Grace," but, for many people unfamiliar with the song until then, it would become the definitive recorded version.

Although the vocal score was her own, she stuck closely to Edwin Othello Excell's 1910 version, using his choice of Newton's first three stanzas plus the "10,000 years" stanza. She also used his arrangement of "New Britain" rather than William Walker's *Southern Harmony* arrangement. The only significant change was the substitution of "we" for "I" in the "Through many dangers" stanza, signaling that she was singing on behalf of her generation rather than just for herself. This was a cleaner and more organized "Amazing Grace" than the one that George Pullen Jackson and the Lomaxes had found in the South; an "Amazing Grace" of marble rather than sawdust, of Italian walnut rather than rough hewn pine.

When Elektra boss Jac Holzman heard the recording, he considered it a wild card as a single because it was so different. "I had been so impressed by 'Hey Jude.' To me it was the Sistine Chapel of rock, and if I was in the dumps I would listen to it through headphones. Now there was 'Amazing Grace.' I was overcome by its purity, the sense of redemption in the words and the elegiac simplicity of the melody."

The timing was right. The war in Vietnam was dragging on and Lieutenant William Calley was in an American court on a charge of massacring civilians at My Lai. In Los Angeles, Charles Manson and his hippie acolytes were also appearing before a judge on murder charges. It seemed that both the American Dream and the hippie dream had ended up in the same place. There was a widespread yearning for less complicated times, for the days before napalm and LSD, for values that had stood the test of time.

Christian themes had appeared more often in pop songs over the past two years. The Edwin Hawkins Singers had a surprise hit in the summer of 1969 with "Oh Happy Day," a gospel song that had its origin in an eighteenth-century hymn by Philip Doddridge, one of Newton's inspirations. Norman Greenbaum's "Spirit in the Sky" ("I got a friend in Jesus") charted in March 1970 and James Taylor's "Fire and Rain," released as a single in October 1970, was the cry of a reforming heroin addict who needed the "helping hand" of Jesus. *Jesus Christ Superstar*, also released in October 1970, was a rock opera written by Andrew Lloyd Webber and Tim Rice.

Two important songs of 1970, "Let It Be" by the Beatles and "Bridge Over Troubled Water" by Simon and Garfunkel, were written in a hymnic style and offered consolation during difficult times. Paul Simon had built his song up from the title phrase, which he'd found in an ad lib made by Claude Jeter during a recording of "Mary Don't You Weep" with the Swan Silvertones. As lead singer Louis Johnson repeatedly called the name of Mary, Jeter cried out: "I'll be a bridge over deep water if you trust in my name."

After years of avoiding commitments there was a generational feeling that it was time to put down roots. The prime indicator of this change was Bob Dylan's abandonment of his drug fueled on-the-road lifestyle in favor of family life in rural upper New York State where he cut his hair, cleaned up, and started writing the songs for *John Wesley Harding*, a record he later described as the first "Biblical rock album."

At his Woodstock home Dylan had a large open Bible prominently displayed on a lectern.

Drugs had also played a part in making the sixties generation more aware of spiritual realms. Musicians such as John Lennon and Paul McCartney who'd previously declared religion to be irrelevant to modern life were now either talking about their personal encounters with God or advocating the practice of Hindu forms of meditation. The Beatles track "Tomorrow Never Knows" drew from Timothy Leary's loose translation of the Tibetan Book of the Dead. "The Inner Light" was borrowed from the Tao Te Ching, and "I Am the Walrus" referred to Krishna.

There had been an unspoken rule in the music industry that religion wasn't a safe subject for pop. It was okay in folk, gospel, or country, but pop was fundamentally secular. References to religious topics had the potential to alienate nonbelievers or upset believers. In 1966 there was record company consternation when the Beach Boys recorded "God Only Knows" because it seemed likely that radio stations would be nervous about playing a pop single with the word *God* in the title. Two years later similar worries surfaced over Simon and Garfunkel's soundtrack song for *The Graduate*, "Mrs Robinson," which had the line "Jesus loves you more than you can know."

By the time "Amazing Grace" was being considered as a single these concerns had diminished. It contained only one overt use of the word *God* ("sing God's praise") and many were now unaware that it was a hymn, let alone one written by an eighteenth-century Calvinist. David Sharp, a Methodist minister from England, was one of those who initially thought that the success of "Amazing Grace" would provide a useful point of contact between trainee ministers and "unchurched" youth. In his 1976 book *No Stained-Glass-Window Saints*, he wrote, "But frequently the college students have found that the hymn is incomprehensible to the young people, because they assume that 'grace' is a girls' name."

Holzman's hunch that it could be the first single from the album was endorsed by Elektra's European label manager, Clive Selwood, who thought it would make an ideal Christmas single. Selwood's enthusiasm led to its being released in Britain in the middle of November 1970 with "Poor Immigrant," a track from her previous album *Who Knows Where the Time Goes,* on the flip side. It immediately received heavy airplay and slowly rose in the charts over the next three months until, in February 1971, it reached number five. "I didn't even know it was a hymn," wrote Roy Hollingworth in Melody Maker. "But it sounded glorious. It sounded like a humble thank you. Against the rash of rebellious rock it was sobering. If it was God rock, then God rock was good."

The song was still in the British charts when it was heard by thirty-seven-year-old Stuart Fairbairn, then bandmaster of the Royal Scots Greys regiment of the British army, who could imagine it being played on the bagpipes. "I kept it at the back of my mind for a while and eventually got an arrangement down on paper," he said. "Then I was made redundant and before I left I gave the pipe melody of 'Amazing Grace' to Pipe Sergeant Tony Crease."

The score he had devised was based on the Judy Collins version: a pipe solo at the beginning following her lead vocal, and the combined pipes, drums, and concert band emulating her small a capella choir. The tune was played in a slower time to accommodate the bagpipes and therefore a stanza was cut. "It's a very simple structure and has to be kept that way because the melody doesn't quite marry up to the actual scale on a bagpipe," said Fairbairn. "There is a similarity but it doesn't quite match, and if you make the background too complicated it produces dissonances."

At the time that Fairbairn produced this score, the regiment had just returned to Scotland after a long posting in Germany and had learned that it was to be amalgamated with a Welsh regiment, the Third Carabiniers, to form the Royal Scots Dragoon Guards. It was suggested that the passing of the Greys, a regiment with a history stretching back to the seventeenth century, should be marked by a recording. The pipe president, Captain Mel Jameson, felt strongly that if it happened it should combine the regiment's two musical groups—its pipes and drums, along with its military band.

The commanding officer contacted Peter Kerr, a freelance producer who'd worked on two previous albums for the Greys, to see if a deal could be struck with RCA. "Basically RCA wasn't interested," said Kerr. "They said that they would only do it if the regiment would guarantee to buy a thousand copies. The regiment agreed and we set to work."

The minuscule budget of only a few hundred pounds meant that it had to be recorded in the Study Centre at Redford Barracks, Edinburgh, a large room with a stage and grey army blankets acting as soundproofing, and that it had to be completed in two three-hour sessions. Peter Kerr operated out of a mobile control room.

At the end of the second session it was realized that the material already on tape was just a few minutes short of the time needed to fill both sides of a long player. "I asked if they had something that could be slipped in to make up the last few minutes," said Kerr. "The new bandmaster said that there was this version of Dvorak's 'Going Home' that they had played when they left Germany and that some of the young pipers had been mucking about with a thing that Judy Collins had recently had a hit with and which Stuart Fairbairn had written a score for. I said we should give it a go. I listened to it and then recorded it in a single take."

Because of the drones and the difference in scales, bagpipes are notoriously difficult to record. The drones emit a fixed note of B-flat, which clashes with chordal changes within the military band. "What we did was to stick a cork in them," said Kerr. "So all you can hear on the record are the chanters which carry the melody. Later we added an introductory drone which was brought in and gradually faded out until the brass took over. It was seamless. It sounds as though there were thirty pipers on it but there were no more than six."

Albums of military music usually sell in modest numbers in Britain—five thousand copies is considered very reasonable—and there was no expectation that *Farewell to the Greys* would be any different. But then a BBC radio presenter, Keith Fordyce, played "Amazing Grace" on his show Late Night Extra, which ran for two hours each Tuesday night on Radio 2 between 10:00 P.M. and midnight and promised "music and news, people and places." The track was chosen by the program's producer, Ian Fenner, who was a fan of military music. Fordyce, who didn't take an immediate liking to it, asked his listeners to write in with their reactions. "The BBC was flooded with letters requesting the track and asking about the record," said Kerr. "RCA then reluctantly put out the single and soon they had to have every pressing plant they used in Britain and Europe working full time to satisfy demand. It is still the best-selling instrumental single of all time in Britain."

"Amazing Grace" had never been recorded on the pipes before and it was considered controversial within the piping community, not just because it covered a recent pop hit but because it combined pipes and drums with a military band. "It was seen as being incorrect," said pipe president Mel Jameson. "I was summoned to see the director of bagpipe music at Edinburgh Castle who said, 'How dare you do this to the bagpipes!' I said, 'I'm sorry. I'm not understanding you.' He said, 'It's sacrilege what you've done. You can't have bagpipes being demeaned in this fashion.' But I said, 'But we've just introduced bagpipes into a million homes in the United Kingdom. Is that a bad idea?'"

A third influential pop version was by Aretha Franklin, known as Lady Soul, whose father the Reverend C. L. Franklin had personally introduced her to Marion Williams, Clara Ward, Mahalia Jackson, and many other great gospel singers of the postwar era when they came to sing at his church in Detroit. At the age of fourteen Aretha recorded Clara Ward's songs and had been taken around the country by her father on preaching tours, at which she would sing before his sermon.

Four years later she was singing pop in a gospel style, a genre of music that had become known as soul, and after a sluggish period with Columbia Records had a string of hits masterminded by Atlantic Records producer Jerry Wexler beginning in 1967. In 1972, Wexler, the man who had coined the phrase "rhythm and blues" when working for *Billboard* magazine and had later said that he really should have called it "rhythm and gospel," persuaded her to return to her gospel roots for a live double album.

He took Aretha to New Temple Missionary Baptist Church on South Broadway in the Watts District of Los Angeles, which had been the scene of extensive rioting in 1965. Performances were scheduled for two consecutive evenings and her backing was to be provided by the voices of the Southern California Community Choir under the leadership of James Cleveland, then the best-known male gospel singer in America.

Aretha used "Amazing Grace" to close both evenings and in doing so produced one of the most impassioned performances of her recording career. Whereas the roots of the Judy Collins version went back through Methodist choirs to Edwin Othello Excell's arrangement, the roots of Aretha's version went back through Marion Williams and Mahalia Jackson to the long meter style of the Holiness churches where the tune is pulled apart wide enough to let the spirit in.

The last voice heard before the vocals kicked in was Cleveland asking, "Can I get a witness here tonight?" and that was the key to the performance. In gospel music the point is not clarity, precision, and faithfulness to the text but witness to personal experience and faithfulness to the movement of the spirit. Judy Collins covered four stanzas and a repeated first stanza in four minutes and four seconds. Aretha took two stanzas and wrung every meaning out of them over a period of fourteen minutes.

To Aretha the truth of the song came out in the singing. She approached every word and syllable with reverence, savoring the sounds and exploring every nuance of emotion. Some words deserved to be whispered, some had to be wailed, some needed to be broken, some needed to hang in the air. "The other day, in rehearsal," Cleveland said during his spoken introduction, "Aretha began to sing it and when she got to the part where it says 'through many dangers' I looked over at her and saw the tears rolling out of her eyes."

After moaning out an introduction she stuck closely to the text of the first stanza but on the second stanza she let go, using key words as the basis for vocal ad libs, adding interjections, feeding off the response of the congregation, tunneling deep into the collective memory. It seemed that the words that John Newton had written in his study in Olney two hundred years ago were being scrutinized while she drew on her own experiences to add a commentary.

Through, through, through, through, through many dangers toils and
    snares,
I—I feel right here in the midst of—have already, already, have
    already—Jesus was with me—have already come—yes I have
It was, it was, it was, it was, it was, it was grace—that saved me—has
    been with me—has brought me safe thus far—don't you know
And that same, that same old grace, they call it God's amazing,
    amazing, amazing grace
[moans the tune out for 85 seconds]
It was, it was—I want the world to know that it was—it was, it was, it
    was grace
It was grace Lord, that brought me—me so safe, so safe, so safe, so safe,
    so safe, so safe—so safe thus far
And it won't be nothing but that same grace—I know that it won't—that's
    gonna lead me and mine right on, right on, right on, right on, right
    on, yeh.

She could have been thinking of the trials facing African Americans but also her own personal problems, including the breakdown of her marriage. "I don't want to sound phony about this but I feel a great kinship with God," she told *Ebony* in 1971. "That's what has helped me pull out of the problems I've faced. Anybody who has kept up with my career knows that I've had my share of problems and trouble, but look at me today. I'm here. I have my health, I'm strong, I have my career and my family and plenty of friends everywhere, and the reason why is that through the years, no matter how much success I achieved, I never lost my faith in God."

Although never a political spokesperson she put out records that often had an unintended poignancy. When her home city of Detroit was torn apart by race riots in the summer of 1967, she had topped the charts with "Respect," which became a black power anthem. Soldiers reluctantly serving in Vietnam took delight in her next year's hit, "Chain of Fools." Two months before his death Martin Luther King came to Detroit and presented her with the Southern Christian Leadership Conference Award.

It wasn't only Aretha who had been brought "safe thus far" but her people, "me and mine." There had been casualties but there had been immense gains. The mood was changing from anger to self-respect. The "niggers" of the 1950s, later the blacks of the 1960s, were about to become the African Americans of the 1970s, who displayed pride both in their Americanness and their Africanness. Marvin Gaye had grown a beard and recorded the classic "What's Going On." Alex Haley had written *Roots.* For the cover photograph of the album, which was released in July 1972, Aretha wore a dashiki-style gown and a tall head wrap.

Rod Stewart, who had inherited a love of gospel vocals from Sam Cooke and an appreciation for American folk after busking on the streets of Paris, recorded a soulful version with blues musician Sam Mitchell on slide guitar for his 1971 album *Every Picture Tells a Story.* Mitchell had been playing regularly at Les Cousins, a folk club in London's Soho, and was spotted one evening by singer Long John Baldry, who took the liberty of taping his set and later playing it to Stewart, who was looking for new material.

"I used to play an instrumental version of 'Amazing Grace' and when Rod heard the tape of it he wanted me to come and play for him," said Mitchell. "I went to his house in Highgate where we rehearsed it and that night we recorded it at Morgan Studios. It only needed a couple of takes to get it right and the reason that Rod only sang one verse is because he only knew one verse! The melody stands on its own. You only need to hear it once and you've got it. Repeated hearings don't make it any better."

Only two minutes long, it was nevertheless a unique country-blues version. Despite its potential it had never been explored adequately by blues musicians, the only recordings of any note being Blind Willie McTell's instrumental for the Library of Congress, a 1955 version by Jesse Fuller, and Mississippi Fred McDowell's recording made in 1966 and released in 1969.

Although he wouldn't have been aware of the appropriateness, Mitchell's acoustic-guitar playing with the notes bending and wailing created an atmosphere that suggested the isolation that Newton must have felt on Plantain Island. Then, after two instrumental stanzas, Stewart's rasping vocal came in, the strain of reaching for words like "wretch" and "lost" again brilliantly appropriate. It was as though he couldn't quite bring himself to admit to his past misery.

In January 1971, during the early sessions, Stewart spoke of titling the album *Amazing Grace* but the unexpectedly huge success of the Judy Collins's single forced him to change and then as the result of a mistake when relaying information to Mercury Records in America the track wasn't listed either on the label or the sleeve. Stewart, however, ensured that Mitchell was registered as a cowriter. "I still play it in my concerts," said Mitchell. "I introduce it as my platinum record. It's the only platinum record I've ever appeared on." When the Faces toured, Stewart would perform it with Ronnie Wood playing Mitchell's slide guitar parts. Wood later used it in his solo concerts.

These four recordings helped turn "Amazing Grace" into a pop standard. They were each aimed at the general pop market where they succeeded but they also appealed to specialized markets. Judy Collins was still thought of as a folksinger and her albums were reviewed on the folk pages of music publications. Aretha was a major figure in soul music, but, especially as she had used James Cleveland, her album sold through gospel outlets. Rod Stewart's audience was young scarf-waving rock fans. The Royal Scots Dragoon Guards would have appealed to an older, more traditional listenership. These vastly different natural fan bases meant that, unusually, the same song was being bought at roughly the same time by elderly conservatives as well as young liberals, white kids from Santa Monica as well as black kids from Harlem.

In America, Judy Collins reached number 15 on the singles charts. In Britain, she sold over a million copies and was second only to Diana Ross as 1971's best-selling female artist. The Royal Scots Dragoon Guards went to 11 in America and to the top spot in Britain, where they had the biggest-selling single of 1972. Worldwide they were eventually to sell more than 16 million copies in all formats.

Commercial success gave "Amazing Grace" a makeover. It had been a worthy song, but ancient. Now it sounded brand-new, and its chart performance proved that it had the quality to compete with the best songs of the day. For many people, especially those outside of America, these pop versions were their introduction to the song. They didn't know its heritage in the church, hadn't heard the story of John Newton, and probably had no clear idea of what grace was.

The cosmetic company Philosophy promotes a line of products named after the song, which, it says, "Was created to ring in a new era of women's fragrances."

Chapter 12

ICON

The Music Educators National Conference has compiled a list of 42 tunes which it says Americans "must continue singing, humming, and strumming to preserve an important part of the national culture." Among the songs suggested for singing and preservation are: "I've Been Workin' on the Railroad," "Oh! Susanna," "Amazing Grace," "Simple Gifts," and "Puff the Magic Dragon."
—*The Associated Press*, NEWS RELEASE, 1996

The song's message—that man is essentially wretched and powerless to effect his own redemption, but with God all things are possible—neatly reflects the stark yet ultimately hopeful tenets of evangelicalism, arguably the quintessential American experience.
—*Benjamin Schwarz*, FOREIGN POLICY ANALYST, 1997

> *They like to take all this money from sin,*
> *Build big universities to study in*
> *Sing "Amazing Grace" all the way to the Swiss banks.*
> —*Bob Dylan*, "FOOT OF PRIDE," 1983

*T*raditionally icons are visual, but the iconography of popular culture is more extensive, embracing living people (Madonna), brand names (Coca-Cola), events (the Woodstock Festival), places (the Alamo), and even historical periods (the Kennedy years). The principle remains the same. An icon is something that represents a larger reality, usually an ideal. There is no reason why a song or a piece of music can't be an icon: "We'll Meet Again" an icon of World War II for the Allies, "All You Need Is Love" an icon of hippie optimism, "We Shall Overcome" an icon of the civil rights movement.

"Amazing Grace" has become such an icon, especially in America. Like the Declaration of Independence or Martin Luther King's "I Have a Dream" speech, it represents a widely shared belief. E. D. Hirsch's 1987 book *Cultural Literacy* included a list of five thousand essential names, phrases, dates, and concepts that he believed every American should know. There were thirty-three songs on the list, five of which were religious. Of these five songs, two were Christmas carols, two were spirituals, and one was a hymn. The hymn was "Amazing Grace."

In a similar spirit the Music Educators' National Conference, in 1996, compiled a list of forty-two songs that it felt it was essential to preserve by ensuring that they were learned by each generation. Again, "Amazing Grace" was on the list. In December 1999, *USA Today* suggested a hundred things that it believed should be preserved in a time capsule to communicate the essence of the twentieth century to future generations. Along with such objects as a can opener, Velcro, Barbie dolls, any Charlie Chaplin movie, a Batman comic book, the polio vaccine, a piece of the Berlin Wall, a Chevy Camero, and a cushioned toilet seat was the song sheet for "Amazing Grace." The only other individual song mentioned was "Auld Lang Syne."

When "Amazing Grace" is sung in America, particularly at times of national mourning or rejoicing, people feel that they are connecting with something that is shared not only by their contemporaries but by their ancestors. In *Atlantic Monthly* (March 1997) the foreign policy analyst Benjamin Schwarz suggested some of these reasons in an article that challenged Conor Cruise O'Brien over his assertion that Thomas Jefferson was so deeply racist that he should be expelled from the American pantheon. Schwarz concluded his argument by suggesting that in the final analysis the creed embodied in "Amazing Grace" may be of more use in reaching a successful interracial society than the creed embodied in Jefferson's Declaration.

"Jefferson's elegant and often abstract Declaration of Independence is, as O'Brien recognizes, a sacred text in America's civil religion," he wrote. "But if we are to overcome our national pathology, perhaps we must look to a simpler text. 'Amazing Grace,' whose tune is based on an American folk melody, was written in England in 1779 [sic], but is not a popular hymn there. It is, however, beloved in this country and has permeated the culture; as with the Declaration, most Americans know its gist. The hymn and the story of its creation both attest to a characteristically American notion—the possibility of emotional and spiritual transformation."

So what is the creed embodied in the song? "Amazing Grace," as sung today, usually consists of Newton's first three stanzas with the "ten thousand years" stanza and can mean so much to so many because it can be read in different, yet not necessarily contradictory, ways. It can be read as the spiritual song that Newton intended, as a more generically spiritual song, as a song of material challenge and conquest, or as a song that unites the spiritual and material.

Most Americans who engage with it are probably thinking of both the material and the spiritual. It's not crudely materialistic like "My Way," which contains no allusion to any divine ordering, but neither is it defiantly Christian like "The Old Rugged Cross," a hymn that it would be difficult to interpret in a purely secular way.

"Amazing Grace" took root in America not only because it articulated the experience of personal conversion but because the trials the song alluded to were so much a part of the archetypal American journey from rags to riches or slavery to freedom. America was a nation built by obstacle overcomers and dreamers of a better tomorrow. Consequently, "Amazing Grace" became the favorite song not only of the dominant white European settlers but of the Native Americans whose land they took and the African slaves whose muscle they used to tame it. It's believed to have been one of the hymns that Cherokees sang to comfort themselves in 1838–39 as they were forcibly marched from their native homelands along the Trail of Tears to Oklahoma.

"That saved a wretch like me": In a spiritual sense this referred to the spoiling effect of sin and of the rescue plan initiated by the death of Christ. Materially and emotionally, wretchedness was a condition you were plunged into, often through no fault of your own. There was the outer wretchedness of poverty, squalor, and persecution, and the inner wretchedness of hopelessness, fear, and a broken spirit.

One of America's goals during the great period of immigration was to provide a refuge for such people, a country where it was possible to begin again. In the hundred years after 1820, around 34 million people immigrated. The words of Emma Lazarus's poem, carved on the pedestal of the Statute of Liberty, have an affinity with some of Newton's phrases:

> *Give me your tired, your poor,*
> *Your huddled masses yearning to breathe free,*
> *The wretched refuse of your teeming shore . . .*

"I once was lost, but now am found": This was the experience of being united with God, but materially it could be about being found by America, about being given a new nationality and, in some cases, a new name. "Was blind, but now I see": the traditional expression of spiritual enlightenment. Everything falls into place. What once seemed irrelevant now seems vital. What once seemed vital now seems irrrelevant. Materially it could have a parallel in the illumination offered by a liberal education and the progress of science, knowledge banishing ignorance and superstition. Liberty carries a flaming torch in her hand.

> *I lift my lamp beside the golden door!*

"And grace my fears relieved": The fear that grace relieved for Newton was the fear of death and punishment. Death is still the ultimate focus of material fears, but its harbingers are poverty, starvation, hopelessness, violence, and oppression. An important part of the American Dream has been the elimination of these fears so that, in the words of President Franklin Roosevelt, the only thing we have to fear is fear itself.

"The hour I first believed": Belief is essential to the spiritual life. Salvation is carried out by God, but faith is the instrument that receives it. Newton stressed the immediacy with which the promises attached to faith took effect. Belief is essential in material matters too: belief in oneself, belief in the product, belief in the nation.

"Many dangers, toils and snares": In a spiritual sense this phrase referred to the temptations that litter the route of the Christian pilgrim. Materially it can refer to the hardships that have to be endured in any life, particularly those that affect a country's pioneers as they cultivate the land, as well as the hardships that have affected America from the War of Independence to the terrorism of September 11, 2001.

"Grace will lead me home": In a spiritual sense home is heaven. In a material sense home could be America or that small piece of America that is yours. The concept of home, of a place that you belong to in a special way, has been particularly important to Americans. The visual image of prosperity and security is so often the family standing by the front gate with the house dominant in the background. "When we've been there ten thousand years": a reference to eternity and the heavenly kingdom. This is the hardest verse to fit into a purely secular interpretation because whereas the phrase "sing God's praise" could be read pantheistically (singing the praise of all matter), it can't be read in a totally nonreligious way.

No one is forced to choose either a spiritual or a material reading of "Amazing Grace," because the spiritual life is lived in the material world. Newton's own life provides an eloquent example. When he was at his most wretched he lived in wretched conditions on Plantain Island. The moment he was spiritually rescued he was physically removed from danger on the Atlantic Ocean. The more he longed for heaven the more he became a believer in the sanctity of his earthly home, resenting having to spend any time away from it.

The iconic status of "Amazing Grace" has been fully realized only in the years following the Judy Collins hit. This was when it began to emerge as a top choice for funeral music and when the title began to be used to name a variety of commercial enterprises from a bakery store in Minnesota and a ship in the Caribbean to a bath gel manufactured in Arizona and a llama farm in Ohio. It is now possible to buy Amazing Grace key chains, fridge magnets, bumper stickers, posters, mugs, and T-shirts. It began to creep into other forms of popular culture, giving its name to a villainous character in Superman comics, being used in video installations in art galleries, and supplying endless newspaper subeditors with captions for photographs of gymnasts and ballet dancers.

This was also the period during which it first became widely covered by other artists. Until this point "Amazing Grace" hadn't been seen as a commercial pop song or even added to a pop album as a hymn with crossover potential. On the rare occasions when nongospel musicians had used it, the context was clearly religious. Chet Atkins, the country musician, recorded an instrumental version in 1962, but only because it was for an album entitled *Down Home Hymns*. The folk group the Limeliters covered it in 1963, but on an album of spirituals called *Makin' a Joyful Noise*. No one saw it as a contender in the league of "You've Lost That Lovin' Feelin'" and there was a reluctance to sell it as a piece of light entertainment.

Once it had made its mark on the charts, though, its qualities seemed obvious to everyone. Almost immediately it was treated as a classic and was included on albums produced for the nonspecialist market, although those who recorded it for the first fifteen years after 1971 actually shared a lot of similarities. The majority of them were white. They were either raised in the South (e.g., Merle Haggard, Charlie Rich, Willie Nelson), had a long-standing interest in historical American music (e.g., Van Dyke Parks, John Sebastian, John Fahey) or were committed Christians (e.g., Glen Campbell, Johnny Cash, Anita Bryant). Because of this they almost all approached the song in a reverential way, as though to depart too drastically from the way that grandma always sang it would be akin to blasphemy.

The most interesting departures were instrumentals by guitarist John Fahey, composer and arranger Van Dyke Parks, and British blues band the Groundhogs. Separated from Newton's text, musicians felt free to experiment. Fahey's acoustic guitar instrumental, recorded in January 1971 and therefore unlikely to have been influenced by the new pop interest, was stately and medieval. Parks, best known as Brian Wilson's songwriting collaborator on the ill-fated Beach Boys album *Smile*, did a "slow version" and a "toe tapper," both featuring an orchestral arrangement with an accordion picking out the melody. The Groundhogs' track, which used a guitar fed through a Mellotron, caused the normally cynical *Rolling Stone* critic, the late Lester Bangs, to say of guitarist Tony McPhee, "He even records an instrumental electro version of that sudden classic 'Amazing Grace' in a move roughly analogous to Hendrix' 'Star Spangled Banner' shuck, and he pulls the damn thing off with aplomb."

Some southern-born recording stars must have kicked themselves for not having realized the potential of a song which they'd known since they were at Sunday school. Elvis Presley, for example, was raised in the Assembly of God denomination, where it was popular. He would also have been familiar with the recording made in 1953 by his favorite white gospel group, the Blackwood Brothers Quartet, some of whose members attended the church the Presley family belonged to in Memphis. He didn't consider "Amazing Grace" for his two albums of hymns and gospel songs in the 1960s, which were designed to appeal to the religious market as well as to his mainstream fans. Yet, within weeks of Judy Collins's version entering the Billboard Top Twenty, he cut a version for his third inspirational album, *He Touched Me*, at RCA Studios, Nashville.

It's the nature of an icon to be used in other art forms as a representation of something much bigger. "Amazing Grace" is typically used in pop culture either as an indicator of populist evangelical religion (e.g., its use in *The Simpsons*), to denote death (e.g., *Coal Miner's Daughter, Star Trek II*), or to suggest core American values that are worth defending and even dying for (e.g., *Memphis Belle*).

The song is now greater than the sum of its parts. In fact, because it is a cultural icon, any one of its parts automatically suggests the whole. The lines of at least half of its stanzas are so widely known that it's possible to allude to them in other songs. White rappers the Beastie Boys quoted "I once was lost but now I'm found" on their album track "Shadrach," Jill Scott quoted "I was blind, now I can see" in her hit single "A Long Walk," and hip-hop artist Afroman quoted the entire first stanza in "The American Dream," a track on his debut album *The Good Times.*

"Amazing Grace" has informed not only music and film. The National Dance Theatre Company of Jamaica choreographed a dance to it that "celebrated the spiritual dimension of the human experience."

Australian-based "sound sculptor" Nigel Helyer had it broadcast from speakers installed in a buoy floating in Liverpool's Albert Dock as part of an exhibit that commented on the history of the port city. Porn star turned performance artist Annie Sprinkle had it performed by her then girlfriend Kimberley Silver for the 1996 show *Hard Core from the Heart* to suggest the finding of true love. "She's really butch and made these orgasmic sounds as she sang it," said Sprinkle. "It was probably the most erotic version that there has ever been."

It's also natural that an icon should be reinterpreted. It wasn't until the mid-1980s that it was recorded by artists with no obvious natural cultural or religious affinity to the song. Janis Joplin, Rod Stewart, and the Byrds, each had earlier connections with folk music and Joplin was a southerner to boot. Chet Baker, however, who taped it for his *Silent Nights* album in 1986, was a Californian jazz trumpet player best known for his finely chiseled features and his relationship with heroin, and the rock band Yes, who included it as a bass guitar solo on *9012 Live*, were English and more likely to sing of cosmic consciousness than born-again experience. The Lemonheads, who recorded it the following year, were an indie band from Boston led by Evan Dando, and the Spotnicks a Swedish instrumental group, which had been recording since 1961.

Guitarist P. K. Mitchell gave it the heavy metal treatment on his album *All Hail the Power*, using the first stanza as a refrain and sounding like Deep Purple, circa 1968. Ras Michael and the Sons of Negus did a reggae version for their *Spiritual Roots* album. KC and the Sunshine Band funked it up for *Get Down Live*; Boston's Dropkick Murphys interpreted it as speed punk, and New York's Vandal (Peter and Vanessa Daou) did a dance version on a twelve-inch single.

For the first time, irony came into play. It wasn't always clear whether the artists had a genuine affection for the song or whether they were doing it because they knew that there was an incongruity between its message and their image. When Johnny Cash sang "Amazing Grace" it seemed appropriate knowing his cultural heritage, his victorious battle with drink and drugs, and his religious affiliation, but not so when Tiny Tim, the freakish singer with a ukulele who came to fame singing "Tip-Toe Thru the Tulips with Me" included it with "Rudolph the Red-Nosed Reindeer" and "I Saw Mommy Kissing Santa Claus" on an album that the *Chicago Tribune* said was either "a camp masterpiece or a nightmare."

Or what about Bryan Ferry, who over the years had carefully nurtured the image of a foppish British lounge lizard primarily interested in style without content and who had never shown the slightest interest, in his songs at least, in matters metaphysical? Hearing him sing "Amazing Grace" was like hearing Noel Coward performing "All To Thee I Surrender" or a reading of the Sermon on the Mount by Marlene Dietrich. The listener was left wondering what the catch was. Apparently he recorded it as an antidote to the current state of pop. "In this world of hideous rap and the horrors of the modern world," he told Anthony Decurtis of *Rolling Stone*, "it seemed very old fashioned, quaint and beautiful. It was something pure."

These are examples of perceived clashes between song content and image rather than song content and privately held beliefs, but there were others who sang "Amazing Grace" who had violently disagreed with the teachings of the Christian faith. Tori Amos, a Methodist minister's daughter from North Carolina, rebuked the church for thwarting spirituality through its dogma and announced that she was on a "mission to expose the dark side of Christianity." She was more attracted to the Native American concept of a spirit that lived in all things. Sinead O'Connor, an Irish Catholic by upbringing, had expressed her disgust with the Roman Catholic hierarchy by tearing up a photograph of the pope on American TV. She had later become an ordained priestess in the renegade Latin Tridentine Church but left when, after three months, she found the vows of chastity too hard to keep. She then studied guided meditations with a view to becoming a psychic medium.

When O'Connor performed the "Amazing Grace" live on Irish radio in April 2000, it was a surprisingly traditional rendition, using four of Newton's stanzas and the "10,000 years" stanza. None of the words had been altered and there appeared to be no hidden agenda, but perhaps because of this it left the listener searching for ambiguity. Surely she couldn't be identifying with such a conventionally Christian expression of spiritual transformation? Or was she doing it for the shock value of hitching herself to tradition?

Tori Amos, on the other hand, was more obviously subversive. She used three of Newton's stanzas but tweaked them enough with references to grace as "she" and "mother" to turn it from a song of praise to the God of the Old and New Testaments into a song for the Earth Goddess, the feminine spirit behind creation.

Because there are so few uniquely Christian buzzwords in the abbreviated four-stanza version, "Amazing Grace" lent itself to adaptations by followers of other religions who had no difficulty attributing the grace of the song to whomever or whatever they worshiped and considered the concept of being lost and then found a universal spiritual experience.

It was even applied to drug-induced revelations. In his book *Ecstasy and the Dance Culture* author Nicholas Saunders cites the experience of a graduating senior from Harvard Divinity School who in 1995 organized a ritual parting, involving the drug Ecstasy. During this ritual someone sang "Amazing Grace," and the student reported: "I was healed. I was strengthened. I was redeemed. 'Amazing grace, how sweet the sound!' It must have been fifty minutes since the ingestion. [The tune of 'Amazing Grace'] was lifting me away into a supernatural dimension and the sacrament was simultaneously making its healing presence known."

"Amazing Grace" became popular with yoga practitioners as music to calm the mind. Musician Krishna Das incorporated the first stanza into an eight-minute rendition of the Hare Krishna mantra set to the melody of an ancient Tibetan chant. In this context, the phrase "how sweet the sound" took on a different meaning because the sound of the mantra supposedly frees the mind from its attachment to the world and allows it to perceive the divinity within. "Chanting is a spiritual practice," said Das. "All the practices help turn us in the right direction, but essentially they open us to grace."

There were even pagan adaptations, the best-known of which is the anonymously written:

Amazing grace, how sweet the Earth
that bore a witch like me!

I once was burned, now I survive,
Was hung but now I sing.

Verna Knapp, who first posted it on the Internet, heard it performed at a Spring Mysteries Festival in the 1980s. "I remember several women singing it at a talent show," she said. "I was in tears, along with several others."

The music is often quoted without the words. The first four notes are usually enough for people to recognize the song. In 1998 the British girl group All Saints had a number one hit single, "Never Ever," built around its distinctive chords played throughout on piano. In a fascinating essay, "The Amazing Grace of Never Ever," the Dutch music critic Ger Tillekens argued that "by using 'Amazing Grace' as a reference to this theme, the composers of 'Never Ever' treat the original hymn as a palimpsest, wiping out the original lyrics and writing their own hasty words over the shadowing remaining blots."

Rick Taube's 1995 electronic fantasy "Amazing Grace," commissioned for the opening ceremony of the Multimedia III Festival in Karlsruhe, Germany, began with the rhythmic contours of the folk melody and progressed toward the finished composition "like a dust cloud spiralling inwards to form a star." For Taube it was about "the processes of becoming." The Canadian trance rock outfit Godspeed You Black Emperor! worked in the other direction in a performance after September 11, tantalizing listeners with unresolved parts of the song. As one reviewer commented, "It was as if they were saying, in these times anything close to amazing grace is far from assured."

The use of "Amazing Grace" in the wake of the terrorist attacks on New York and Washington illustrated its power to unite Americans and those around the world who felt sympathy for America. Somehow "Amazing Grace" could embrace core American values without ever sounding triumphalist or jingoistic. It was a song that could be sung by young and old, Republican and Democrat, Southern Baptist and Roman Catholic, African American and Native American, high-ranking military officer and anticapitalist campaigner.

It had been used in the same way after other national tragedies; the failed *Challenger* space launch, the Oklahoma City bombing, the Columbine High School massacre. When *Los Angeles Times* religion correspondent Mary Rourke published her illustrated gift book *Amazing Grace in America* in 1996 she subtitled it "Our Spiritual National Anthem."

It has gained a place in America's political life. It was declared a favorite hymn by Presidents Jimmy Carter and Bill Clinton. But no president has shown as much affection for it as George W. Bush, who gave it prominence in his inauguration ceremony and used phrases from it in his autobiography to describe his personal commitment to Christ. Before he was president, when he visited Israel with a group of fellow senators, Bush chose the words of "Amazing Grace" for a reading that he gave on the slopes of Galilee at the spot where tradition has it that Jesus delivered the Sermon on the Mount.

Congressional records show that "Amazing Grace" has been referred to or quoted from an average of fourteen times a year since 1994. Often this is a reference to the song. Sometimes it is used to define God as "the God of amazing grace." When Georgia governor Roy Barnes defended the decision to change the Georgia state flag to reduce the proportion of it featuring the Confederate battle flag, he declared his southernness and ended: "My heart swells with pride when I see a football game on a crisp fall Saturday. I still cry when I hear 'Amazing Grace.' My great-grandfather was captured at Vicksburg fighting for the Confederacy, and I still visit his grave in the foothills of Gilmer County. . . ."

"Amazing Grace" has now circled the globe. This journey began in the nineteenth century when it was exported by missionaries and has been continued by record and radio. Its simplicity and memorability have given it a universal appeal. Among overtone singers in Mongolia it is one of the most popular melodies used for a style in which several musical notes are sung simultaneously. Taught the tune by a Christian friend, a Nepalese nun, Ani Choying Drolma, has set a Tibetan Buddhist chant to it.

Many moving stories about "Amazing Grace" have come from Westerners who have been surprised to encounter it in remote locations. American climbers scaling Mount Kilimanjaro who traded songs with their Tanzanian porters around the fire at night performed "Amazing Grace" and then heard it spontaneously and unexpectedly being sung back to them in Swahili. Western visitors to a Chinese church service held in a cramped hotel room sang it and noticed the locals eagerly joining in even though it was not in their hymnal and could only have survived by being handed down from missionary days.

There was a similar experience in Kenya for students from Earlham College, Indiana. While working on a community project in Kenya their hosts entertained them with displays of traditional dance and they tried, unsuccessfully, to reciprocate with American and English folk songs. "Then, in a moment of silence, we quietly began 'Amazing Grace,' " reported one student. "The room listened to our honest, humble, English style rendition with the rain still falling in the background. As the last refrain died, a wonderful thing happened. Spontaneously, the men and women in the room began to sing 'Amazing Grace' back to us, with their own words, but the same familiar tune, filling that small room with booming, rich harmonies and in uncompromising African style. It was a powerful, and connecting few minutes."

One of the most distinctively different recordings of recent years was by Ladysmith Black Mambazo, the South African vocal group that first came to international prominence after collaborating with Paul Simon on tracks for his 1986 album *Graceland*, where black South African sounds were fused with Western pop. The ten-member group, already popular as the leading practitioners of Zulu isicathamiya music, were led by Church of God pastor Joseph Shabalala. In 1988 he worked with Paul Simon on a new arrangement of "Amazing Grace," which linked it to the nineteenth-century hymn "Nearer My God to Thee." For the recording, Simon took the lead vocal on words of "Amazing Grace."

For many black South Africans the words articulated their feelings as they approached the longed-for release from the rule of apartheid, just as over a century before the same words had articulated the aspirations of American slaves. For Joseph Shabalala it encapsulated his own amazement at being chosen to be an international mouthpiece for native South African music after previously only having been allowed to play in his hometown of Natal. When Nelson Mandela's release from jail was celebrated with a rock music festival at London's Wembley Stadium, one of the most powerful moments came when the opera singer Jessye Norman stilled the crowd that had been fired up with hours of pumping rock music, with a rendition of "Amazing Grace." Lines such as "Through many dangers, toils and snares / I have already come" took on a new poignancy with the image of Mandela walking to freedom still so fresh in the public mind. Norman again performed the song in September 1998 when Mandela was awarded an honorary Doctor of Laws degree by Harvard University. The only other songs used in the ceremony were the South African National Anthem and "Fair Harvard."

A good example of the iconic status of "Amazing Grace" was the *New Amazing Grace* project organized by writer and political activist Ed Sanders, a member of the avant-garde sixties poetry and politics band the Fugs and later the author of *The Family*, the first book about the Charles Manson killings. Describing the project, the *Village Voice* said, "equal parts whimsy and social commentary [this evening out] offers original verses of the 18th-century classic by poets, songwriters, activists, scientists and schoolchildren."

Sanders asked more than two hundred American authors, poets, and musicians to submit contemporary stanzas that fitted the "New Britain" tune. He then had the stanzas performed in two musically augmented shows at the St. Mark's Poetry Project in New York's Bowery. It was a respectful treatment of the song and its reputation, updated for the secular, liberal, ecologically conscious late twentieth century. He elicited contributions from writers such as Robert Bly, Anne Waldman, Allen Ginsberg, Pete Seeger, Robert Hunter, Michael McClure, and Lawrence Ferlinghetti. "The only proviso was that there had to be a faint ray of hope or expectation," said Sanders. "There had to be a glimmer of light through the keyhole."

As might be expected, the new stanzas contained a variety of perspectives: praise for the Earth Mother, haiku-like observations on nature, praise for the DNA code from a professor in human genetics, ruminations on the possibility of grace extending to other planets, cosmic speculations, wordplay, jokes, a protest at a Jewish day school's refusal to let a poet's daughter sing the traditional words at a talent show, and only one disparaging comment ("Amazing Grace—I loathe the sound / Of that old mournful dirge . . .").

Anne Waldman added two stanzas to her poem about the muse and included it in her collection *Fast Speaking Woman*. Allen Ginsberg's five stanzas about homelessness are in *Selected Poems 1947–1995* as "New Stanzas for Amazing Grace." In 1996 he recorded it with Lenny Kaye of the Patti Smith Group on bass and David Mansfield and Marc Ribot on guitars, and it was released on a CD single with "Ballad of the Skeletons."

Although the song still holds its original meaning for millions of Christians around the world, it now has a parallel existence outside the church, where often the only link is a shared belief that it is a song about hope, a song that gives voice to the conviction that it is possible to rise from the depths of confusion, despair, and evil and to become a new person.

" 'Amazing Grace' is perhaps the most terse explanation of redemptive power," said Sanders. "It's used by people of all political persuasions under almost every circumstance. You don't have to be religious to appreciate it. You can just believe in a biomedical entity called the human being."

AMAZING
GRACE...

DON'T LET IT
VANISH WITHOUT
A TRACE.

1.800.CALL.WWF
www.worldwildlife.org/act

*The World Wildlife Fund's ads broadened
the meaning of grace.*

Chapter 13

UNDERSTANDING GRACE

Could Paul have done anything, Jesus would not have had
the honour of doing all. This way of being saved entirely by
grace, from first to last, is contrary to our natural wills. It
mortifies self, leaving it nothing to boast of and, through
the remains of an unbelieving, legal spirit,
it often seems discouraging.
—*John Newton*, 1775

God never regenerates a man until he reforms himself.
There is nothing in grace that will make you a sober man,
with a quart of whiskey in your stomach.
—*Sam Jones*, 1895

For hundreds and even thousands of years before the
scientific conceptualization of such things as immune
globulins, dream states, and the unconscious, this force
has been consistently recognized by the religions,
who have applied to it the name of grace.
—*M. Scott Peck*, 1978

*T*he spread of *"Amazing Grace" could be viewed as*
slow but relentless, the natural consequence of being in a growing
number of hymnals and of being conveniently positioned when significant forms of communication were invented. In the early part of the
nineteenth century it was included in an average of two new hymnals
each year: By the end of the century this had increased to an average of

eight. Since 1900 it has benefited from advent of the phonograph, radio, television, and portable tape recorder.

A more accurate picture would be to see its development as episodic; the writing of the words in 1772, the addition of the music in 1835, and the absorption into secular culture in 1970. Significantly, these stages coincided with major spiritual upheavals in American life, each of which resulted in "Amazing Grace" being understood in a different way.

The first of these was the revival later known as the Great Awakening, which started in Massachusetts under the preaching of Jonathan Edwards and continued under George Whitefield and others. Although Newton wasn't one of its converts, the Calvinistic theology that was its heritage had a profound effect on his intellectual and spiritual development, and in this respect "Amazing Grace" was a product of the Great Awakening.

Whitefield, whom Newton admired so much, died before "Amazing Grace" was written, but he would have approved its theme of salvation through the undeserved favor of God. Yet while Whitefield was quite aggressive in denouncing non-Calvinistic theology as not merely off the mark but "anti-Christian," Newton showed a generosity of spirit, believing that "hatred of sin, thirst after God, poverty of spirit and dependence on Christ" were the marks of a believer regardless of their position on secondary theological issues. "If I thought a person feared sin, loved the word of God, and was seeking after Jesus," he wrote in 1775, "I would not walk the length of my study to proselyte (sic) him to the Calvinistic doctrines. Not because I think them mere opinions, or of little importance to a believer—I think the contrary—but because I believe these doctrines will do no one any good till he is taught them of God."

The next boost to "Amazing Grace" had come during the Second Great Awakening, when it appeared in *Southern Harmony* attached to "New Britain" and became part of the shape-note music revolution. Despite being known as the Second Great Awakening this revival was not a replica of what had happened under Edwards and Whitefield. The leaders tended to be less educated (and often proud to be so since they thought it showed their power as preachers came directly from God rather than from natural gifts), the sermons less scholarly and the responses to them more extremely physical and emotional. It was also guided by a different theology. The emphasis had subtly shifted from God choosing people to people choosing God, from Calvinism to Arminianism.

The knock-on effect of this change would be profound, leading in the twentieth century to the worst excesses of televangelism, audience manipulation, and bumper-sticker theology. If the task of the preacher was not merely to present the gospel and allow the spirit to convict but to elicit a decision, then any technique that changed minds was legitimate. Under these circumstances the "altar call" and the "anxious seat" were introduced. Preachers became more theatrical. Music began to play an important part in working on the emotions. Gipsy Smith, the evangelist that Edwin Othello Excell worked with after the death of Sam Jones, was given the following advice early in his ministry: "Always sing before you preach. The song is the gimlet that makes the hole for the nail to go in. Sometimes if you don't sing you might split the board."

Although "Amazing Grace" was Calvinistic, the theological distinctives were buried in its sinews rather than tattooed on its skin. There was nothing in it that an Arminian would find objectionable. When Newton referred to himself as a "wretch" it was with total depravity in mind but an opponent of this doctrine, such as the evangelist Charles Finney who called it "anti-scriptural and nonsensical dogma," could take it to mean a feeling of despondency. Likewise, "I once was lost, but now am found" was meant by Newton to emphasize his inability to save himself and therefore his utter dependence on God, but it could be taken to mean "I once felt confused and unsure of my direction in life but now I feel as though I am on the right path."

The Second Great Awakening occupied the first half of the nineteenth century, its effects were felt throughout. Sam Jones, an evangelist who stressed moral reformation more than spiritual regeneration, was a direct descendent as were Moody and Sankey with their carefully stage-managed campaigns. During this period Excell removed Newton's most explicitly Calvinistic lines ('But God, who called me here below . . .') and replaced them with the "10,000 years" stanza. As the Methodist son of a German Reformed Church pastor, it's hard to believe that he wasn't aware of the theological significance of his editing.

The most recent fillip to "Amazing Grace" came not in the midst of a Christian revival but during the new consciousness movement that gathered momentum in the 1960s and 1970s. Embracing disciplines as varied as yoga, sound-color healing, geomancy, astrology, rebirthing, and Mind Control, there was no single worldview, as there had been with the Awakenings, but there was a basic shared belief in the need for personal transformation through accessing a higher source of energy. The human problem was not original sin but limited consciousness. Salvation came not through divine rescue but through mind expansion and the awareness of previously hidden powers.

Converts to New Age practices were excited by the prospect of tangible, speedily obtained results. Astrological guidance, unlike prayer, didn't require holy living to be effective. Yogic bliss, unlike the biblical "peace that passeth all understanding," could be achieved through correct technique rather than repentance and obedience. The salvation offered by Christ was only fully realized at death, whereas inner healing could only be fully realized in life. Tom Wolfe, in his classic essay "The Me Decade," called it "the third great religious wave in American history, one that historians will very likely term the Third Great Awakening."

It was in this climate that "Amazing Grace" first flourished as a pop song, and it's surely no coincidence that the story of Judy Collins's recording begins at an encounter group in New York. In the era of transformative therapies "Amazing Grace" was no longer automatically perceived as a song about the mercy of God but as a celebration of human potential. Wretchedness was no longer a fatal spiritual condition leading to exclusion from heaven but an inability to realize self-worth. (Joan Baez and Odetta had already switched to singing "saved a soul like me.") Grace was not an amazingly supernatural act but a perception-shaking jolt, one frequently induced by altering the body's chemistry.

Newton had written it as a testimony to his own rottenness and God's graciousness. It was now being interpreted to mean that we can achieve whatever we want given the right degree of determination. This view was promoted by the psychologist M. Scott Peck in his phenomenally popular *The Road Less Traveled* (1978), in which he combined psychological insight with pseudo-Christian spirituality. The concept of grace was important to Peck and he devoted a quarter of his book to a discussion of it, prefacing the section with four stanzas of "Amazing Grace."

A Christian vocabulary was used and Bible verses were quoted but Peck's analysis of the human condition was far from Christian. In his opinion, the central human problem was laziness. We could receive grace if only we did something about it. Pure evil, he argued, was merely "laziness carried to its ultimate, extraordinary extreme." He sounded almost orthodox when stating that grace was a gift of God, but then he qualified it by claiming that we were all potential gods. So where was the gift of grace to be found? The answer was that it is hidden in the 95 percent of our consciousness of which we are unaware. "If you want to know the closest place to look for grace," he wrote, "it is within yourself. . . . To put it plainly, our unconscious is God. God is with us. We were part of God all the time."

Although released two years before Peck's book was published, the "Amazing Grace" rewritten by New Wave singer Jonathan Richman captures the same spirit. Newton was lost, but Richman just feels that way. Newton gets saved, but Richman just gets to feel good. Grace pursues Newton, but it's inside Richman all along.

> *Well, amazing grace, how sweet the sound*
> *Which brings my joy back again.*
> *Sometimes I've worried so much, felt so lost, but then I always feel found*
> *And I should know by now that grace is something that's always within.*

If we all possess grace and yet it remains hidden from most of us, an effort of the will or a sudden illumination is required to access it. If Peck is right, grace will favor those who are determined and resilient, those who are able to focus their energies to embark on the journey within. This thinking gave rise to the assumption that grace is something bestowed upon those with grit and self-control, life's champions rather than life's losers. Grace is the overcoming of obstacles, the rising to any challenge, the fulfilling of potential.

A TV commercial for the John Hancock Mutual Life Insurance Company used during the opening and closing ceremonies of the 1996 Atlanta Olympics emphasized this understanding. It told the stories of four American athletes who had triumphed over adversity to become Olympic gold medalists. Brief sequences of each athlete were followed by captioned details of the hardships they had overcome. "One of twenty-two children, Wilma Rudolph wore a leg brace from age six to ten, a victim of rheumatic fever," said one. "Incredibly, she became the world's fastest woman, winning three gold medals at the 1960 Rome Summer Games." The only sound during the whole commercial was an edited recording of Judy Collins singing "Amazing Grace."

The implication was clear. The wretchedness each one had experienced was a physical or social handicap and the grace that had saved them was contained within their own determination to succeed. That's what made a champion. All that was required was a vision and the inner strength to follow it. A quote from Jesse Owens, which closed the sequence, said, "Everybody should have a dream."

The commercial won praise from the advertising industry and according to a *USA Today* viewers' poll was the third most popular spot in the Olympic coverage. To Steve Burgay, John Hancock's head of advertising, it was an inspired choice not only because it was a song that already had a deep resonance but because it embodied the Olympic ideal. "If you look at what these athletes accomplished, it had to do with amazing grace," he said. "It had to do with more than just their bodies. It had to do with their spirits. I think that's why people felt that it was a perfect match. You have to have a certain kind of spirit and spirituality to accomplish what these people accomplished. That's why 'Amazing Grace' seemed to go hand in hand with their stories."

Some felt "Amazing Grace" was not so much about inner resolve as it was about a moment of mental clarity when a person sees his or her life's meaning and purpose. Often they related it to forms of intense awareness, such as those experienced during Zen satori, trance states, and drug highs; Joan Baez, who has been performing the song for almost forty years, confessed that she was not sure what the word *grace* meant. "I've never thought about it, but it sounds like the loveliest way to say a form of enlightenment or a form of real gratitude, of giving. It's a state I would like to be in for more than thirty seconds a day."

If *grace* is another word for this kind of illumination, the blindness of "Amazing Grace" must refer to our limited consciousness. Normal life has a dulling effect. The range of small things that we have to deal with each day clutters our perceptions. Grace has a neurological effect on us, allowing us to see clearly, even if only momentarily. During this time we perceive things as they really are and are able to make the appropriate decisions.

In a sermon on "Amazing Grace," Unitarian Universalist minister Roberta Finkelstein of Sterling, Virginia, asked what grace is for those who don't believe it originates with God. "Grace is still a very personal and subjective experience. It is something indescribable that happens to us when we least expect it, when we haven't asked for it, and certainly when we don't merit it. Whatever it is, we are transformed by the experience in the here and now, and sustained by its memory later on. It is what life surprises us with."

A related understanding was that "Amazing Grace" is about the loss of ego and the recognition that we are all part of an energy force. What that force is, was of no great concern. This was the thinking of liberal Protestant theologian Paul Tillich who wrote: "It (grace) strikes us when, year after year, the longed-for perfection of life does not appear, when the old compulsions reign within us as they have for decades, when despair destroys all joy and courage. Sometimes at that moment a wave of light breaks into our darkness, and it is as though a voice were saying: 'You are accepted, accepted by that which is greater than you, and the name of which you do not know.' Do not ask for the name now; perhaps you will find it later." In what appears to be a similar spirit Judy Collins declared, " 'Amazing Grace' is a song about letting go, bottoming out, seeing the light, turning it over, trusting the universe, breathing in, breathing out, going with the flow."

This is grace as the experiencing of the interconnectedness of things, the mystical state in which the individual sees herself as a molecule in a universal dance of molecules. In her book *States of Grace: The*

Recovery of Meaning in the Postmodern Age, Charlene Spretnak defines a state of grace as "consciousness of the unity in which we are embedded" and argues that people can experience this either unexpectedly or through performing a ritual that invites it. "Experiencing grace involves the expansion of consciousness of self to all of one's surroundings as an unbroken whole, a consciousness of awe from which negative mind-states are absent, from which healing and groundedness result. For these reasons grace has been deemed 'amazing.'"

Understood like this the force that we are to submit to is anonymous. Grace comes by admitting our limitations and abandoning ourselves to the energy that suffuses the universe in the belief that it has our best interests at heart. This involves total trust because the energy that creates and nurtures may turn out to be the same energy that destroys and inflicts suffering. Judy Collins: "We're always in the path of this power and my own feeling is that agnostics, atheists, spiritual people and devoted churchgoers alike all have the same experience because it is talking about forces unseen which are always around us."

"Amazing Grace" had global implications for some. They considered it anthropocentric to think of grace only in terms of how it benefits us as humans. There needed to be consideration of how all life could be transformed through international peace, animal welfare, and environmental protection. This touched on the meaning of grace as "elegance of proportion." Amazing grace would take place when everything was in its right relationship with everything else. "Grace means harmony," said Pete Seeger. "Isn't the law of gravity throughout the universe a kind of harmony or the way the ninety-three elements combine throughout the universe or the way that mathematics works? There's harmony there."

Seeger's contribution to Ed Sanders's *New Amazing Grace* consisted of four lines that expressed this view:

From quarks to stars, there's grace we know
The grace of MC square
And endless more, above, below
We feel the grace is there.

A campaign by the World Wildlife Fund used photographs of dolphins, penguins, a polar bear, and a panda with the slogan, "Amazing Grace . . . Don't Let It Vanish Without a Trace." As a magazine ad, this was perplexing. Was Grace the name of the penguin or the polar bear and was this a campaign to prevent their extinction? But a supporting sixty-second TV commercial in which the opening of "Amazing Grace" was played over a collage of images of the natural world made the intention clear. Over dissolving shots of giraffes and African sunsets an unidentified voice described how the planet has given life to more than 10 million species: "An amazing place. Truly amazing grace." *Grace*, in this sense, was not a supernatural rescue but a balanced and unexploited natural world. The commentary ends by appealing for help so that "we can keep this planet in a state of grace."

The most widespread understanding of "Amazing Grace" was that it celebrated a general sense of preservation; it was a song about being kept from danger and blessed with good things. The most common contemporary uses of the word *grace* is in the phrase "There but for the grace of God go I," said on seeing someone fall victim to a misfortune. The person saying it usually means: "It could have been me. But it wasn't. And I'm grateful."

What would John Newton think of these contemporary interpretations? As someone keen to endorse the good, even if eventually pointing out the bad, I think he would agree that grace bears all of the above characteristics. Grace had opened his eyes. Grace had motivated him. "How unspeakable our obligations to the grace of God!" he wrote to a friend shortly after moving to Olney. "What a privilege it is to be a believer! They are comparatively few, and we by nature were no nearer than others. It was grace, free grace, that made the difference."

Grace restrained evil and promoted harmony. He could see examples of God's wisdom and love in nature. After visiting a museum display of then-remarkable mechanical toys, he commented: "Not withstanding the variety of their motions, they were all destitute of life. There is unspeakably more wisdom and contrivance in the mechanism of a butterfly or a bee, that flies unnoticed in the fields, than in all his apparatus put together. But the worlds of God are disregarded, while the feeble imitations of them which men can produce gain universal applause."

Grace had protected him before his conversion in his narrow escapes from death. "It extends to the minutest concerns," he wrote to a young girl in 1783. "He rules and manages all things, but in so secret a way that most people think he does nothing when, in reality, he does all."

But he would have made an important distinction. General, or "common," grace, extended to all creation but it was special grace that "saved a wretch like me." Although both came from God, they were not to be confused. The grace that through conscience stopped people being as evil as they could be, would not inevitably lead on to repentance. For that to take place required saving grace. "The convictions of natural conscience, and those which are wrought in the heart by the Holy Spirit, are different, not only in degree, but in kind. The light of a glow-worm and of the sun do not more essentially differ."

He believed that everyone benefited from common grace but relatively few benefited from saving grace. He used his own conversion as an example of the difference. His crewmates on the *Greyhound* endured the same Atlantic storm and were brought safely to Loch Swilly (common grace), but only for Newton did the experience lead to spiritual transformation (saving grace). "No one else on board was impressed with any sense of the hand of God in our danger and deliverance," he wrote. "No temporal dispensations can reach the heart unless the Lord himself applies them. My companions in danger were either quite unaffected, or soon forgot, but it was not so with me. I was not any wiser or better than they, but the Lord was pleased to vouchsafe me peculiar mercy."

Of all the recent understandings of grace, the two that are most similar in appearance to saving grace, or "amazing grace" as Newton phrased it, are the relinquishing of the ego and mental clarity. Grace, Newton frequently stressed, can only begin when efforts to save ourselves have been abandoned. Yet "throwing yourself on the mercy of God" is not the same as blind surrender to the powers of the universe. Newton saw his submission as being to a knowable being, with a personality and a will, who, because of the crucifixion, had the power to forgive and restore.

"We are never more safe, never have more reason to expect the Lord's help, than when we are most sensible that we can do nothing without him," he wrote. "This was the lesson Paul learnt—to rejoice in his own poverty, and emptiness, that the power of Christ might rest upon him. Could Paul have done anything, Jesus would not have had the honour of doing all.

"This way of being saved entirely by grace, from first to last, is contrary to our natural wills. It mortifies self, leaving it nothing to boast of, and, through the remains of an unbelieving legal spirit, it often seems discouraging. When we think of ourselves so utterly helpless and worthless, we are too ready to fear that the Lord will therefore reject us whereas, in truth, such a poverty of spirit is the best mark we can have of an interest in his promises and care."

Spiritual illumination came as a result of this saving grace and wasn't a requirement for it. You were enlightened because you were saved, not saved because you were enlightened. He didn't discount the value of reason but believed that because it had been corrupted it was unable to accept the verdict that it was corrupt. Only a mind renewed by grace could agree with the doctrine of total depravity and want to repent and follow Christ. Without this renewal, the teachings of Christianity not only appeared ridiculous but were morally offensive. "When the heart is changed, and the mind enlightened, then reason is sanctified," he argued. "[It] renounces its curious disquisitions, and is content humbly to tread in the path of revelation. This is one difference [between faith and rational assent]—assent may be the act of our natural reason, faith is the effect of immediate Almighty power."

Grace wasn't a onetime experience for Newton. He attributed his daily protection, his desire to live obediently, and his future hopes to grace. "Amazing Grace" began with the hour he first believed but continued through the dangers, toils, and snares, through death and on into eternity. "The grace of God has a real influence upon the whole man," he once wrote. "It enlightens the understanding, directs the will, purifies the affection, regulates the passions, and corrects the different excesses to which different persons are by constitution or habit inclined."

When Newton preached to inmates of a London prison in 1775, he took as his text the words of Paul "Here is a trustworthy saying that deserves full acceptance: Christ Jesus came into the world to save sinners of whom I am the worst." Some of the men were awaiting execution. He told them the story of his life and "gained their attention more than I expected" (1 Timothy 1:15).

As he preached he found himself crying and noticed many of the prisoners also in tears. "Had you seen their present condition and could you hear the history of some of them, it would make you sing, 'O to grace how great a debtor!' " he later wrote. "By nature they were no worse than the most sober and modest people, and there was doubtless a time when many of them little thought what they should live to do and suffer. I might have been, like them, in chains, and one of them have come to preach to me, had the Lord so pleased."

This is the paradox at the heart of "Amazing Grace." Someone as naturally corrupt as any condemned prisoner "sunk in sin, and lost to shame" had been chosen to be blessed. If he had possessed an unimpeachable reputation or had lived the life of an ascetic, he might have been tempted to think that salvation was his just desert. But he was running from all that was good and godly when he was finally forced to his knees. He had been given what he didn't deserve. This was, by definition, amazing. This was, by definition, grace.

Two years after composing "Amazing Grace" he wrote: "That I was ever called to a knowledge of his salvation, was a singular instance of his sovereign grace. That I am still preserved in the way, in defiance of all that has arisen from within and without to turn me aside, must be wholly ascribed to the same sovereignty. If, as I trust, he shall be pleased to make me a conqueror at last, I shall have a peculiar reason to say, 'Not unto me, not unto me, but unto thy name, O Lord, be the glory and the praise!' "

It's fitting that of all the millions of words that Newton spoke, preached, and wrote (his selected works alone total almost four thousand pages) it should be the handful that make up "Amazing Grace" that have endured because this was not only the story of his life but the essence of his message. He was a man appalled at the depths of his sinfulness and amazed at the heights of God's mercy.

It's impossible to know his story and not to wonder how he would feel if he were to be transported into the twenty-first century and hear the lines he wrote in his attic at Olney being sung on the street corners of London, in the folk clubs of New York, at the Brandenburg Gate in Berlin, on the mountainsides of Kenya, and in the secret churches of China; to hear the phrases he put together coming from the mouths of rock singers, mourners, antiglobalization protesters, and Christian worshipers of every denomination in every country in the world.

What he might say is indicated, I believe, in a passage he wrote toward the end of his life. "Perhaps the annals of thy church scarcely afford an instance in all respects so singular. Perhaps thy grace may have recovered some from an equal degree of apostasy, infidelity, and profligacy: but few of them have been redeemed from such a state of misery and depression as I was in, upon the coast of Africa, when thy unsought mercy wrought for my deliverance.

"But, that such a wretch should not only be spared and pardoned, but reserved to the honour of preaching thy gospel, which he had blasphemed and renounced, and at length be placed in a very public situation, and favoured with acceptance and usefulness, both from the pulpit and the press; so that my poor name is known in most parts of the world, where there are any who know thee, this is wonderful indeed! The more thou hast exalted me, the more I ought to abase myself."

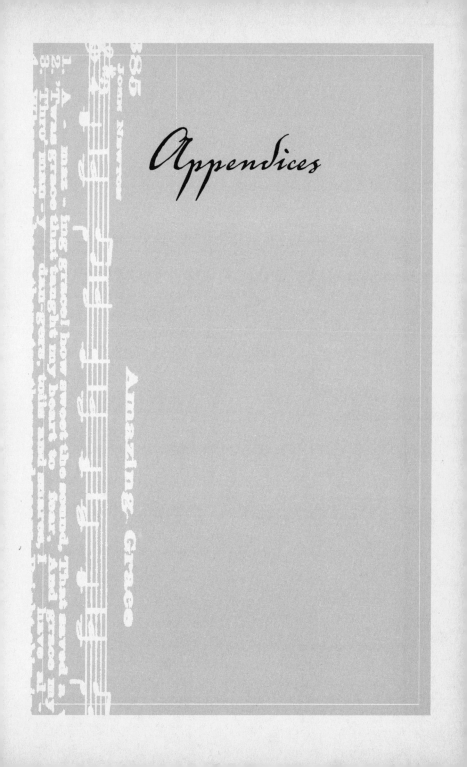

Appendices

Appendix 1: "Amazing Grace" Lists

TEN FILMS FEATURING "AMAZING GRACE"

1. *Alice's Restaurant,* 1969
2. *Invasion of the Body Snatchers,* 1978
3. *Coal Miner's Daughter,* 1980
4. *Star Trek II,* 1982
5. *Silkwood,* 1983
6. *Dudes,* 1988
7. *The Handmaid's Tale,* 1990
8. *Memphis Belle,* 1991
9. *Cry, the Beloved Country,* 1995
10. *Entertaining Angels,* 1996

TEN SONGS CONTAINING REFERENCES TO "AMAZING GRACE"

1. " 'Amazing Grace' Used to Be Her Favorite Song," Amazing Rhythm Aces, 1975
2. "Foot of Pride," Bob Dylan, 1983
3. "You Brought the Sunshine (Into My Life)," The Clark Sisters, 1983
4. "Shadrach," The Beastie Boys, 1989
5. "(I've Got to) Stop Thinking 'Bout That," James Taylor, 1991
6. "She Sang 'Amazing Grace,' " Jerry Lee Lewis, 1992
7. "A Long Walk," Jill Scott, 2000
8. "The Crawl," Placebo, 2001
9. "The Bravest," Tom Paxton, 2001
10. "American Dream," Afroman, 2001

TEN CELEBRITY FUNERALS TO USE "AMAZING GRACE"

1. Stevie Ray Vaughan, musician (performed by Stevie Wonder, Jackson Browne, and Bonnie Raitt), 1990
2. Albert King, blues guitarist (performed by Joe Walsh of the Eagles), 1992
3. Alex Haley, author of *Roots* (played on flute), 1992
4. Richard Nixon, former U.S. president (played as his coffin was loaded on plane), 1994
5. Bill Monroe, bluegrass musician (sung a cappella by Ricky Skaggs), 1996
6. Sonny Bono, singer and congressman (sung by choir), 1998
7. Barry Goldwater, senator and presidential nominee (sung by Renee Morgan-Brooks), 1998
8. Joe DiMaggio, baseball player (sung by two vocalists), 1999
9. John Kennedy, Jr., publisher (sung at memorial mass by O Freedom Choir), 1999
10. Pete Conrad, astronaut (performed by Willie Nelson), 1999

TEN ARTISTS WHO HAVE PERFORMED "AMAZING GRACE"
BUT HAVE NOT RELEASED IT ON RECORD

1. Bob Dylan (1975, New York, N.Y.)
2. Everly Brothers (1981, *Rock 'n' Roll Odyssey* video)
3. Phish (1993, Poughkeepsie, N.Y.)
4. The Eagles (1994, Irvine, Calif.)
5. Shelby Lynne (1995, Nashville, Tenn.)
6. Deep Purple (1999, Brisbane, Australia)
7. Sinead O'Connor (2000, *Mystery Train* radio show, Dublin, Ireland)
8. Mary J. Blige (2001, Los Angeles, Calif.)
9. U2 (2001, Portland, Ore.)
10. Whitney Houston (various dates and venues)

AMAZING GRACE, HOW SWEET THE PRODUCT

1. Amazing Grace Bakery (Duluth, Minn.)
2. Amazing Grace's Bar BQ (Kansas City, Mo.)
3. Amazing Grace Bath Gel (philosophy brand of products, Ariz.)
4. MV *Amazing Grace* (a ship registered in Equatorial Guinea)
5. Amazing Grace Whole Foods (Louisville, Ky.)
6. Amazing Grace Flowers (Jakarta, Indonesia)
7. Amazing Grace Llamas (Perrysville, Ohio)
8. Amazing Grace Custom Upholstery (Toronto, Ontario, Canada)
9. Amazing Grace Cleaning (Laconia, N.H.)
10. Amazing Grace Hair Styling (Norfolk, Va.)

TEN FAVORITE HYMN POLLS

1. *Cyber Hymnal* (2001), "Amazing Grace" #1
2. *Baptist Standard*, Texas (2001), "Amazing Grace" #1
3. *Christian Reader* (2001), "Amazing Grace" #1
4. *The Hymn* (1991), New England United Methodists, "Amazing Grace" #2
5. *The Hymn* (1991), New England Episcopal, "Amazing Grace" #1
6. Newspaper Enterprise Association (1990), "Amazing Grace" #1
7. Southern Baptists (1988), "Amazing Grace" #1
8. United Methodists (2000), "Amazing Grace" #1
9. Membane United Methodist Church, N.C. (2001), "Amazing Grace" #1
10. St. Andrews Presbyterian, Windsor, Ontario (2001), "Amazing Grace" #2

Appendix 2: Select Discography

1 9 2 6

> The Wisdom Sisters (single), Columbia 15093D
> Rev. H. R. Tomlin (single), OKeh 74291
> Rev. J. M. Gates (single), Victor 20216

1 9 2 8

> Friendship Four (single), Victor 21287

1 9 3 0

> Fiddlin' John Carson (unreleased track), OKeh W404624-B (available
> on *Fiddlin' John Carson, Vol. 6*, Document DOCD-8019)

1 9 3 5

> Aunt Molly Jackson (field recording), Library of Congress, 821 B2

1 9 3 6

> Gilbert Fike (field recording), Library of Congress 3189 B6
> Mrs. Henry Garrett (field recording), Library of Congress 3175 A3

1 9 3 7

> Bill & Pauline Garland (field recording), Library of Congress 1394 A1
> Pine Mountain Settlement School (field recording), Library of
>   Congress 1383 B1
> Lucy McKeever & Friends (field recording), Library of Congress 917 B2

1 9 3 8

> Rev J. C. Burnett (single), Decca 7494

1 9 3 9

> Mary Shipp (field recording), Library of Congress 3005 A1
> Jesse Allison (field recording), Library of Congress 2684 A1
> New Hope Baptist Church (field recording), Library of Congress
>   3042 A2

Mr. and Mrs. Braley (field recording), Library of Congress 2638 A2
Mr. and Mrs. Walker (field recording), Library of Congress 3104 A2
Vera Kilgore (field recording), Library of Congress 2939 B4
Mrs. Martin (field recording), Library of Congress 2748 B1 & 2

1940

Blind Willie McTell (field recording), Library of Congress 4071 B3
    (available on Masters of the Country Blues Yazoo BCD 144)
Blind Gipson (field recording), Library of Congress 3981 A1
Huddie "Leadbelly" Ledbetter (field recording), Library of Congress
    (available on *Go Down Old Hannah,* Rounder 611099)
Granny Reid (field recording), Barnicle-Cadle Collection BC-341

1941

Robert R. Pierce (field recording), Library of Congress

1942

William Floyd Parton (field recording), Barnicle-Cadle Collection
    BC-550

1946

Ernestine Washington (single), Jubilee 2502
Dixie Hummingbirds (single), Apollo 108

1947

Fairfield Four (single), Bullet 292
Mahalia Jackson (single), Apollo 194, B side of "Tired"

1949

Golden Gate Quartet *Our Story,* Columbia Col 494053
Sammy Bryant (single), Sacred 6008
Sister Rosetta Tharpe (single), Decca 14575, B side of "Blessed
    Assurance"

1950

Five Blind Boys of Mississippi (single), Peacock 1536

1952

Aunt Martha Wiltz (single), Flame 1005
Pilgrim Travelers (single), Specialty 847

1953

Jones Brothers (unreleased but later included on), *Sun Gospel*, Sun
BCD 16387

The Blackwood Brothers Quartet, *1953, Vol. 1* Bibletone BCD-10030

1954

Five Trumpets (single), Savoy 4060

Maceo Woods (single), Vee-Jay 122

Paul Robeson, *Solid Rock*, Othello Records R-201A-F

Mahalia Jackson (unreleased), Columbia 14031

The Georgia Peach, *Gospel in the Great Tradition*, Classics Editions, CE
5001

1955

Harmonizing Four (single), Gotham 779

Jesse Fuller *Frisco Bound!* Cavalier CAV 5006

1957

Harry & Jeanie West, *Favorite Gospel Songs*, Folkways FA 2357

Famous Ward Singers, *Meeting Tonight on the Old Camp Ground*, Savoy 14015

1959

Sacred Harp Convention, *Southern Journey: And Glory Shone Around*,
Rounder CD 1710 (1998 release)

Clara Ward, *In the Garden*, Dot 3223

The Stars of Faith (single), Savoy 4128 (moaned-out version by
vocalist Frances Steadman under the title "Moan Frances")

1960

Highway QCs, *Jesus Is Waiting*, Vee-Jay 5007

Frank Boggs, *Songs from the Heart*, Word W-3110

Old Regular Baptist Church Congregation, *Mountain Music of
Kentucky*, Folkways FA 2317

Brother Joe May (single), Nashboro 677

J. Robert Bradley, *God's Amazing Grace*, Decca DL 4043

1961

Mighty Clouds of Joy, *Family Circle*, Peacock 114

Johnny Duncan, *Beyond the Sunset*, Music for Pleasure MFP 1032

1962

    Caravans, *Seek Ye the Lord*, Vee-Jay 5026

    Roy Rogers, *The Bible Tells Me So*, Capitol ST 1745

    Swan Silvertones (single), Vee-Jay 909

    Chet Atkins, *Back Home Hymns*, RCA Victor LSP2601

    Horton Barker, *Traditional Singer*, Folkways FA 2362

    Bessie Jones, *The Long Road to Freedom* (Harry Belafonte project not
        released until 2001), Buddha 99756

    Swan Silvertones, *Savior Pass Me Not*, Vee-Jay 5013

1963

    Soul Stirrers, *Encore*, SAR 504

    Weavers, *The Weavers at Carnegie Hall, Vol. 2*, Vanguard VMD 79075

    The Limeliters, *Makin' a Joyful Noise*, RCA LPM/LSP-2588

    Jean Ritchie and Doc Watson, *Jean Ritchie and Doc Watson at Folk City*,
        Folkways FA 40005

    Doc Watson, *Old Time Music at Clarence Ashley's, Part 2*, Folkways FA 2359

1964

    Cotton Brothers (single), Songbird SB 1099

    Pete Seeger, *Pete Seeger in Prague* (released 2001), Flyright 68

    Lucille Marley (single, B-side) Vee-Jay 944

1965

    Marion Williams, *When Was Jesus Born?* CBS 52.054

    Bernice Reagon, *Folk Songs: The South*, Folkways FA 2457

1966

    Patti Page, *Patti Page Sings America's Favorite Hymns*, Sony/Legacy
        65199

1967

    Burl Ives, *I Do Believe*, Word 3391

    Rev. Sammy Lewis (single), Halo 19

    Janis Joplin, *Farewell Song* (released 1982), CDL 01-484458-10

1968

    Southern Hummingbirds (single), Fink 305

1969

    Mississippi Fred McDowell, *Amazing Grace*, Testament 2219

    Arlo Guthrie, *Alice's Restaurant*, United Artists RCD 10737

    The Great Awakening (single), London HLU 10284

1970

    Judy Collins, *Whales and Nightingales*, Elektra 75010-2

    Byrds, *Untitled/Unreleased* (released 2000), Sony Legacy 65847

    Jerry Lee Lewis, *Church* (released 1989), Lection Records 841 032

1971

    John Fahey, *America* (not released until 1998), Takoma CDTAK 8903

    Rod Stewart, *Every Picture Tells a Story*, Mercury SRM-1-609

    Skeeter Davis, *Love Takes a Lot of My Time*, RCA LSOP 4557

    Anita Bryant, *Love Lifted Me*, Word WST 8540

1972

    Royal Scots Dragoon Guards, *Farewell to the Greys*, RCA NL 25212

    Elvis Presley, *He Touched Me*, RCA LSOP-4690

    Merle Haggard, *Land of Many Churches*, Capitol SWBO-803

    Aretha Franklin, *Amazing Grace*, Atlantic 2-906

    Van Dyke Parks, *Clang of the Yankee Reaper*, Warner B-2878

    Vera Lyn, *20 Family Favorites*, EMI TV 28

    Groundhogs, *Who Will Save the World*, BGO CD 77

    Andy Williams, *Alone Again, Naturally*, Columbia LPA 25431

    Betsy Rutherford, *Traditional Country Music*, Biograph RC 6004

1973

    Glen Campbell, *I Knew Jesus (Before He Was a Star)*, Capitol SW-11185

1974

    The Faces, *Coast to Coast*, Mercury 832 128

    Cliff Richard, *Help It Along*, EMI, EMA 768

    Ike and Tina Turner, *The Gospel According to Ike and Tina Turner*, UA
        29626

1975

    Johnny Cash, *Johnny Cash Sings Precious Memories*, Columbia C-33087

1976

>Jonathan Richman, *Jonathan Richman and the Modern Lovers*, Beserkeley, B2 0048
>
>Charlie Rich, *Silver Linings*, Epic KE–33545
>
>Willie Nelson, *The Sound in Your Mind*, Columbia 34092
>
>Joan Baez, *From Every Stage*, A & M 216 506

1977

>Paul Butterfield and John Sebastian, *Woodstock Mountains*, Rounder 3018
>
>Charlie McCoy, *Country Cookin'*, Monument MC 7612
>
>Ralph Stanley, *Clinch Mountain Gospel*, Rebel 1571

1978

>Stanley Brothers, *Beautiful Life*, Old Homestead, OHCS 119

1980

>Pete Seeger, *Singalong: Live at Sanders' Theatre*, Folkways 40027

1981

>Al Green, *Higher Plane*, Myrrh MSB 6674

1982

>Tammy Faye Bakker, *Tammy Sings the Old Hymns*, PTL 1829

1984

>George Beverly Shea, *Looking Homeward*, Worldwide, LHCO 386
>
>Meryl Streep, *Silkwood*, DRG 6107

1985

>Statler Brothers, *Pardners in Rhyme*, Mercury 824-420-1

1986

>Chet Baker, *Silent Nights*, GSRCD 87
>
>Yes, *9012 Live*, Atco 90474

1987

>Lemonheads, *Hate Your Friends Taang!* 15
>
>Spotnicks, *Love Is Blue*, Europa 100 423.9

1988

    Ladysmith Black Mambazo, *Journey of Dreams*, WEA 7599257532

1989

    Randy Scruggs, *Will the Circle Be Unbroken, Vol. 2*, Universal 12500

    Daniel Lanois, *Acadie*, Warner 25969

    Marion Williams, *Surely God Is Able*, Spirit Feel 1011

    Martha Bass, *Mother Smith and Her Children*, Spirit Feel 1010

1990

    Arlo Guthrie, *Precious Friend*, Warner Bros. 3644

    Vandal, *Decoded and Danced Up* (compilation), RCA 3083

1991

    Throwing Muses, *Counting Backwards* (4 track), 4AD

    Jessye Norman, *Amazing Grace*, Phillips 2PH 432–546

    Acker Bilk, *Golden Instrumental Hits*, Laserlight 55506

    Boots Randolph, *Homer Louis Randolph III*, Monument 47070

    James Cleveland, *Amazing Grace*, Savoy 14260

1992

    Diamanda Galas, *Vena Cava*, Mute CDSTUMM119

    Jordanaires, *Jordanaires Sing Gospel*, Arrival 4339

1993

    Bryan Ferry, *Taxi*, Virgin 7243 8 47712 2 5

    Jerry Garcia, *The Pizza Tapes* (issued 2000), Acoustic Disc ACD-41

    Eternal, *Always and Forever*, EMI 7243 8 28212 2 9

    Diana Ross/Jose Carreras/Placido Domingo, *Christmas in Vienna*, Sony 5358

    Fats Domino, *Christmas Gumbo*, Right Stuff 27753

    Marion Williams, *Can't Keep It to Myself*, Shanachie, 6007

1994

    Pete Seeger and Arlo Guthrie, *More Together Again*, Rising Son RSR-0007

    Neville Brothers, *Live on Planet Earth*, A & M 31454 02252

    Jimmy Swaggart, *The Best of Jimmy Swaggart*, Jim-Records 03-158

Tramaine Hawkins, *To a Higher Plane*, Columbia 57876

Herbie Mann, *Deep Pocket*, Kokopelli 1296

P. K. Mitchell, *All Hail the Power: The Rock Hymns Project*, Rugged 91872

The Beat Daddys, *South to Mississippi*, Waldoxy 2807

1995

Robson and Jerome, *Robson and Jerome*, RCA 74321323902

Kronos Quartet, *White Man Sleeps*, Warner/Nonesuch 79163

Bob Snyder, *Sunday at the Grand*, Saxy Records 103

Tiny Tim, *Tiny Tim's Christmas Album*, Durto 029

Kristin Hersh, *The Holy Single* (4 track), 4 AD TAD 5017

Ray Stevens, *Ray Stevens Live!* Curb D2–77662

B. J. Thomas, *Precious Memories*, Warner 45952

K. C. and the Sunshine Band, *Get Down Live*, Intersound 8124

Elder Roma Wilson, *This Train*, Arhooolie 429

Lee Greenwood, *God Bless the USA*, MCA 20605

Sydney Ellis, *Amazing Grace*, Black Wallet P1003A

Sean Kelly, *Lighthouse Rocket*, What Are Records 60009

Crystal Gale, *Someday*, Intersound 9315

1996

Tori Amos, *Talula* (3-track single), East West A8512CD1 (UK only)

Ani Difranco, *Dilate*, Righteous Babe Records 008

Allen Ginsberg, *Ballad of the Skeletons* (4 track), Mercury 697 120
101-2

Blind Boys of Alabama, *I Brought Him with Me*, House of Blues 51416
1274 2

Cissy Houston, *Face to Face*, House of Blues, HOBME 700108

Bela Fleck and the Flecktones, *Live Art*, Warner 46247

Kitty Wells, *One Day at a Time*, King 490

Jose Carreras/Natalie Cole/Placido Domingo, *A Celebration of
Christmas*, Erato 620000

1997

Leanne Rimes, *You Light Up My Life*, WEA/Atlantic/Curb 73027

Jeff Beck, *Merry Axemas* (compilation), Sony EK 67775

Martin Speake, *Amazing Grace*, Spotlite SBJ-558

Glenn Miller Orchestra, *Live in Europe*, Laserlight 17114

Walela, *Walela* (in Cherokee), Triloka 85208

Laura Love, *Octoroon*, Mercury 3145346492

Fairfield Four, *I Couldn't Hear Nobody Pray*, Warner 46698

1998

Charlotte Church, *Voice of an Angel*, Sony Classical SK 60957

Pras, *Ghetto Supastar*, Columbia COL 491489 2

Nana Mouskouri, *Gospel*, Mercury 314 558 095-2

Odetta, *To Ella*, Silverwolf 1012

Pat Boone, *The Inspirational Collection*, Varese Vintage 5903

Third Man (Dana Gillespie), *Dream On*, Siva 108

Mark O'Connor, *Midnight on the Water*, Son 62862

Loretta Lynn, *All-Time Gospel Favorites*, Time-Life Records 18118

1999

Destiny's Child, *The Writing's on the Wall*, Sony 4943942

Dolly Parton, *Precious Memories*, Blue Eye Records

Robbie Robertson, *Any Given Sunday, Vol. II* (soundtrack), Warner Sunset/Atlantic 83390-2

Ras Michael, *Spiritual Roots*, VP 2090

Carreras, Domingo, Pavarotti, *The Three Tenors' Christmas*,

R. Carlos Nakai, *Inner Voices*, Canyon 7021

Dropkick Murphys, *The Gang's All Here*, Hellcat 80413

2000

Chuck Mangione, *Everything for Love*, Chesky JD199

Mormon Tabernacle Choir, *Amazing Grace*, Avalon 9602

2001

Blind Boys of Alabama, *Spirit of the Century*, Real World CDRW95

Wycliffe Gordon, *Slidin' Home*, Nagel-Hayer 2001

Lou Rawls, *I'm Blessed*, Malaco 4517

Charles Littleleaf, *Ancient Reflections*, Redwood Productions

Ray Charles, *Music of Hope* (compilation), Koch TJE 1901

Tramaine Hawkins, *God Bless America* (compilation), Sony 86300

Colin Pryce-Jones, *Guitar Heaven*, Fury, FCD 3055
Marcus Miller, *m2*, Telarc, 83534

2 0 0 2

Krishna Das, *Pilgrim Heart*, Karuna 7 93018 56062
BeBe Winans, *Live Up and Close*, Motown 016 705
Matt Harris, *Slighty Eliptical Orbit*, Leon Russell Records 30015
Spiritualized, *Do It All Over Again* (3-track single), Spaceman 0PM007
   (UK only)

2 0 0 3

Aaron Neville, *Believe*, EMI Gospel EGD 20381

Appendix 3: Who's Who

Baez, Joan 1941–
Leading lady of the urban folk boom of the 1960s, she introduced spirituals and hymns into her performance during the civil rights movement. "Amazing Grace" became one of her most requested songs although she didn't record it until the mid-1970s as a track on a live album.

Caesar, Shirley 1939–
She began singing as part of the Caesar Sisters as a child. Cut her first record in 1951. Joined the all-female Caravans in the late 1950s and left in 1967 to record alone. She recorded "Amazing Grace" with the Caravans in 1962 and later as a solo artist. She now combines singing with being the pastor of her own evangelistic organization.

Carrell, James P. 1787–1854
He used the tune of "Amazing Grace" as "Harmony Grove" in *Virginia Harmony*, the tune book he edited with Presbyterian elder David L. Clayton in 1832. For many years this was thought to be the first publication of the tune. Carrell lived his whole life in Lebanon, Virginia, and was a Methodist lay preacher, farmer, and county clerk.

Carson, Fiddlin' John 1868–1949
Born in Fannin County, Georgia, he was one of the first performers of what later became known as "country music" to appear on radio and phonograph. He was a traveling musician, house painter, and brewer of moonshine whiskey. His broadcasting debut was on the radio station WSB started by the *Atlanta Journal*. He recorded his first songs for OKeh in June 1923. For his version of "Amazing Grace," recorded in Atlanta in 1930, he was accompanied by the Virginia Reelers.

Clow, Patrick ?–1763

In the journals that Newton kept as a slave trader in the 1750s, he mentions Clow a dozen times, and by this time he appears to have been trading from Plantain Island. Nicholas Owen and his brother Blayney also mention Clow. Because Clow knew P. I. it has often been assumed by biographers, wrongly I believe, that Clow was the slave trader who kept Newton imprisoned on Plantain Island. Born and raised in Scotland, his brother James Clow succeeded Adam Smith as professor of logic at Glasgow University. Clow never married or had children and died in London in 1763.

Clunie, Alexander ? –1770

Clunie, a sea captain and Christian, was a huge influence on Newton shortly after his conversion and introduced him to Calvinistic ideas. The two men met in St. Kitts in 1754, where Newton was delivering slaves, and they stayed close friends until Clunie's death. Some of their correspondence was published as a book in 1790. At the time that they first met, Clunie was living in Wapping and belonged to an independent chapel in Stepney.

Cohen, David 1942–

A Los Angeles session musician who had worked with Sonny and Cher, Bobby Darin, and Tim Hardin (it's his twelve-string finger-picking on "If I Were a Carpenter"). Cohen recorded the first rock version of "Amazing Grace" under the pseudonym of the Great Awakening in 1969. It became an underground hit in Britain after repeated plays by London deejay Jeff Dexter at the 1970 Isle of Wight Festival.

Coleman, Robert Henry 1869–1946

An independent publisher of hymnals and gospel songbooks from 1909 to 1939, and all that were designed for congregational singing included Edwin Othello Excell's arrangement of "Amazing Grace." These books were particularly influential on Baptists. For many years Coleman led the singing at the annual meetings of the Southern Baptist Convention and was assistant to George W. Truett at the First Baptist Church, Dallas.

Collins, Judy 1939–

Her 1970 recording of "Amazing Grace," included on the album *Whales and Nightingales* and later released as a single, was a watershed event in the life of the song, introducing it to a fresh audience around the world, reviving its life as a hymn and establishing it as a classic that would eventually be covered by all types of musicians.

Cooper, Anthony Ashley (Lord Shaftesbury) 1671–1713

Grandson of the first Earl of Shaftesbury, his 1711 publication *Characteristicks of Men, Manners, Opinions, Times* was influential on Newton's teenage thinking, breaking the dominance of his early Christian upbringing and turning him into a freethinker. He spent much of his life out of England living in Holland and Italy.

Cowper, William 1731–1800

Coauthor of *Olney Hymns* (1779), the book in which "Amazing Grace" was first published, and Newton's closest friend for more than thirty years, Cowper suffered from bouts of mental instability that caused him to doubt the security of his own salvation but managed to write some of the most enduring Christian hymns, including "There Is a Fountain Filled with Blood" and "God Moves in a Mysterious Way." Although he stopped attending church in 1773, he continued to vehemently defend its doctrines. His poetry, especially "The Task," was influential on such English romantic movement poets as Wordsworth, Coleridge, and Blake.

Crease, Major Anthony J. 1946–

A pipe sergeant with the Royal Scots Dragoon Guards in 1971, he played the first stanza solo when the regiment recorded "Amazing Grace," being joined on the other stanzas by fellow pipers and the military band. When released as a single in 1972, the recording became an international hit, selling more than 16 million copies in various formats.

Dartmouth, Lord (William Legge) 1731–1801

Dartmouth financed the publishing of Newton's autobiography, convinced the bishop of Lincoln that he should be ordained by the Church of England and offered him the curacy at Olney. He also renovated the vicarage in Olney and gave Newton the use of the unoccupied Great House, the building where Sunday evening meetings were held and where "Amazing Grace" would have first been presented on New Year's Day, 1773. Dartmouth was, at various times, President of the Board of Trade and Foreign Plantations, Lord Keeper of the Privy Seal, Colonial Secretary and High Steward of Oxford University. Dartmouth College in New Hampshire is named in his honor.

Doddridge, Philip 1702–51

Doddridge's hymn writing was very influential on Newton, particularly on "Amazing Grace." His biography *The Life of Colonel James Gardiner* (1747), which Newton read while captain of a slave ship, also impressed him, causing him to read it "more frequently and sensibly than all the books I ever read." Although he died before Newton was ordained, his effect was still felt in the Midlands, where he had set up several dissenting academies in his name. He had been the pastor of the Independent Congregation at Castle Hill, Northampton (close to Olney), and was a friend to Newton's childhood pastor David Jennings as well as to Isaac Watts. His book *The Rise and Progress of Religion in the Soul* played a part in the conversion of William Wilberforce.

Edwards, Jonathan 1703–58

Between 1735–37 his preaching in Northampton, Massachusetts, inspired the beginning of a revival that became known as the Great Awakening. He attended Yale at the age of twelve and earned his master's degree at nineteen. He was a pastor in Northampton for twenty-three years, a missionary to the Housatonic Indians for six years, and had just accepted the presidency of the College of New Jersey (now Princeton) when he died of an infection. His best-known and most frequently published sermon is "Sinners in the Hands of an Angry God."

Excell, Edwin Othello 1851–1921

His arrangement of "Amazing Grace" with the addition of the "10,000 years" stanza has become the standard form of the song performed and published today. Excell was a musician, singer, choir leader, and publisher of hymns who accompanied the evangelist Sam Jones for twenty years as musical director and then Ronald "Gypsy" Smith for fifteen years. He died in Louisville, Kentucky, while accompanying Smith on a crusade.

Fairbairn, Stuart 1934–

When bandmaster of the Royal Scots Dragoon Guards, Fairbairn was responsible for the arrangement of "Amazing Grace" that was later used for the recording. He left the British army before the album and single were released and moved to New Zealand to become director of music for the Royal New Zealand Air Force. He now lives in western Australia.

Fountain, Clarence 1929–

Fountain started singing with George Scott and Jimmy Carter at the Talladega Institute for the Blind in Alabama in the late 1930s, and this group became the nucleus of the Blind Boys of Alabama, a gospel outfit that is still recording and performing today. They recorded "God's Amazing Grace" in the early 1950s, a traditional version of "Amazing Grace" in the 1990s, and then set it to the tune of "House of the Rising Sun" for their 2001 album *Spirit of the Century*.

Franklin, Aretha 1942–

Daughter of the Reverend C. L. Franklin, Aretha grew up surrounded by gospel music and met many of America's leading gospel singers, including Mahalia Jackson, Clara Ward, and James Cleveland at her home during her teenage years. Her 1972 version of "Amazing Grace," recorded live at a church in Los Angeles, was one of the most impassioned performances of her career and became the title track of a bestselling album.

Gates, Rev. J. M. ?–?

Although the Reverend Gates made one of the first recordings of "Amazing Grace," very little is known about him other than that he was a black preacher who recorded "sermons with singing," starting in the mid-1920s and specialized in working up themes suggested by the titles of blues songs. When Document Records compiled his *Complete Recorded Words* it stretched to nine volumes.

Gother, Anthony ?–?

Gother was a Liverpool captain employed occasionally by Joseph Manesty. He was in charge of the *Greyhound*, which rescued Newton from Sierra Leone and which was the ship caught in the mid-Atlantic storm that marked the beginning of his Christian conversion. Gother must have continued sailing for many years because Nicholas Owen's journal for January 1758, written in Sierra Leone, mentions the arrival of "Capt. Gauthers from Liverpool."

Guthrie, Arlo David 1947–

Son of the folksinger Woody Guthrie, Arlo began singing in the mid-sixties and was taught "Amazing Grace" by Pete Seeger who was a long-standing friend of his father's. He included several different versions of the song on the soundtrack of his film *Alice's Restaurant* (1969) and the same year performed it at the Woodstock Festival. It has since become a popular song in his concerts and is available on his album *Precious Friend* (1990) and with Pete Seeger on *More Together Again* (1994).

Haweis, Thomas 1734–1820

He read Newton's letters to the Baptist minister John Fawcett in which Newton told his life story and as a result asked him to expand on them. These letters became the basis for Newton's autobiography. When Haweis was offered the curacy at Olney by Lord Dartmouth he suggested that Newton be given the position.

Hays, Lee 1914–81

The son of a Methodist minister from Arkansas he became a singer of labor songs and together with Millard Lampell and Pete Seeger formed the Almanac Singers. He taught "Amazing Grace" to Pete Seeger and sang it with the Weavers, a group that he and Seeger formed with Fred Hellerman and Ronnie Gilbert. The Weavers were blacklisted because of their left wing views and disbanded in 1952, reforming in 1955. Although they continued to be banned from radio and TV they were pop-

ular in concert halls, folk clubs, and on college campuses, spearhead-
ing the urban folk revival of the 1950s and inspiring future folksingers
such as Joan Baez and Bob Dylan.

Huntingdon, Countess (Selina Hastings) 1707–91

A hugely influential figure in Britain's evangelical movement during the
eighteenth century, she established her own network of chapels to provide pulpits for those excluded from the established church. She was a
tireless reformer and encourager and after the publication of *Olney Hymns*
was the first person to include "Amazing Grace" in a hymn collection.

Jackson, George Pullen 1874–1953

His 1933 book *White Spirituals in the Southern Uplands* revived the
shape-note tradition and provided a history of William Walker's
Southern Harmony, the first collection to match the words of "Amazing
Grace" to the tune "New Britain." Jackson, who was born in Maine, was
a professor of German who taught at several universities before becoming an associate professor at Vanderbilt University, Nashville. He
retired in 1943. His main interest outside of his university subject was
American folk music, particularly southern spirituals about which he
wrote a number of books.

Jackson, Mahalia 1911–72

Born in New Orleans, she later moved to Chicago and in 1946 signed
with Apollo Records in New York. Her third release for Apollo, "Move
On Up a Little Higher" became the first million-selling gospel record
and established her as the best-known gospel singer in America. She
recorded "Amazing Grace" for Apollo Records in 1947 and then again
for Columbia in 1954.

Jennings, David 1691–1762

Jennings was the minister at the Independent Meeting House (est. 1680)
in Old Gravel Lane, Wapping, when Newton was born, having started
there in 1718. He pastored Newton's mother, who was a member of the
chapel until her death in 1732. Newton, after his conversion, struck up a
strong friendship with Jennings and corresponded with him regularly.

Jennings had been a friend of two of the songwriters who had the greatest effect on Newton—Isaac Watts and Philip Doddridge.

Jones, Sam 1847–1906

Jones was a flamboyant evangelist who in 1886 chose Edwin Othello Excell to be his musical director. Excell went on to arrange what has become the standard version of "Amazing Grace."

Joplin, Janis 1943–70

Before becoming a rock star with Big Brother and the Holding Company, Joplin had played Texas folk clubs accompanied by an autoharp. She sang "Amazing Grace" in emulation of the traditional mountain singer Jean Ritchie and in 1966 began singing a version with Big Brother.

Kerr, Peter 1940–

Kerr produced the Royal Scots Dragoon Guards version of "Amazing Grace" in 1971. Prior to becoming a record producer he had been an executive officer in the Civil Service, then a jazz musician with the Clyde Valley Stompers. In the early 1980s he abandoned record production to become a beef and barley farmer in Scotland and then an orange farmer on the Spanish island of Majorca. He wrote two books about his experiences in Majorca—*Snowball Oranges* and *Mañana Mañana*.

Lewis, Job ?–1754

Lewis was the first victim of Newton's virulent anti-Christian attacks when he was a midshipman on the *Harwich*. Years later, when Newton was a captain, he offered Lewis a job on board his ship to try to mend the damage he believed he had inflicted on him. Lewis died on the journey. These experiences affected Newton deeply and the memory of them kept him constantly aware of his earlier apostasy.

Ligon, Joe 1941–

Born in Alabama, Ligon moved to Los Angeles in the 1950s. There he formed the Mighty Clouds of Joy with his school friend Johnny Martin in 1959. The group, with Ermant and Elmer Franklin, Leon Polk, and Richard Wallace, started recording in 1960 and cut a live version of

"Amazing Grace" in 1963. In the 1970s they became an opening act for the Rolling Stones, Marvin Gaye, and Paul Simon. Although the group membership has changed, Ligon still performs with the Mighty Clouds of Joy.

Lomax, Alan 1915–2002

Son of legendary music collector John Lomax, he began making field recordings with his father in 1932 and in 1934 became the coauthor of the book *American Ballads and Folk Songs*. In the same year he became honorary consultant and curator of the Archive of American Folksong at the Library of Congress.

Lomax, John Avery 1867–1948

The most significant collector of American folk songs in the twentieth century, Lomax pioneered the preservation of America's musical heritage through recording the music of ordinary Americans. Over the years, with his wife, Ruby, he recorded a number of versions of "Amazing Grace."

Manesty, Joseph ?–1771

Manesty was a prominent Liverpool merchant and shipowner who was a friend of Newton's father. It was Manesty's ship the *Greyhound* that rescued Newton from Sierra Leone and Newton later became captain on two of Manesty's ships, the *Duke of Argyl* and the *African*. His company went bankrupt in 1766, causing Newton to lose all his savings.

McGuinn, Roger 1942–

McGuinn was the spiritually sensitive member of the Byrds who converted to Sufism in the 1960s and then became a Christian in the 1970s. The group had scored a hit with Pete Seeger's adaptation of a passage for Eccelesiastes "Turn! Turn! Turn!" and began performing "Amazing Grace" in 1970, recording it during sessions for the *Untitled* album but not releasing it until 2001.

McTell, William Samuel "Blind Willie" 1901–59

Born in Thomson, Georgia, blues musician and singer McTell had a sporadic recording career that started in 1927 and ended in 1956. Between times spent as a recording artist he became a street corner musician. This is how he was spotted by John and Ruby Lomax in 1940, when the music collectors were in Atlanta. McTell recorded a number of tunes for them, including an instrumental version of "Amazing Grace" on his guitar. His work had an effect on the white blues and folk of the 1960s.

Mitchell, James ?–?

Mitchell was Captain Philip Carteret's clerk on board the *Harwich* and was characterized by Grace Irwin in her biographical novel *Servant of Slaves* (1960) as the midshipman who converted Newton to freethinking, although Newton had never named him or anyone else as that individual. Mitchell kept a journal during his time on the *Harwich*. It was published in 1933 in an obscure Indian magazine. He left the *Harwich* to join the *Medway's Prize* as purser.

Moody, Dwight 1837–99

The best-known evangelist of the late nineteenth century, Moody organized campaigns on a scale never seen before and recognized the potential for using music to make an audience more receptive to his message. He was responsible for making the musician and singer Ira Sankey a household name.

Nelson, Rev. David 1793–1844

Nelson, as pastor of the Presbyterian church in Danville, Kentucky, encouraged Charles Spilman to put together the tune book *Columbian Harmony*, which contains the earliest known publication of the music now associated with "Amazing Grace." Nelson campaigned for the emancipation of slaves and was later involved in helping escaped slaves travel safely from the South to Chicago along the Underground Railroad.

Newton, Captain John 1700?–50

Possibly the son of a London sailor himself, Captain Newton, John Newton's father, was involved in the Mediterranean trade before becoming a land-based agent for the Royal African Company. His final job was as governor of Fort York on Hudson's Bay, a position he held at the time of his death by drowning.

Owen, Nicholas ?–1759

Irish-born Nicholas Owen was working as a slave trader in Sierra Leone in the 1750s and kept a journal, which wasn't published until 1930. He mentions many of the traders that Newton knew and the places, including Plantain Island, that Newton visited.

Reagon, Bernice Johnson 1942–

As Bernice Johnson, she was a member of the Freedom Singers, a group created by the Student Nonviolent Coordinating Committee to perform during the civil rights movement. She recorded "Amazing Grace" as a solo artist in 1965 and later founded the a cappella ensemble Sweet Honey in the Rock. She is now Distinguished Professor of History at American University and Curator Emeritus at the Smithsonian Institution National Museum of American History. Her special area of interest is African American oral, performance, and protest traditions.

Ritchie, Jean 1922–

Born in Viper, Kentucky, she brought mountain songs to New York in the 1950s, "Amazing Grace" among them. She first performed it on a record with Doc Watson in 1962.

Robeson, Paul Leroy 1898–1976

An actor and singer, Robeson was also a campaigner for left wing causes and had a deep interest in folk music from around the world. The son of a preacher, he introduced spirituals and hymns into his performance at a time when this was considered controversial and in 1954 recorded "Amazing Grace."

Sanders, Ed 1939–

Born in Kansas City, Missouri, Sanders studied at New York University and in 1965 formed the rock group The Fugs with poet and singer Tuli Kupferberg. He is the author of *The Family* (1971), a study of Charles Manson, *Tales of Beatnik Glory*, and a number of other books. He lives in New York State with his wife Miriam where they publish the *Woodstock Journal*. He intends to publish the 150 stanzas contributed by various writers to his project *New Amazing Grace in 2002*.

Sankey, Ira 1840–1908

Through his appearances at the meetings of evangelist Dwight Moody, Sankey became one of the best-known singers of his era. He included "Amazing Grace" in three of his collections, which helped popularize the song during the late nineteenth century, especially among the new urban middle classes.

Seeger, Pete 1920–

One of the pioneering urban folksingers of the 1940s and 1950s, Seeger was taught "Amazing Grace" by Lee Hays, his partner in the Almanac Singers and later in the Weavers. He started performing it in the 1940s and continues to do so today.

Spilman, Charles Harvey 1805–92

While a student at Centre College, Danville, Kentucky, Spilman was encouraged by his pastor, Rev. David Nelson, to put together a tune book. Published in Cincinnati, *Columbia Harmony* is the first known collection to contain the music to the tune now used with "Amazing Grace." Spilman, who spent the rest of his life in Kentucky, worked as a doctor.

Stewart, Rod 1945–

Stewart recorded a brief version of "Amazing Grace" on his 1971 album *Every Picture Tells a Story*. He was originally going to title the album *Amazing Grace*, but in the end he didn't even list the track on the album cover. Slide guitar on the track was played by Sam Mitchell.

Stowe, Harriet Beecher 1811–96

She wrote her novel *Uncle Tom's Cabin* to further the cause of emancipation and included a version of "Amazing Grace" as one of the songs that Tom would sing to comfort himself. This included the earliest known printing of the song with the additional "10,000 years" stanza.

Thornton, John 1720–90

Thornton, who was a director of the Bank of England, supported Newton financially and put up the money for the first printing of

Olney Hymns. He had been converted through the preaching of George Whitefield, and was a friend to Lord Dartmouth. His half sister, Hannah, was the aunt who cared for William Wilberforce as a child.

Tomlin, Rev. H. R. ?–?

Among the first of the "shouting preachers" to be recorded and the first to record "Amazing Grace," Tomlin was probably from Atlanta, Georgia. He was accompanied on the record by the Rigoletto Quintette from Morris Brown University.

Torrey, R. A. 1856–1928

Born in Hoboken, New Jersey, Torrey was an evangelist, teacher, and author who was educated at Yale and became superintendant of the school that is now Moody Bible Institute and pastor of Chicago Avenue Church, which is now Moody Memorial Church. Between 1902–06 he preached in Australia, New Zealand, India, China, Japan, Britain, Germany, and Canada as well as in America. His 1909 hymnal *World Renowned Hymns* was the first to include the definitive Edwin Othello Excell arrangement of "Amazing Grace."

Tucker, Ira 1925–

Born in Spartanburg, South Carolina, home to William Walker a century before, Tucker joined the Dixie Hummingbirds in 1938 and recorded his arrangement of "Amazing Grace" in 1946 when he was nineteen years old. The Dixie Hummingbirds played at the Newport Folk Festival in 1966 and recorded with Paul Simon on his 1973 album *There Goes Rhymin' Simon*. The Dixie Hummingbirds, with Ira Tucker, are still performing.

Unwin, Mary 1724–96

Unwin met the poet William Cowper through her son, William, and he became a permanent houseguest. Cowper stayed on when her husband, Morley, died, and in 1767 she moved with Cowper to Olney. In 1786 they moved to Weston Underwood. It's unlikely that they had a sexual relationship, but they were inseparable companions.

Walker, William 1809–75

Walker was the first person to put the words of Newton's "Amazing Grace" to the tune we now associate with it, which he titled "New Britain." This took place in 1835 for his tune book the *Southern Harmony*, which was to become one of the best-known shape-note books ever. He later included it in another collection, *Christian Harmony*.

Watson, Arthel "Doc" 1923–

Doc Watson, who was born and raised in Stoney Fork, North Carolina, learned "Amazing Grace" from William Walker's *Christian Harmony*, which his family used to sing from at home. His father was a farmer who also led the singing at the local Baptist church. Watson was almost forty years old when he was "discovered" by the urban folk crowd and began recording and touring. He included "Amazing Grace" in his set starting during the early 1960s because he said he believed in the message of the song and thought it was something that people should hear.

Watts, Isaac 1674–1748

Watts was brought up in Southampton and became a pastor of an Independent Meeting. Newton read his children's poems as a child and also learned his catechism. Watts's hymns encouraged the switch from the exclusive use of metrical psalms to a mixture of psalms, hymns, and spiritual songs. George Whitefield introduced his hymns to America and they became so popular that all eighteenth-century English hymns came to be referred to as "Dr. Watts's hymns," and still are in some African American churches.

Wesley, Charles 1707–88

He was possibly the most prolific of the eighteenth-century hymn writers and brother to John. He tried to incorporate profound theology in his words while making the hymns memorable. Many of his works are still sung today.

Wesley, John 1703–91

Along with Whitefield, the greatest of the English evangelists of the eighteenth century. He helped pioneer large outdoor meetings, and although he never left the Church of England he was described as a "Methodist." Those who later followed Wesley's approach became known as Methodists. He met and corresponded with Newton, reading Newton's autobiography several times and adding in his journal, "something very extraordinary therein, but one may account for it without a jot of Predestination."

White, Benjamin Franklin 1800–79

White was William Walker's uncredited collaborator on *Southern Harmony*, and after splitting with Walker went on to produce the *Sacred Harp*, which also included "Amazing Grace" and has proved to be the most enduring of the shape-note tune books.

Whitefield, George 1714–70

Newton heard Whitefield preach in Liverpool shortly after leaving the sea, and the man and his message had a great impact on him. He was also able to meet him in Liverpool. He was strongly influenced by Whitefield's doctrinal emphasis, and many in Newton's close circle of Christian friends were either people who knew Whitefield or who had been converted through his preaching. It was Whitefield who along with Jonathan Edwards created the environment for the Great Awakening, which in turn prepared people for the theology of "Amazing Grace."

Wilberforce, William 1759–1833

Wilberforce first met Newton when he was a child and became reacquainted with him in his twenties, when he was on the brink of an illustrious political career as a British MP. He was the politician who drew up the bill to abolish slavery in Britain and was involved in establishing Sierra Leone as a settlement for freed slaves. His outspokenness on the abolition issue may well have prompted Newton to make his first public confession of guilt over his past involvement in the slave trade.

Woods, Maceo 1932–

Woods played the Hammond Organ. He recorded the first commercially available instrumental version of "Amazing Grace" in 1954, and it became a gospel hit. He became a minister in 1960 and is currently minister of Christian Tabernacle Church in Chicago.

Select Bibliography

Alldridge, Thomas. *The Sherbro and Its Hinterland* (London: MacMillan, 1901).

Allen, William Francis, et al. *Slave Songs of the United States* (Mineola, N.Y.: Dover Publications, 1995).

Anon. *Check-List of Recorded Songs in the English Language in the Archive of American Folk Song* (Washington, D.C.: Library of Congress Music Division, 1942).

Baez, Joan. *And a Voice to Sing With* (New York: Summit Books, 1987).

———. *The Joan Baez Songbook* (New York: Ryerson Music Publishers, 1964).

Ball, Edward. *Slaves in the Family.* (New York: Farrar Straus & Giroux, 1998).

Bargar, Bradley Duffee. *Lord Dartmouth and the American Revolution* (Columbia: University of South Carolina Press, 1965).

Beale, John. *Public Worship, Private Faith: Sacred Harp and American Folksong* (Athens, Ga.: University of Georgia Press, 1997).

Beecher, Henry Ward. *The Plymouth Collection of Hymns and Tunes* (New York: A. S. Barnes, 1855).

Bego, Mark. *Aretha Franklin* (London: Robert Hale, 1990).

Benson, Louis F. *The English Hymn* (London: Hodder & Stoughton, 1915).

Broughton, Viv. *Black Gospel* (Poole, Dorset: Blandford Press, 1985).

Brownlie, John. *The Hymns and Hymn Writers of the Christian Hymnal* (London: Henry Frowde, 1899).

Bull, Josiah. *John Newton of Olney and St. Mary Woolnoth* (London: Religious Tract Society, 1868).

Burdett, Staunton S. *Baptist Harmony* (Philadelphia, Penn.: T. W. Ustick, 1832).

Bush, George W. *A Charge to Keep* (New York: Morrow, 1999).

Campbell, John, ed. *Letters and Conversational Remarks of the Rev. John Newton* (London: Religious Tract Society, 1808).

Carrell, James P., and David L. Clayton, *The Virginia Harmony* (Winchester, Va.: Samuel H. Davis, 1831).

Cecil, Richard. *The Life of John Newton*, ed. Marylynn Rouse (Fearn, Ross-shire: Christian Focus Publications, 2000).

Clark, Rufus W. *The Work of God in Great Britain under Messrs. Moody and Sankey* (New York: Harper and Bros, 1875).

Clay, Eleazar. *Hymns and Spiritual Songs* (Richmond, Va.: John Dixon, 1793).

Cobb, Buell E. *The Sacred Harp: A Tradition and Its Music* (University of Georgia Press, 1978).

Collins, Judy. *Amazing Grace* (New York: Hyperion, 1991).

Cooper, Anthony Ashley. *Characteristicks of Men, Manners, Opinions, Times, 3 Volumes* (London, 1714).

Coupland, Reginald. *Wilberforce* (London: Collins, 1945).

Cowper, William. *Letters* (London: MacMillan, 1914).

Craig, Robert, and James Rupert. *Liverpool Registry of Merchant Ships* (Manchester: Manchester University Press, 1967).

Cross, F. L., ed. *The Oxford Dictionary of the Christian Church* (London: Oxford University Press, 1974).

Damer-Powell, J. W. *Bristol Privateeers and Ships of War* (Bristol: J. W. Arrowsmith, 1930).

Daniel, Darrin. *Fragments of a Northwest Life* (Seattle: Elbow Press, 2000).

Darby, Madge. *Waeppa's People* (Colchester: Connor & Butler, 1988).

Davies, K. G. *The Royal African Company* (London: Longmans, 1957).

DeMaray, Donald E. *The Innovation of John Newton (1725–1807)* (Lewiston, N.Y.: Edwin Mellen Press, 1988).

Denisoff, R. Serge. *Great Day Coming: Folk Music and the American Left* (Chicago: University of Illinois Press, 1971).

Dixon, Goodrich, and Rye Dixon. *Blues and Gospel Records 1890–1943* (Oxford: Oxford University Press, 1997).

Doddridge, Philip. *Hymns Founded on Various Texts in the Holy Scriptures* (Salop: J. Orton, 1759).

Donnan, Elizabeth. *Documents Illustrative of the History of the Slave Trade to America*, 4 vols. (Washington, D.C.: Carnegie Institution of Washington, 1930–34).

Edwards, Brian H. *Through Many Dangers: The Story of John Newton* (Darlington, County: Durham Evangelical Press, 1975).

Edwards, Paul, and David Dabydeen, ed. *Black Writers in Britain 1760–1890* (Edinburgh: Edinburgh University Press, 1991).

Ella, George Melvyn. *William Cowper: Poet of Paradise* (Darlington, Co.: Durham Evangelical Press, 1993).

Equiano, Olaudah. *The Interesting Narrative of Olaudah Equiano* (London: T. Wilkins, 1789).

Excell, Edwin Othello. *Coronation Hymns* (Chicago: E. O. Excell, 1910).

Excell, Edwin Othello. *Make His Praise Glorious* (Chicago: E. O. Excell, 1900).

Forucci, Samuel L. *A Folk Song History of America* (New York: Prentice Hall, 1984).

Fountain, David. *Isaac Watts Remembered* (Worthing: Henry E. Walter, 1974).

Funk, Joseph. *Genuine Church Music* (Winchester, Va., N.P., 1832).

Fyfe, Christopher. *A History of Sierra Leone* (Oxford: Oxford University Press, 1962).

Genovese, Eugene D. *Roll, Jordan, Roll: The World the Slaves Made* (New York: Pantheon Books, 1974).

Goodspeed, Edgar Johnson. *The Wonderful Career of Moody and Sankey* (New York: Henry S. Goodspeed & Co., 1876).

Hall, H. U. *The Sherbro of Sierra Leone* (Philadelphia: University of Pennsylvania Press, 1938).

Hammond, John. *John Hammond on Record* (New York: Ridge Press, 1977).

Hancock, David. *Citizens of the World* (Cambridge: Cambridge University Press, 1994).

Harris, Michael W. *The Rise of Gospel Blues* (Oxford: Oxford University Press, 1992).

Hastings, Selina. *A Select Collection of Hymns* (London: Hughes & Walsh, 1780).

Heilbut, Anthony. *The Gospel Sound* (New York: Doubleday, 1975).

Hindmarsh, Bruce. *John Newton and the English Evangelical Tradition* (Oxford: Clarendon Press, 1996).

Holzman, Jac, and Davis, Gavan. *Follow the Music: The Life and High Times of Elektra Records* (Santa Monica: First Media, 1998).

Hughes, Langston. *Famous Negro Music Makers* (New York: Dodd, Mead & Company, 1963).

Irwin, Grace. *Servant of Slaves: A Biographical Novel of John Newton* (Grand Rapids, Mich.: William B. Eerdmans, 1961).

Jackson, George Pullen. *White Spirituals in the Southern Uplands* (Chapel Hill: University of North Carolina Press, 1933).

Jackson, George Pullen. *White and Negro Spirituals* (New York: J. J. Augustin, 1943).

James, Joe S. *A Brief History of the Sacred Harp* (Douglasville, Ga.: New South Book & Job Print, 1904).

Johnson, James Weldon. *American Negro Spirituals* (New York: Viking, 1969).

Johnson, W. A. B. *A Memoir* (London, N.P., 1852).

Jones, Charles C., Jr. *The Dead Towns of Georgia* (Savannah, Ga.: Morning News Steam Printing House, 1878).

Julian, John. *A Dictionary of Hymnology* (New York: Dover Publications, 1892).

King, James. *Anglican Hymnology* (London: Hatchards, 1885).

Kup, A. P. *Sierra Leone: A Concise History* (Newton Abbot: David & Charles, 1975).

Langford, Paul. *A Polite and Commercial People: England 1727–1783* (Oxford: Oxford University Press, 1989).

Laurens, Henry. *The Papers of Henry Laurens*, ed. George C. Rogers (Columbia: University of South Carolina Press, 1978).

Law, Robin. *The Slave Coast of West Africa* (Oxford: Clarendon Press, 1991).

Legge, William Walter. *The Manuscripts of the Earl of Dartmouth*, 3 vols. (London: H.M.S.O., 1876–96).

Lomax, Alan. *The Land Where Blues Began* (New York: Pantheon, 1993).

Lloyd, A. L. *Folk Song in England* (London: Panther Books, 1969).

Madan, Martin. *A Collection of Psalms and Hymns* (London, N.P., 1760).

Manly, Basil. *The Choice* (Louisville, Ky.: 1891).

Martin, Bernard. *John Newton: A Biography* (London: Heinemann, 1950).

Martin, Bernard, and Mark Spurrell. *The Journal of a Slave Trader (John Newton) 1750–1754* (London: Epworth Press, 1962).

Martin, Geoffrey Thorndike. *Aveley Church and Parish* (Ramsgate: Graham Cumming, 1957).

Mason, Lowell. *A Yankee Musician in Europe: The 1837 Journals* (Ann Arbor, Mich.: Studies in Music, 1990).

Mackee, William. *History of the Sherbro Mission in West Africa* (Dayton, Ohio: United Brethren Publishing House, 1874).

Minnix, Kathleen. *Laughter in the Amen Corner: The Life of Evangelist Sam Jones* (Athens: University of Georgia Press, 1993).

Morgan, Kenneth. *Bristol and the Atlantic Slave Trade in the Eighteenth Century* (Cambridge: Cambridge University Press, 1993).

Murphy, Martin. *St Gregory's College Seville 1592–1767* (Wolsingham, County Durham: Catholic Record Society, 1992).

Myers, Peter D. *The Zion Songster* (New York: J. S. Redfield, 1829).

Nason, Elias. *The American Evangelists Moody and Sankey* (Boston: D. Lothrop, 1878).

Nelson, David. *The Cause and Cure of Infidelity* (New York: John S. Taylor, 1837).

New, A. H. *The Coronet and the Cross* (London: Partridge & Co., 1857).

Newton, John. *The Works of John Newton,* 6 vols. (Edinburgh: Banner of Truth, 1985).

Newton, John. *An Authentic Narrative of Some Remarkable and Interesting Particulars in the Life of* **** (London, N.P., 1764).

Newton, John. *Letters* (Edinburgh: Banner of Truth, 1960).

Newton, John. *The Searcher of Hearts* (Fearn, Ross-shire: Christian Heritage, 1997).

Newton, John, and William Cowper. *Olney Hymns* (London: W. Oliver, 1779).

Norris, Kathleen. *Amazing Grace: A Vocabulary of Faith* (Oxford: Lion, 2000).

Owen, Nicholas. *Journal of a Slave-Dealer* (New York: Houghton Mifflin, 1930).

Patterson, Robert. *The Wonders of Redeeming Love* (Lexington, Ky.: 1801).

Plomer, Bushnell, Dix, eds. *A Dictionary of Printers and Booksellers 1726–1775* (Oxford: Oxford University Press, 1932).

Plumb, J. H. *England in the Eighteenth Century* (London: Pelican Books, 1950).

Pollock, John. *Amazing Grace: The Life of John Newton* (London: Hodder & Stoughton, 1981).

———. *Wilberforce: God's Statesman* (London: Constable, 1977).

Quinlan, Maurice J. *William Cowper* (Minneapolis: University of Minnesota Press, 1953).

Reagon, Bernice Johnson. *We'll Understand It Better By and By* (Washington, D.C.: Smithsonian Institution Press, 1992).

Reynolds, William J. *Companion to the Baptist Hymnal* (Nashville, Tenn.: Broadman Press, 1976).

Richardson, David. *Bristol, Africa, and the Eighteenth-Century Slave Trade to America*, vols. 2 and 3 (Bristol: Bristol Records Society, 1987).

Richardson, David. *The Bristol Slave Traders: A Collective Report* (Bristol: Bristol University Historical Association, 1985).

Rodger, N. A. M. *The Wooden World: An Anatomy of the Georgian Navy* (London: HarperCollins, 1986).

Root, George. *Story of a Musical Life* (Cincinnati: John Church, 1891).

Rourke, Mary, and Emily Gwathmey. *Amazing Grace in America: Our Spiritual National Anthem* (Santa Monica, Calif.: Angel City Press, 1996).

Sanger, Kerran L. *"When the Spirit Says Sing!" The Role of Freedom Songs in the Civil Rights Movement* (New York: Garland, 1995).

Sankey, Ira. *Sacred Songs and Solos* (London: Morgan and Scott, 1874).

——. *Sankey's Story of the Gospel Hymns* (Philadelphia, Penn.: Sunday School Time, 1906).

Schilling, Sylvester Paul. *The Faith We Sing* (Philadelphia, Penn.: Westminster Press, 1983).

Schwerin, Jules. *Got to Tell It* (New York: Oxford University Press, 1992).

Seeley, Mary. *The Later Evangelical Fathers* (London, 1879).

Smith, Harry. *Think of the Self Speaking* (Seattle: Elbow Press, 1999).

Smith, Ronald "Gipsy." *The Beauty of Jesus* (London: Epworth Press, 1932).

——. *Gipsy Smith: His Life and His Work* (London: National Free Church Council, 1925).

Smith, William. *A New Voyage to Guinea* (London: J. Nourse, 1744).

Snelgrave, William. *A New Account of Some Parts of Guinea* (London: J. & P. Knapton, 1734).

Spilman, Charles, and Benjamin Shaw. *The Columbian Harmony* (Cincinnati: Lodge, L'Hommedieu & Hammond, 1829).

Spretnak, Charlene. States of Grace: *The Recovery of Meaning in the Postmodern Age* (San Francisco: HarperCollins, 1991).

Stanhope, George, trans. *The Christian's Pattern, or a Treatise on the Imitation of Jesus Christ* (Dublin: Boulter Grigson, 1766).

Stow, John. *Survey of London* (London, 1720).

Stowe, Harriet Beecher. *Uncle Tom's Cabin* (Boston, Mass.: John P. Jewett, 1852).

Strong, Nathan. *The Hartford Selection of Hymns* (Hartford, Conn.: John Babcock, 1799).

Swift, Catherine. *John Newton* (London: HarperCollins, 1991).

Taylor, Thomas. *A Biographical Sketch of Thomas Clarkson* (London: Joseph Rickerby, 1839).

Thomas, Hugh. *The Slave Trade* (New York: Simon & Schuster, 1997).

Tick, Judith, and Ruth Crawford. *Seeger* (New York: Oxford University Press, 1997).

Tindall, George Brown, and David Emory Shi. *America: A Narrative History, Brief Fifth Edition* (New York: W. W. Norton, 2000).

Torrey, R. A. *World Renowned Hymns* (Montrose: Penn.: Montrose Christian Literature Society, 1909).

Tower, Lionel R. *A Short Story of the Kagbor Chiefdom* (Shenge, Sierra Leone: private printing, 1994.)

Turner, Steve. *Hungry for Heaven: Rock 'n' Roll and the Search for Redemption* (Downers Grove, Ill.: InterVarsity Press, 1995).

Van der Merwe, Peter. *Origins of the Popular Style: The Antecedents of Twentieth-Century Popular Music* (Oxford: Clarendon Press, 1989).

Von Schmidt, Eric, and Jim Rooney. *Baby Let Me Follow You Down* (New York: Anchor Books, 1979).

Wakefield, Samuel. *The Christian's Harp* (Pittsburgh, Penn.: Johnson and Stockton, 1887).

Walker, William. *The Christian Harmony* (Philadelphia, Penn.: E. W. Miller, 1866).

——. *The Southern Harmony* (New Haven, Conn.: Nathan Whiting, 1835).

Waller, Maureen. *1700: Scenes from London Life* (London: Hodder & Stoughton, 2000).

Walvin, James. *Black Ivory: A History of British Slavery* (London: Harper-Collins, 1992).

Watts, Isaac. *Divine Songs* (Oxford: Oxford University Press, 1971).

Wheatley, Phillis. *Poems on Various Subjects* (London, 1773).

White, Benjamin Franklin, and E. J. King. *The Sacred Harp* (Philadelphia, Penn.: 1844).

Whitefield, George. *Select Sermons* (Edinburgh: Banner of Truth, 1958).

Wilberforce, Robert, and Samuel Wilberforce. *The Life of William Wilberforce* (London: John Murray, 1838).

Willens, Doris. *Lonesome Traveler: The Life of Lee Hays* (New York: Norton, 1988).

Williams, Gomer. *History of the Liverpool Privateers* (London: Heinemann, 1897).

Williamson, R. *The Liverpool Memorandum Book* (Liverpool: R. Williamson, 1753).

Winterbottom, T. *An Account of the Native Africans in the Neighbourhood of Sierra Leone* (London, 1803).

Wright, Thomas. *The Life of William Cowper* (London: T. Fisher Unwin, 1892).

Yancey, Philip. *What's So Amazing About Grace?* (Grand Rapids, Mich.: Zondervan, 1997).

Zook, G. F. *The Company of Royal Adventurers* (Lancaster, Penn.: 1919).

ARTICLES, UNPUBLISHED PAPERS

"100 Things for a Time Capsule," *USA Today*, 20 December 1999.

"Chapelle Senior Sings at President's Inauguration," *Clarion* (New Orleans) *Herald*, 1 February 2001.

House of Commons Sessional Papers of the 18th Century, Reports and Papers 1790, vol. 73.

"Dr. Charles Harvey Spilman," in *Kentucky: A History of the State* (Mercer County, Ky., 1887).

"James P. Carrell (1786–1854)," in *Russell County Heritage Book*, vol. 2.

"Disco Nun Chants the Hip Hop Way," *Asian Age Online*, 5 October 2001.

Burlington, Charles, *Slave Narrative from the Rawick Papers*, ser. 5, Western Historical Manuscript Collection, University of Missouri, Columbia, Missouri.

Decurtis, Anthony, "Bryan Ferry Interview," *Rolling Stone*, 4 July 1993.

Ella, G. M., "Selina Countess of Huntingdon," *New Focus*, February/March 2001.

Eskew, Harry, *The Life and Work of William Walker*, unpublished master's thesis, New Orleans Baptist Theological Seminary, 1960.

Eskew, Harry, "James P. Carrell," in *The New Grove Dictionary of American Music* (New York, Macmillan, 1986).

Fulgham, Richard, "In Search of Lost Lebanon," *Lebanon News*, 18 August 1999.

Goldstein, Richard, "Radicals Rising," *Village Voice*, 19–25 July 2000.

Hatchett, Marion J., "Amazing Grace! How Sweet the Sound," in *The Hymnal 1982 Companion*, vol. 1, ed. Raymond F. Glover.

Hatchett, Marion J., "Benjamin Shaw and Charles H. Spilman's Columbian Harmony, or, Pilgrim's Musical Companion," *The Hymn* 42:1 (1991).

Henderson, Connie, "They Called Him Singing Billy," *Mountain Life and Work*, Fall 1962.

Hindmarsh, Bruce, "Amazing Grace: How Sweet It Has Sounded," unpublished paper delivered at Wheaton College for Hymnody in American Protestantism conference, May 2000.

House, H. Wayne, "M. Scott Peck: Traveling Down the Wrong Road," *Christian Research Journal*, Spring 1996.

Justice, Eva T. C., "Singin' Billy Walker Wrote Song Book 100 Years Ago," *Charleston News & Courier*, 15 April 1934.

Leoudak, Zoe, "Hearing the Noise," *Sculpture Magazine* 18:4 (1999).

Leaver, Robin A., "Olney Hymns 1779," *The Churchman* 93:4 (1979); 94:1 (1980).

Leaver, Robin A., "Olney Hymns: A Documentary Footnote," *The Churchman* 97:3 (1983).

Mitchell, James, "Voyage of H. M. S. *Harwich* to India in 1745–1749," *Bengal Past and Present*, vol. XLV, part II, April–June 1933.

Pearl, Susan, "Britain's Black Ancestors," *Family Tree*, October 1995.

Perez, Marvette, "Interview with Bernice Johnson Reagon," *Radical History Review* 68 (1997).

Piper, John, "John Newton: The Tough Roots of His Habitual Tenderness," unpublished paper, January 2001.

Reynolds, William J., "B. F. White: The Sacred Harp Man," *Away Here in Texas*, March–April 1997.

Reynolds, William J., "Tunes for Amazing Grace," unpublished document.

Reynolds, William J., "Amazing Grace: A 20th Century Icon," unpublished paper delivered as a Hugh T. McElrath Lecture in 1999 at the Southern Baptist Theological Seminary's School of Church Music and Worship.

Sanders, Edward, "New Amazing Grace II," unpublished manuscript "conceived, gathered, and sequenced" by Sanders. A published version will be available in 2002 from Edward Sanders, Box 729, Woodstock, NY 12498.

Schwarz, Benjamin, "What Jefferson Helps to Explain," *Atlantic Monthly*, March 1997.

Spilman, Charles H., "Record of Facts and Events and Reminiscences of Early Life," Transylvania University Special Collection.

Steel, David Warren, "Big Singing Day," review of unpublished thesis, *Southern Baptist Church Music Journal* 9 (1990).

Steel, David Warren, "Shape-Note Singing in the Shenandoah Valley," unpublished lecture given to Singers Glen Music and Heritage Festival, August 1997.

Tillekens, Ger, "The Amazing Grace of 'Never Ever,' " *Soundscapes* (online), November 1999.

Whisnant, David E., "The Whitetop Festival and What We Have Learned," paper given to Virginia Highlands Festival, 1998.

Wilcox, Glenn C., Introduction to the 4th edition of *The Southern Harmony and Musical Companion* (Lexington: University Press of Kentucky, 1987).

Grateful acknowledgment is made to the following for permission to reprint from published and unpublished material: Lambeth Palace Library for extracts from John Newton's sermon notes and letters. Special Collections, Transylvania University Library, Lexington, K.Y. 40505, for extracts from unpublished autobiographical notes of Dr. Charles Harvey Spilman. The Albert and Shirley Small Special Collections Library, University of Virginia Library, Charlottesville, V.A., for extracts from the John and James Booker Civil War Letters Collection. Great Honesty Music for a quote from "Spirit in the Sky" by Norman Greenbaum. Special Rider Music for a quote from "Foot of Pride" (1983) by Bob Dylan; copyright 1983 by Special Rider music. All rights reserved. International copyright secured. Reprinted by permission. A. S. Saunders and www.ecstasy.org for a quote from *Ecstasy and the Dance Culture*, by Nicholas Saunders, Simon & Schuster Adult Publishing Group for an extract from *The Road Less Traveled* by M. Scott Peck, M. D. Modern Love Songs, administrated by Joel S. Turtle, for a quote from "Amazing Grace" by Jonathan Richman. Roberta Finkelstein for a quote from her sermon. Pete Seeger for his stanza from *The New Amazing Grace* (1995) compiled by Edward Sanders. Charlene Spretnak for a quote from her book *States of Grace* (San Francisco: HarperCollins, 1991). Jac Holzman for an extract from his book *Follow The Music: The Life and High Times of Elektra Records* (Los Angeles: First Media, 1998). Hudson's Bay Company Archives, Provincial Archives of Manitoba, for an extract from the York Factory Journal of 1750 (B. 239/a/33). Jay Ungar for a quote from his parody "Amazing Grass." Chappell & Co for a quote from "God's Amazing Grace" by Roberta Martin (copyright 1938, renewed 1965), used by permission of Warner Bros. Publications. Benjamin Schwarz for quotes from "What Jefferson Has To Explain," by Benjamin Schwarz (*The Atlantic Monthly*, March 1997).

ABOUT THE AUTHOR

STEVE TURNER is the author of *Trouble Man: The Life and Death of Marvin Gaye*, *A Hard Day's Write: The Story Behind Every Beatles Song*, *Hungry for Heaven: Rock and Roll and the Search for Redemption*, *Jack Kerouac: Angelheaded Hipster*, and *Van Morrison: Too Late to Stop Now*. His articles have appeared in *Rolling Stone*, *Mojo*, *Q* and the *London Times*. He lives in London with his wife and two children.